EDUCATORS, PARENTS, AND EXCEPTIONAL CHILDREN

A Handbook for Counselors, Teachers, and Special Educators

Robert L. Marion
University of Texas, Austin

AN ASPEN PUBLICATION®
Rockville, Maryland
London
1981

Library of Congress Cataloging in Publication Data

Marion, Robert L.
Educators, parents, and exceptional children.

Bibliography: p. 231.
Includes index.

1. Exceptional children—Education.
2. Home and school.
I. Title.
LC3965.M278   371.9   80-24701
ISBN: 0-89443-334-2.

Library of Congress Catalog Card Number: 80-24701
ISBN: 0-89443-334-2

Printed in the United States of America

1 2 3 4 5

Table of Contents

Preface

Parent involvement in special education has been an evolving process. It can be traced from limited contact in early years to maximum involvement under the Education for All Handicapped Children Act of 1975 (Public Law 94-142). Under this act, parent involvement in special education is predicated on the premise that educators and parents will work together as allies for the betterment of exceptional children and youth.

Bound together by the law, both parties are attempting to renegotiate their roles in the educational process. Special education teachers, especially, have had to make adjustments in their professional roles as they seek ways to cement effective working relationships with parents. Sometimes teachers have felt that they have been thrown into combat situations, ill-equipped, and with their lives on the front lines. At other times special educators have contended that they are not teachers but rather have been relegated to the roles of testers, receptionists, writers of Individualized Education Programs (IEPs), and paper pushers.

This book describes roles that teachers can adopt to fulfill meaningful functions while seeking to involve parents of exceptional children and youth in special education. By adopting the roles of advocate, case manager, and ombudsman, special education teachers can find their involvement with parents less stressful as the personal contact between the two allies increases.

While this book was written specifically with special educators in mind, it should interest other professionals who have contact with the exceptional child. The disciplines of medicine, counseling, psychology, social work, guidance, psychiatry, and nursing that come into contact with parents of exceptional children because of P.L. 94-142 can determine better how special educators can use their help as together they assist exceptional children and parents in carrying out

---

Note: This book follows the standard practice of using a "masculine" pronoun wherever the pronoun refers to both males and females. "Feminine" pronouns appear only where antecedents are exclusively female.

the IEP. Some of these parents might find the book a useful complement to their involvement with special educators and other helping professions.

At this point, as the author, I have several acknowledgments to make. Collectively, I owe my family a debt of gratitude. My wife, Irene Marion, especially was a pillar of support and contributed greatly in creating an environment in which I could work. I will be forever in her debt. My children, Renee and Robert, Jr., understood when I wrestled with manuscript problems instead of with them. The other person I wish to thank is Curt Whitesel, my editor, who suggested the topic and supported my efforts until completion of the project.

Robert L. Marion, Ph.D.

Chapter 1

Families and Schools

Many things can be said about families and schools. However, regardless of which entity is being discussed, considerable debate regarding the merits and/or failures of each institution is certain to result. Some concerned family experts (Bronfenbrenner, 1977; Hobbs, 1975, 1966) argue that families are in trouble. They point to a spiraling divorce rate and an increase in single-parent families, then emphasize the fact that these same single-parent families are poor and most are headed by women. Other critics of family solidarity (Shane, 1973; Clark, 1974) also decry the unavailability of mothers, either by economic or career choice, in the home. As evidence of the negative outcomes of these absences, they offer the increasing numbers of troubled, abused, and illegitimate children that result from the disintegration of the family unit.

Conversely, proponents of family unity are equally as passionate in their advocate roles. They stress the adaptability of families to changing times and denounce the prophets of doom concerning American family life. Bane (1977) rejects the notion that the family is falling apart. She reports that the modern American family is less mobile than its predecessors and that the extended family concept is higher in percentage in the 1970s than in the eighteenth and nineteenth centuries. Vincent (1966) argues that family adaptability to other institutions is indisputable proof that the family, as an institution, is not dying. Earlier, Parsons and Bales (1955) made the point that changing family functions actually "free" the family circle by allowing the group to use the additional energy and time on behalf of individual members.

The same dichotomy surrounding the family unit also is in the minds of those who view the instrument of formal education for their children—the schools. Advocates of the present system point with pride to the role that education played in the assimilation of immigrants into the mainstream of American life. Cubberly (1909) wrote that "knowledge is power" and that a good education was needed if persons were to succeed in an industrial society such as the United States. The *Brown* v. *Board of Education* (1954) decision and the Sputnik

1

debates further established this tenet in education. Later, others extended the "knowledge is power" ideology to imply that education was the key to individual social and economic status. Myrdal (1962), Jensen (1969), Coleman (1966), and others directly equated equality of educational opportunity with quality of life. These ideas about schooling, in this context, were then argued as a remedy for inequalities of social and economic opportunity (Cohen, 1970). Compulsory education laws, compensatory education programs, court decisions, and legislative mandates in the area of civil rights all have tended to support this contention over the last decade or so.

Education, however, has not been without its critics. Professional educators have been challenged often by parental voices of dissatisfaction to protest against schools and their offerings. Hickerson (1966), Coleman (1966), and Glazer (1965) speak of the alienation that the poor, culturally different, and disenfranchised feel with the formal education system. Hurley (1969) and Miller (1967) compare the school to great sorting and labeling factories where members are credentialed by race, creed, handicap, and socioeconomic status. Opponents of present-day schools sometimes propose two alternatives. (1) Many want to return to the "good old days" of the three Rs—reading, 'riting, and 'rithmetic. (2) Others seek more extreme remedies and demand that the entire system be overhauled. For these citizens, the schools have failed. These persons form the nucleus of a concerned group seeking to reform the schools (Gallup, 1973; Passow, 1976; Brown, 1975).

All of the preceding data point to the clouded and confused issues confronting two established and related institutions—families and schools. The question is: Have the obstacles become so insurmountable that neither can survive? Historically speaking, have both been weakened, strengthened, or just adapted through time? This chapter examines what a family is and what its role is in society and education. The debate about schools is narrowed to focus upon their programs in special education. These parameters permit centering attention on the involvement of parents and families in special education. Through a historical perspective, the functions of each are considered to determine if and how functions have changed. The concept of families and special education as separate systems is compared to illustrate how interactions between the two affect exceptional children.

THE FAMILY: SOCIAL INSTITUTION AND SYSTEM

Often cherished, sometimes attacked, but nevertheless maintaining its position as one of the most resilient systems in the world is the family. Throughout history families have reared their children, have protected them against danger, and have resisted attempts to shatter the emotional bonds that bind them together. Moreover, although child-rearing practices have varied throughout the world, families have managed to survive the holocausts of wars; the terrors of religious, racial, and ethnic persecution; the ravages of childhood diseases, and the devastation of infant mortalities. Therefore, when viewed over time, the family can be considered as a primary institution from the Stone Age to today's twentieth century America (Ackerman, 1966).

If the family is to be perceived in terms of an institution and a system, these terms must be defined and discussed. But first, a more basic question: What is a family? Families can be defined by number, affiliation, or type of structure. Numerically speaking, the U.S. Bureau of the Census describes a family as a group of two or more persons related by blood, marriage, or adoption and living together. Family also can be defined by affiliation. For instance, the family of origin refers to the unit into which one is born and from which roles and behaviors are molded (Ackerman). Another definition is the family of procreation; this unit is recognized after adults marry and produce children. Generally, the family of origin provides personal affiliation for children while the family of procreation fulfills the same function for adults.

Families also have been described by their type of structure. Two types have appeared to dominate the structural composition of families. The first type is the family nucleus consisting of the husband and wife and their offspring. The second is the extended family composed of the nuclear family plus lineal kinsfolk (those related by blood) and collateral kinship (those related through marriage or adoption,) (Murdock, 1949). Another rapidly growing type now appearing in the United States is the one-parent family. The formidable growth is expected to continue in 1980; 48 percent of all children born in 1980 will live "a considerable time with only one parent before they reach the age of 18" (p. 537). Divorces, death of spouses, and adoptions are all family circumstances contributing to this phenomenon.

These multiple criteria help define the family to a degree. However, these definitions still limit the parameters in which families can be viewed. Therefore, additional definitions of institution and system must be explored to allow a holistic perception of family development, structure, interactions, functions, and adaptability. This also permits inclusion of several of the concepts in the previous definitions. In this process, the family unit as an institution is examined initially.

Webster defines an institution as an organized pattern of group behavior, well established and well accepted as a fundamental part of a culture. Many social scientists support this interpretation and describe an institution as something that is regarded by society as proper and necessary, and as displaying predictable activity (Goldberg & Deutsch, 1977). Therefore, three basic tenets of institutions can be extracted:

1. The patterns of behavior regulated by institutions ("institutionalized") deal with perennial basic problems of any society.

2. Institutions involve the regulation of behavior of individuals in society according to some definite, continuous, and organized patterns.
3. These patterns involve a definite normative ordering and regulation; that is, regulation is upheld by norms and by sanctions legitimized by these norms (Sills, 1968).

Having established the legitimacy of institutions, can educators apply their basic characteristics to families? The reply is yes. Satir (1967) listed seven functions of the family that definitely stamp the unit as an institution:

> the heterosexual union of the mates; the division of labor between adults and between children; the maintenance of a generational boundary; the transmission of culture; the producing and nurturing of children to perpetuate the race; the teaching of the child to communicate; the recognition of adulthood and the provision for the eventual care of parents by their children (p. 21).

In this functional definition, the term family becomes infused with meaning and becomes a social institution. Moreover, all of the functions Satir (1967) attributed to families meet the requirements set by the social scientists. Thus, by definition and function families possess the necessary qualifications to be called an institution.

On the other hand, do families also function as systems? Bell and Vogel (1960) advance the proposition that families function not only as a single system operating as a whole, but also can be viewed as a system consisting of several subsystems (i.e., husband-wife, parent-child, and sibling systems). They perceive the family as a social system and believe that it is an organization of individuals who stand in dynamic interchange with one another and who, as a system, stand in similar interchange with the environment (Bell & Vogel, 1960). Mills (1959) provides the ultimate framework in which families should be viewed:

> One is a child in a certain kind of family, one is a playmate in a certain kind of child's group, a student, a workman, a foreman, a general, a mother. Much of human life consists of playing such roles within specific institutions. To understand the biography of an individual, we must understand the significance and meaning of the roles he has played and does play; to understand these roles we must understand the institutions of which they are a part (p. 161).

Mills's summarization characterizes the family relationships that are explored following discussion of another established institution—education.

EDUCATION: ANOTHER INSTITUTION AND SYSTEM

Education as an institution must be examined because it affects families and children. Since this effect is systematized in society, it is necessary first to establish education as an institution. To meet the test of being an institution, education must: regulate behavior; deal with perennial, basic problems of society; and invoke norms and sanctions to regulate the desired behavior. Again the basic question arises: Does education qualify to be called an institution? The functions of education supply an answer.

The primary function of education in the United States is to prepare citizens for occupational roles. Expanded technology and industrialization have increased greatly the need for semiskilled, skilled, and professional workers. Conversely, the demand for unskilled laborers has decreased. In today's society, most of the occupational roles thus require some degree of specialized training and literacy. Consequently, the primary purpose of education is, in fact, the preparation of the citizenry for occupational roles.

Another function of education is the preservation of culture by passing it from one generation to another. Still others are: to encourage democratic participation by teaching students to think rationally and independently; to produce citizens who understand their nation's history and who are dedicated to its future; and to build "character," however that may be interpreted, in a given time and place (Hobbs & Blank, 1975). All of these functions provide an ideology for education and fulfill the requirements for being designated an institution.

The codes of behavior expected of their members also are unique features of institutions. Education embraces this aspect. There are organizational patterns (K-12, elementary, secondary, postsecondary), compulsory attendance laws, and a formal system of education that place the participants in predetermined situations causing people to act in defined roles. In the United States, children are expected to attend school until they reach the age of 16 (Salmon, 1973; Brubacher, 1973). Different kinds of degrees and certificates help determine when children can enter and leave the system, and degrees are given to those who complete specific knowledge requirements. Parents condone this system by their acquiescence to these rules and expectations and continue to abide by the expectations imposed by the educational system.

Another significant trait of an institution is that the behavior patterns involve norms and are given additional weight through sanctions. Education is the accepted vehicle for citizens to use for upward mobility and to change their status quo. The prevailing theory behind behavior follows this line of thinking. The more education people have, the more it enhances their chances for a better job. Parents are expected to sacrifice to enable their children to obtain more education and the perpetuation of the "American dream" passes from generation to generation.

According to these criteria, education is institutionalized. This can be documented by the fact that education can organize human activity into predictable behavioral patterns and make the biological, social, and cultural continuity of society possible (Goldberg & Deutsch, 1977).

However, the similarities that mark families and education do not end here. Education also is very much a system since it contains a formal and informal learning network. The formal component contains schools—the major subsystem of this learning system. This subsystem consists of public elementary and secondary school populations organized from the kindergarten level through high school. It also requires that schools educate children between the ages of 5 and 18 based on the various combinations and groupings of grade levels. The schools' character is evidenced by trained intelligence as indicated by IQ tests, is easily identifiable through classroom attendance, and awards diplomas and other formal credentials (Marion, 1976).

The boundaries of this subsystem approach are limited here to special education. Special education is the subsystem that operates schools to meet the needs of students with special needs. This approach was described by Cruickshank (1967):

> Exceptional children, defined as children with differences, have both the same needs as do their peers and some different needs pertinent to their type of exceptionality. Special education must meet both needs in its effort to bring exceptional children and youth to the maximum of their developmental potential, and to prepare them adequately for a satisfactory life adjustment as adults who may also have differences (p. 22).

Discussion focused on the family and education is necessary to ensure that the parallel comparisons as institutions and systems are clear. However, this parallel approach does not provide a convincing picture of the linkage that exists between two comparable and established entities. Therefore, it is important at this point to discuss this interaction.

FAMILY AND SCHOOL INTERRELATIONSHIPS

This linkage is effectuated when the child enters school. By giving the child leave from the family circle, the parents have accorded the schools equal status for the pupil's well-being. This concession by parents to schools has not been effected without some uneasiness. The scenarios played out by parents and children on the first day of school each year are classic examples. Separation from children at this juncture is an emotionally stressful time in parents' lives.

Parents and children are not certain about their acceptance in an alien environment. Thus both are filled with apprehension upon arrival at the school.

Parents of handicapped children are undergoing these emotional stresses at the same time. From the day of handicapped children's birth, not many of their families have lived without crises. The apprehension that they feel is heightened by the addition of the child's handicap.

Teachers, too, are not without their uneasy moments. Many ponder over, "I wonder who I'll get new this year," or pray for "just some of the good group that I had last year." In any event, teachers enter a period of anxiety until they get to know their class.

Most teachers and parents have survived the uneasiness of these opening days and have gone on to experience good and bad days and times in their interactions involving the children. The stresses have remained, however, since differences have surfaced that at times have strained the normal working relationships between the two parties. From the time of entry until the young adult leaves the world of formal schooling, parents and teachers negotiate an uneasy truce in the interests of the child. Most parents have accepted the role of the school as a primary caretaker in the welfare of the child. Schools have tended to regard parents with mixed feelings as they attempt to fulfill the roles of primary caregivers and educators.

In effect, the schools constitute a system that starts out by synchronizing its activities with those of parents having children in schools. This unified effort produces some desired behavioral results in children during the elementary years and parents are pleased. Parents see their children imitating their own behavior and therefore encourage schooling.

However, as parents watch their children pass into the adolescent grades, some (or many) begin to experience dissatisfaction with the products that their children have become through schooling (Passow, 1976; Brown, 1975). Consequently, teachers and families become antagonists rather than allies. Parents working within their informal family circle fail to understand why the tried and proved way of teaching parenting skills no longer is operative. They tend to blame schools and seek to effect change. In fact, they have been called the "third force" in education, school board members and teachers ranking first and second (Brown, 1975). Schools, on the other hand, react with apprehension, dismay, or anger to charges that they are not educating children to be good parents. As the argument rages, those who suffer most are the children. In the United States, neither parents nor schools are allowed to hurt children, so both parties are obligated to settle their differences for the good of society.

However, this story is not complete because it omits families and children with special needs. The revolution in education of the 70s was fought by the third force (families) on behalf of their children with special needs. Although they believed in the developmental stages proposed by Freud and Erickson

(1967), they failed to see the school as a partner in the process for their children. They watched their children contained in special classrooms enjoying second-class citizenship away from the mainstream of public school life. Parents experiencing all the effects of a sometimes hostile society felt they were being asked to do the job of educating alone, without much help from school. Perhaps more importantly, they wondered if their children's bleak present was their career option for the future. So they requested arbitration. National arbitration came in the form of legislation for the exceptional child.

The past may have been bleak but the Education for All Handicapped Children Act of 1975 (P.L. 94-142), which was signed into law November 29, 1975, has brightened the future for parents and families with exceptional children. This law has encouraged teachers and parents to become partners in the educational process. It also has encouraged the two groups to reevaluate the parent-teacher involvement process, not only because of its relationship to learning but also because of the total emotional atmosphere that had existed between the two systems—families and schools. The next chapter examines further the atmosphere surrounding exceptional children and their families.

Chapter 2

Effects of the Exceptional Child on the Family

As stated at the end of Chapter 1, an emotional atmosphere surrounds the family with an exceptional child in its midst. Ross (1964) reported that "it matters not whether an exceptional state exists in the child's condition or in the parents' perception." In essence, he reaffirmed the fact that the exceptional child cannot be viewed in isolation and should be perceived within the context of the family system. Ross also perceived that certain psychosocial changes occurred in the family and that the child passed through designated developmental changes. What was important was the parents' perception of the quality and quantity of the change in that development. If this reasoning is applied to the normal family, it indicates that both the parents and the child are expected to pass through such developmental stages. These developmental tasks as conceptualized by Freud, Erickson, and others are universal in nature. From these points of view, the child can be described as having an "identity" or a state of being.

While Ross was describing the state of *being,* there is another perception that alters the dynamics of the family with an exceptional child. This view is related to the verb *to be.* The importance of this verb is that it introduces the factor of genetics into the interaction patterns of family systems. The outcome of this process has enabled parents with exceptional youngsters who might be caught in high risk situations to make decisions concerning having any more children.

It should be noted that while "genetic disorders diagnoses" techniques have reassured some families, they also have caused disharmony in others. The genetic factor also has introduced moral questions concerning how the information is to be used. Consequently, high risk parents often find themselves caught in the dilemma of to be or not to be since all too often they must face the question of whether to have children. Other secondary concerns such as family stock and religious and cultural factors enter the picture. These, too, tend to supersede the primary birth defect question. Secondary considerations have obscured intrafamily and interfamily relationships to the extent that disruptions in the form of

9

separation, divorce, and isolation between or from families and friends have occurred. Thus, primary and secondary parental concerns about the possibility or reality of a handicapping condition in the child has characterized the "to be" or "being" family circle.

VARIABLES AFFECTING PARENTS' REACTIONS

Genetics

While birth-defective children have long been a fact of life, only recently have many parents of these children become knowledgeable enough to seek counsel concerning future pregnancies. Some newlyweds have become sufficiently concerned about their ability to conceive a normal child that they seek prenatal diagnoses. The outcome of both of these deliberations has had an impact on the reactions of the couples.

In some cases, the information has brought some parents to the realization that they never could conceive a healthy child. This knowledge sealed the fact that they never could fulfill the societal function of normal parenthood. Many young couples who received such information experienced problems of adjustment. Some were affected so deeply that they divorced or separated. Others turned to extramarital affairs. Many sought solace in the comfort of alcohol and drugs (Marion & McCaslin, 1977). Couples who already had a defective child also had family disequilibrium burdens. The disclosure that a mate was the precipitator of the exceptional child led to questions about the integrity of that marriage partner. Changes in attitudes and feelings toward the opposite mate also have been reported (Schilds, 1968). Full disclosure of adverse genetic information has led to divorce or to a change of spouse. Changes in the marriage partners' self-image have led to feelings of isolation, bitterness, bewilderment, and confusion. Therefore at onset (before birth) or when anticipating another child (prenatal diagnosis), the expectancy of a birth-defective infant becomes a factor for disequilibrium in the family circle.

Social Acceptability of the Handicap

Historically, societies have not dealt fairly with defective children. In ancient civilizations, children were destroyed if they were not physically and mentally ablebodied. The medieval ages saw mentally defective people become the court jesters or become subjected to ridicule and scorn. The movie, *The Hunchback of Notre Dame,* was a prime example of the fate of the physically defective person. In later civilizations, defective people sometimes were believed to have magical powers or were regarded as the devil's handiwork. The former were called "les enfants du bon Dieu" while Luther and Calvin thought of them as "filled with Satan" (Mandelbaum & Wheeler, 1963).

Until Clifford Beer's memorable book *(A Mind That Found Itself)* appeared, nineteenth century Americans tended to confuse mental retardation with mental illness and with insanity. Modern attitudes toward the handicapped in the 1970s were shaped and changed only through the tireless efforts of parents and professionals in the courts, legislatures, and public forums. Although the extremely negative attitudes of earlier years are not considered dominant in today's society, certain feelings of fear, anxiety, and embarrassment still consume parents and professionals alike when they view defective persons.

Mothers and fathers still are shamed by the birth of Down's syndrome (mongoloid) children, more so than are the parents of a learning disabled child. In the case of the latter, learning disabled is viewed as more socially acceptable than mental retardation, which carries a connotation of dumbness. The blind child can become an object of instant pity while the hyperactive, emotionally disturbed child can elicit fear and anxiety in the onlooker (witness the increase in the use of Ritalin). Most people today respect crippled or blind persons and do not believe their intelligence is limited. These same persons might regard the multihandicapped child as a "vegetable" and feel pity for the parents. A definite stigma is attached to some forms of exceptionalities that does not extend to all kinds of handicapping conditions.

Degree or Severity of the Handicap

Parents may become upset if they discover that their child has been born with an afflicted extremity. They could be overwhelmed if their child is born without a leg or arm. A mildly retarded child regarded as "slow" with no physically distinguishing features might be more acceptable than the Down's syndrome child, who is instantly recognizable by the "fold" in the eyes. However, the degree or severity of handicap often is not directly proportional to the reactions of parents. Barsch (1969) indicated that there were no significant differences among parents that could be attributed simply to the child's disability category. On the other hand, some parents of severely retarded children testified that since the severity of the handicap was obvious at birth, they were better able to handle the feelings and emotions evoked by the condition.

Socioeconomic Level of the Family

Family socioeconomic levels have had an impact on the perception of handicapping conditions. Some lower socioeconomic families regard a birth-defective child as an "act of God." If the child is "marked," parents and family members are not overly concerned and tend to take care of "their own." Another family at the same point on the socioeconomic scale may not regard mental retardation as a debilitating condition but may consider a physical handicap as an extreme limitation in the child's functioning. These conflicting feelings may be congruent with the stance that strength is to be desired and those who do not have it are at a disadvantage, and that mental ability (or lack of it) has nothing to do with strength since their jobs involve hard manual labor.

By comparison, families higher on the socioeconomic ladder may view the presence of a mental handicapping condition as a real limitation. They may be convinced that the child has little chance of equalling or surpassing their socioeconomic status and has punctured the "American dream" syndrome of a better life for succeeding generations held by many parents. If achievement is held in high esteem by these family members, anything less than a child of average intelligence can cause dissonance because his cognitive limitations prevent him from achieving the goals projected by the parents. Since the child manifests mental deficiencies, he is not perceived as positive reflection on the parents and therefore the handicap is identified as a source of frustration and disillusionment to them.

GENERIC REACTIONS OF PARENTS

In the final analysis, the birth of an exceptional child certainly has had an impact on the psychosocial interactions of the family system. The degree of that impact varies according to many of the factors mentioned earlier. Categorically or generically, parents' reactions to the birth of a handicapped child are similar. Within this framework, the following parental reactions have been identified and linked with the attitudes often expressed by families with exceptional children.

Projection (of Blame)

One of the most frequently expressed emotions of parents with a defective child is the feeling that someone else is at fault for their misfortune (Cohen, 1963). This defense mechanism takes many forms and directions. Parents direct their anger at one another. Those who previously expressed mutual feelings of love vent their hostility upon each other. These feelings are sparked by some of the factors cited previously that persuade couples to have children. The child is the object of a dual sharing; he is the creation of their joint efforts to produce the "perfect being." Since the need for a healthy child is not fulfilled, the parents become angry over a dream deferred.

At other times, their frustration may be directed at the attending physician over an imagined insensitivity to the mother's need or the incapability to respond to the diagnosed deficiency. Hostility may be directed toward support personnel (social worker, nurse) as the parents' feelings about the child begin to consume them. Finally, anger can take the form of self-pity as parents continue to wonder why a defective child is their form of "punishment."

Guilt

Closely associated with the feeling of anger is the parental reaction of guilt. Much has been written of this reaction. However, guilt is a complex emotion that can take many forms. Sometimes it emerges in the form of punishment. A parent by self-incrimination feels that the defective child is the adult's reward for sinful acts. Some parents may have been responsible unintentionally for the defective child through their own failure to obtain adequate medical care (Richmond, 1972). A classic example is the parent who unwittingly has been exposed to rubella, resulting in a child that is deaf-blind or multihandicapped. Guilt takes another equally destructive form: parents may abuse a defective child physically if they view that child as an abnormal being and feel that he needs to be punished.

Since guilt is such a complex phenomenon, its outward manifestations may be cloaked in martyrdom, overprotectiveness, or depression. It is not uncommon for the mother to expend enormous amounts of time with the handicapped child to the exclusion of other family members. Other mothers become so protective that the child is not provided the developmental opportunities or stimulation needed for growth. Depression is another manifestation of grief. This climax of the grief process can be temporary or long-term and may result in an unresponsive parent. When that happens, the byproduct may be a psychologically and physiologically neglected child.

Denial

Parental use of denial causes many family conflicts since it appears so early in the reaction process. It can be destructive and useless or it can be a useful mechanism as parents seek to find a neutral ground for their feelings about the exceptional child. If the parents refuse to believe that their offspring is handicapped, the child may be prevented from receiving an appropriate education and supportive services under current legislation. Uselessness lies in the fact that the problem will not go away simply because the parents decline to accept or realize the handicap. Denial is destructive because it places the child in a quandry between fact and fantasy in his everyday world. The child is further precluded from functioning as a full participant in the world of school activities.

Outwardly, parents manifest this mechanism by giving inappropriate explanations of the child's developmental lag. They speak of their child's development as being slow now but hope it will become normal in time. Another expression of denial may be centered on a gross misunderstanding of the physician's explanations. The family is repulsed by the doctor's comments and develops a blind spot concerning the exceptional child. This leads into the third form of denial—the incapacity to discuss the problem outside the family. In this atmosphere, the persistent use of the defensive mechanism of denial can lead to a serious break in the family's lifestyle.

However, manifestation of denial is not always destructive or useless. Often, it helps parents at the outset when they are attempting to get a grip on the exceptionality. It can sustain a fantasy until they can cope with the full realization of a less than perfect child. Physicians, teachers, and other professionals can use the opportunity afforded them through consultation to assist parents in understanding the long-range implications of the handicapping conditions.

Sorrow, Grief, or Mourning

The three emotions—sorrow, grief, or mourning—in this section are linked closely by one denominator: sadness. They can be considered the natural responses to the loss that parents feel. Humans always have grieved over the loss of a loved one. So it is with the birth of a handicapped child. Parents recognize the presence of the exceptional child as the loss of the perfect being, a disappointment to their dream of personal fulfillment. It is an oversimplification to observe that everyone grieves when a loved person is lost. Parents of a handicapped child recognize that their moment of despair will last a lifetime. Therefore, their emotions of sorrow, grief, and mourning are for the child who will never be. To these parents, these emotions may be therapeutic or may be the forerunners of more serious problems.

If the parents need time to recover, the intense feelings of sadness and grieving may have a healing effect. After a time, they may become calm and begin to see the child as a youngster with a handicap rather than as an albatross. Only when parents continue to be despondent over an extended period are they likely to be overrun by their feelings of grief and sorrow and succumb to an escape into despair and worthlessness.

Withdrawal

One of the most common characteristics of persons who have been hurt, frightened, saddened, or denied has been a retreat from reality and a move toward isolation. Withdrawal is resorted to frequently by parents of handicapped children who feel that other relatives, friends, or professionals may not understand their situation. Other parents may adopt this defense mechanism because of the intense feelings of guilt and shame that consume them. Some parents choose to isolate themselves from others to shield themselves from the scrutiny of outsiders.

In essence, withdrawal can be viewed as parents' preoccupation from an internal or external standpoint. Internally, they attempt to handle emotions such as fear, grief, and anger by retreating from their normal states of mental health (Hammer, 1979). Thus they submerge themselves in their other children or assume a martyr's role as they withdraw from normal activities. Externally, they plunge into their work or stop going out or eating out. Refraining from these social functions helps them to keep the eyes of the public away from the family and the exceptional child.

Rejection

Everyone has a desire to be somebody. Achievement of this goal has assured persons a sense of belonging and has served to satisfy a fundamental need (Maslow, 1954). One of the prerequisites of good parenting is that adults be loving and accepting human beings. Therefore, when parents treat children unduly harshly or are inattentive to their needs, others are quick to point out the inhumanity of their actions. In fact, if normal children are subjected to severe neglect and abuse, society admonishes the parents. Rejection of children is not viewed in a favorable light.

On the other hand, parents expect to produce a perfect infant. Failing to do so, a couple may use this imperfection as an excuse to reject the child. Many parents reject the child just because of his appearance. Some are reluctant to hold the infant or do not include him in family activities. Still others exhibit rejection by conflicting expressions of love and acceptance. They declare strong feelings of warmth and affection for the child but their real feelings are exactly to the contrary, and they do not dare express their real sentiments to others. If they had done so, they would have contradicted society's expectations of "good" parents. With such high expectations placed on good parenting, and on a sound mind in a sound body, it is easy to see how parents can succumb to helplessness and reject the less-than-perfect child.

In summary, a word of caution: recognizing that all of these defense mechanisms can be therapeutic as well as harmful, the professional must guard against being caught in the "negative tide." Because of these emotions, parents of handicapped children have long been viewed in a negative light. The true picture that emerged in the 70s was of parents' passing through different periods of developmental and emotional crises not dissimilar to those experienced by other parents. However, society's attitudes, molded inappropriately until of late, contributed heavily to an unfavorable perspective of parents of exceptional children.

CRITICAL NEEDS OF PARENTS

While parents of normal children pass through crises precipitated by developmental periods and psychosocial events, parents of exceptional children are more likely to experience uncommon stress at certain periods. At such times, the parents' needs can be expected to escalate as the additional stress is introduced into the family unit and threatens their mental health. Barraga (1966) identified six needs that must be met for parents of cerebral palsied children. Hammer (1972) generalized these needs to parents of multihandicapped and deaf-blind. These six needs can be expanded to apply to all families of exceptional children. Parents need:

1. emotional understanding and support
2. information and facts
3. a greater degree of active participation in the planning of habilitation
4. to maintain an identity of themselves as parents, as participating members of the community, and as competent individuals within themselves
5. a thorough and dynamic understanding of their role in the habilitation process
6. to know the present and future expectations of the handicapped child (p. 10).

The meeting of these needs has served a complementary purpose for individual parents in the family unit. Marmor (1974) has illustrated the interaction between variables that have an impact on mental health. An understanding of the variables of personality and stress has helped scholars assess the mental health of individuals. This interaction demonstrates that mental health is related to personality and stress. All individuals have the potential for mental health and for mental illness.

As each of the critical needs in the lives of parents of exceptional children is examined, it is possible to relate them to the stress caused by these offspring. (See Figure 2-1.) Additional comparisons can be drawn concerning the mental health of individual family members. These can be reviewed in light of the actions and reactions of the parents in critical periods in their lives.

CRITICAL PERIODS IN PARENTS' LIVES

Recognizing that stress occurs in the lives of all families, Hammer (1972) noted there were certain situations in the lives of parents with exceptional children that precipitated stress:

Figure 2-1 Variables Affecting Mental Health

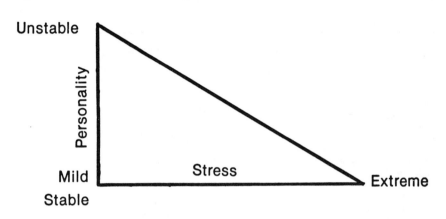

Source: Judd Marmor, *Psychiatry in Transition,* Bruner/Manzel, Inc. © 1974. Reprinted with permission.

1. at birth or upon suspicion of the handicap
2. at time of diagnosis and treatment of the handicapping condition
3. as the child nears age for school placement
4. as the child nears puberty
5. as the child nears the age of vocational planning
6. as parents age and the child may outlive them (p. 10).

A graphic chronology delineating when threatening conditions occur and when stress results in the family is shown in Figure 2-2. Since the diagram is designed to demonstrate the relationship between crisis periods and critical needs of parents, the following section discusses patterns of family adjustment.

Crisis Periods and Critical Needs of Parents

The first crisis time is the birth of the handicapped child or the point when an exceptional condition is suspected. During this period of anxiety, parents are consumed by strong feelings and emotions of fear and apprehension. There is a critical need for them to receive emotional understanding and support. Professionals should interpret this need within the framework of normal parental reactions.

It is to be expected that parents of exceptional children will experience mourning, guilt, depression, and other emotions as normal expressions of a loss.

Figure 2-2 Crisis Periods and Parents' Critical Needs

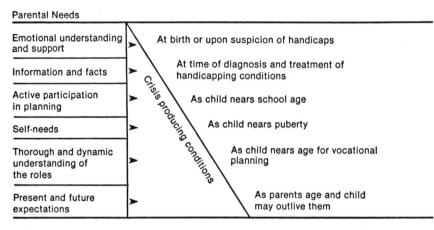

Parental Needs

Emotional understanding and support	At birth or upon suspicion of handicaps
Information and facts	At time of diagnosis and treatment of handicapping conditions
Active participation in planning	As child nears school age
Self-needs	As child nears puberty
Thorough and dynamic understanding of the roles	As child nears age for vocational planning
Present and future expectations	As parents age and child may outlive them

Source: Ed Hammer, *Families of Deaf–Blind Children: Case Studies of Stress,* from a paper presented at the American Ortho-Psychiatric Association, Dallas, © 1972. Reprinted with permission.

Mourning especially is not solely the province of those with disabled family members. From the beginning of time, civilizations have observed periods of mourning for their lost loved ones. More importantly, parents must be accorded the opportunity to run the full gamut of emotional reactions. If professionals provide support and understanding, they will have assisted parents in achieving a satisfactory state of mental health that produces equilibrium in the family and results in a positive self-concept in individual parents. Professionals can help parents by allowing them to proceed in unhurried fashion through these negative reactions. Although there has to be movement both ways, (Figure 2-3), the support and understanding helps parents to conquer the negative feelings and to function in a relatively normal state of mental health.

The second of these crisis periods arises at the time of diagnosis and treatment of the exceptional child's disabilities. In this time of need, parents search for a way to understand why an exceptional child was born to them and why their child is defective. They seek facts to explain their dilemma and the conflicting emotions that engulf them. Parents are confused and stress develops as they and other family members attempt to gain a proper perspective of the effect of the handicapped child.

Parents face several dilemmas during this period. They have sought answers and information. However, the physician may have become angry, annoyed, or impatient with parents who return visit after visit with the same questions (Richmond, 1972). Consumed by anxiety, and bolstered by such defense mechanisms as denial, projection of blame, mourning, and guilt, the parents ''shop around''

Figure 2-3 Professionals and Parents: A Two-Way Street

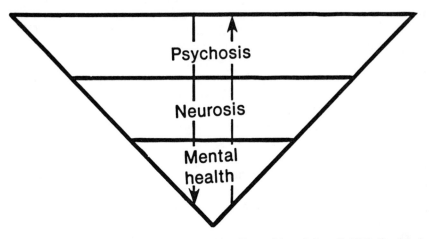

Source: Judd Marmor, *Psychiatry in Transition,* Bruner/Manzel, Inc. © 1974. Reprinted with permission.

for assistance. Their dilemma often was compounded in previous years by a lack of established places to seek information (Klein, 1971). Thus, while parents were being viewed in a less than favorable light by some professionals, they were sincerely seeking assistance. Stress, therefore, was a way of life with these families until their anxieties were diminished and were dealt with by thorough assessment and explanation to their satisfaction. Failure to do so by the helping professionals could move parents and other family members to the right of the Marmer triangle (Figure 2-4) and away from a degree of normalcy in their state of mental health. The ultimate result of such nonresolution eventually can lead to such discord that divorce and family dissolutions occur (Ohshansky, 1963).

A third time of crisis arises when the exceptional child approaches the age for school placement, either preschool or elementary. Anxieties reach another height when parents become overwhelmed by the questions of whether their child will be accepted by school personnel and other children or considered a "funny looking kid;" whether their child will receive an appropriate education or be placed in educational "isolation;" and, most importantly, whether the school will be able to "understand" the child and to meet needs as perceived by the family.

Two Kinds of Families

Professionals face two kinds of parents at this juncture. One is the parent who has lived with the handicap since the child's birth and has an awareness about the exceptionality. The other kind involves those who for the first time confront the knowledge that their child is "different" (Barsch, 1969). The "labeling" process often is bewildering to parents and tends to obscure the other, more pertinent concerns mentioned earlier. Parents, faced with the vast array of educational decisions and tempered by their own conditioning to schools, again are besieged with strong feelings and emotions. These questions and anxieties produce stressful situations that force families to find coping mechanisms to survive. Again, the ability of individual members to resolve intrafamily conflicts produced by an external force (school) can influence their mental health.

Parents, therefore, must be involved actively in planning the rehabilitation and education of their children. While P.L. 94-142 requires parents' active participation, they often come to school with dreadful anticipation and foreboding. They need understanding and support to decrease their anxieties and feelings of isolation. Parents also need information and facts about the school program, about their role, and about the extent of their involvement in the home-school relationship.

The age of puberty, the fourth time of crisis, can be a trying time for all involved—parents and adolescents. Disability or multiple handicaps do not stop the exceptional adolescent from undergoing some, if not all, of the emotional,

Figure 2-4 The Marmor Triangle of Stress and Personality

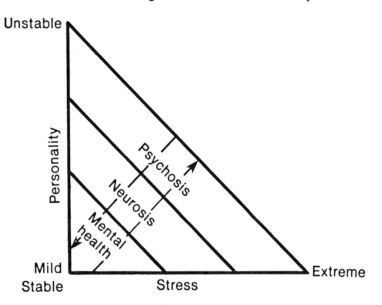

Source: Judd Marmor, *Psychiatry in Transition,* Bruner/Manzel, Inc. © 1974. Reprinted with permission.

social, and physiological changes that emerge with puberty. Difficult as the period may be for "normal" adolescents and parents, it increases the stresses on the families of exceptional children. The parents are faced with a bewildering array of questions and crisis-evoking situations that call for adjustments within the family structure. How does the family cope with the mythology of sex and handicaps if even professional workers are unable to provide satisfactory answers? Questions about conflicting sex mores continue to plague society in general and are a source of continued worry for these parents. They often resist the question of whether they wish their children to be reproductive.

On the other hand, the handicapped adolescents face a time when differences between their peers and themselves are accentuated acutely. Faced by discrimination and conflicting parental and peer behavior directed toward other siblings and themselves, they find themselves in a period of isolation, loneliness, and frustration (Hammer, 1972). Emotions and feelings that arise during this period can be destructive to their parents and families.

Emotions and feelings run especially high when talk turns to the sex education of handicapped adolescents. Parents are distraught because the subject matter is different (Johnson, 1973). They do not regard sex education as a subject matter in the usual educational sense. This also causes a furor in the schools. Study committees have considered its desirability in the curriculum. Objective knowledge still is tied up with moral values and religious attitudes in both families and schools.

Attitudes notwithstanding, exceptional adolescents for the most part still have a broad range of sexual vigor and interest equal to other teenagers. Johnson (1973) outlined these learner characteristics. Although he restricted them to the mentally retarded, they can be equated with those of other handicapped teenage populations:

1. Labels like "mentally retarded" tend to create and to conceal the individuals under them.
2. The so-called "mentally retarded" like the so-called "normal" person is likely to, but does not necessarily have a strong interest in sex.
3. The mentally retarded do indeed tend to be mentally retarded with respect to sex education.
4. The retarded, like the rest of us, tend to decline in level of functioning intelligence as emotional upset increases.
5. Like the verbally normal, the mentally retarded have to deal with a language barrier when confronted with sex education.
6. Mentally retarded people, like most other people, are interested in sex primarily for its potential sensual gratification.
7. The mentally retarded also share with the "normal" population a lack of virtually anything in the way of systematic training in child

rearing or any other orientation as to what having children might
be all about in either a personal or broad sense (pp 58–60)

Caught in the middle of these feelings are exceptional adolescents who need
guidance at this crucial juncture in their lives. Equally distraught are parents
who are concerned over activities such as masturbation, orgasms in sleep, premarital petting, and premarital sex. Johnson (1973) advises these parents to:

1. know the basics of the subject matter
2. be informed of the characteristics of the particular learner population
3. come to terms with his or her own sexuality
4. come to terms with the languages of sex, both the technical and
   the vulgar
5. be aware that the goal of sex education is not to eliminate all sexual
   responses and that sexual interest or behavior is not sinful, intrins-
   ically evil or sick (pp 63–64)

Since the subject of sex education tends to distress parents, Gordon (1973)
suggested basic points that parents should attempt to communicate to teenagers:

1. Masturbation is a normal sexual expression no matter how frequently it is done and at what age.
2. All direct sexual behavior involving the genitals should take place
   only in privacy.
3. Any time a girl and boy who are physically mature have sexual
   relations, they risk pregnancy.
4. Unless both members of a heterosexual couple clearly want to have
   a baby and understand the responsibilities involved in child-rearing,
   they should use an effective method of birth control.
5. Until a person is 18 years old, society holds that he or she should
   not have intercourse. After that age the person can decide for
   himself.
6. Adults should not be permitted to use children sexually.
7. The only way to discourage homosexual expression is to risk heterosexual expression.
8. In the final analysis, sexual behavior between consenting adults
   (regardless of their mental age and of whether their behavior is
   homo or hetero) should be no one else's business, providing there
   is little risk of bringing an unwanted child into this world (p. 69).

Parents need understanding as they face the threatening situation of watching
the handicapped child become an adult. Professionals must lend support and

provide information and facts to parents and to adolescents who are frustrated at this juncture in their lives. Parents especially need help as they seek to maintain an identity as concerned adults whose actions toward their newly emerging adolescents will not be condemned as poor parenting practices by society. Professional understanding and support can assist these parents in a movement away from viewing their children in protective light to a view of self-actualization (Maslow, 1954).

The fifth crisis period occurs when the parents and the young exceptional adult are faced with the problem of making vocational choices. Nonimpaired young adults find this a difficult time. It becomes an even more stressful situation for handicapped persons and their parents, who must face the problem of choosing an appropriate career. Another difficulty revolves around the question of employment and training. Is immediate employment available or must training be provided? Is the job dead end or is there an opportunity for advancement? Will worker job satisfaction correlate to the employer's? These and other questions must be addressed from a continuum that reaches from a sheltered workshop context to an independent worker concept.

Parents need understanding and support at this stage because they have lived for a long time with the handicap. They need information and facts so they can separate the reality of the situation from an emotional wish list of possible career choices for their sons and daughters (Alexander & Clements, 1975). Parents need involvement in the rehabilitation process in order to become active and intelligent participants in the educational and career choice processes with their young adults.

Alexander and Clements (1975) have pointed out another dilemma that accentuates this crisis period for parents: many parents believe that their children's disabilities will disappear after they participate a given number of years in special education. Parents with these kinds of expectations are shocked to learn that progression through the school environment with minor adaptations often does not lead to employability. Parents of some populations (learning disabled and emotionally disturbed) are more vulnerable to this expectation than others. Therefore, parents at this time of crisis need information as well as understanding as they begin to revise their perceptions concerning their child's future.

It is this need that precipitates the final crisis period and enlarges the scope of parental problems. The time of crisis is the realization that the child may outlive parents as they grow old and move into the twilight years.

There have been many reasons why parents are fearful of this period. For one, the worth of a person in society is measured by that individual's ability to hold a job. If disabled individuals are poorly equipped to obtain and sustain themselves in jobs, they often suffer a demoralizing blow because of the loss of the position. Braginsky and Braginsky (1975) spoke to the loss of self-concept that occurs when a person suffers from the inability to hold a job and also reported on the high cost of wearing a label (handicapped). The label plus the prospect of unemployment or underemployment of their young adult progeny create a serious source of concern to parents.

For a second reason, many parents of exceptional adolescents are not sure of the present and are even more skeptical of the future. Parents need facts and information so that the future is not a nebulous picture. They need the opportunity to communicate with professionals concerning their hopes and fears for the adolescent. Similar communication with the youth also is desired, if possible. Parents need understanding and support when their fear of the future is that their children may outlive them. So great is this concern that some parents express the hope that the child "dies before I do."

A great need also arises for parents to have their self-needs fulfilled. Satisfaction of these needs can help them to see the adolescent as a person rather than as an inanimate object. Those with a positive self-concept are likely to be better able to function as parents and as participating members of the whole community and to have reality-based perspectives of the present and of the future. Realistic goals can be set and parents can assist professionals in working toward achievement of goals and career aspirations. At this stage, parents need to be reinforced over and over again about the positive aspects of the child's present and future.

SIBLINGS AND OTHER FAMILY MEMBERS

Parents face several key periods in their lives that can be identified as crisis times. Satisfaction of needs that coincide with these stages consumes much of the parents' energy within the family. However, the family circle often is not confined to the parents and the exceptional child. When examined from the perception of the other family members, the dimensions of needs can be illustrated by the use of Maslow's (1954) hierarchy of needs model. Through this model, the total needs of the family can be viewed.

CONCERNS OF THE NORMAL SIBLINGS

Need To Belong

A phrase often quoted by parents of exceptional children is: "It is not the quantity of time that I spend with my children but the quality that counts." While many parents subscribe to this philosophy, there is limited evidence that it is their actual practice. Too many parents fail to recognize that the normal siblings are beset with feelings, anxieties, and strong emotions about the brother or sister with the handicap. Normal siblings are caught between the parents' desire to give quantitative attention both to them and to the exceptional child. Perhaps the handicapped child needs extensive medical care or a series of related services such as physical or occupational therapy. Parents can have a love for their normal siblings but can be thought of as uncaring by these same individuals. A seeming lack of attention, real or imagined, due to the parental involvement required by the exceptional children can be interpreted by the normal child into a feeling of not belonging.

Some parents deliberately neglect their normal children and become martyrs for the exceptional child (Ross, 1964). As other siblings react to this parental role, they have been known to develop somatic complaints in their attempts to gain attention from their parents (Cohen, 1963). Unhealthy concerns and anxieties about the handicapped child can have the effect of causing parents to become oblivious to the needs of nonhandicapped children. Faced with these apparent expressions of inattentiveness, normal siblings often translate their feelings of being left out into antisocial behavior. Therefore, parents are confronted with sibling-parent situations that either transcend the traditional child-parent issues or introduce conflict into an already tenuous situation.

Need for Working Through Feelings and Emotions

Normal siblings have feelings about the handicapped child that often are translated into negative reactions that affect their state of mental health. In the event that the normal children feel that the handicapped sibling is the center of family attention at their expense, they may have strong feelings of hostility, anger, and resentment. Parents may think they are giving quality treatment to the normal sibling but that child may have a different perception of the situation. Quality time may be viewed as "less" time to the normal sibling and "more" time to the handicapped peer. This situation can leave the normal child with a feeling of being left out (Cohen, 1963).

A feeling of guilt may be aroused when normal siblings find themselves resentful about the amount of attention given to their handicapped counterpart. This feeling may develop from the ambivalence that normalcy brings. Looking at the handicapped sibling, the normal child may have a feeling of relief that he is not the person with the handicap. On the other hand, the normal child's feeling of good fortune is balanced by a resentment that the parents are capitulating to the handicapped sibling's every wish.

Closely allied with guilt may be a feeling of fear in the normal child. Younger normal siblings may have anxieties that they will become blind or deaf in the future. As they are growing into young adults, adolescents may fear that they might become the parents of a defective child. That fact can be substantiated by the large number of adolescents who are seeking genetic counseling (Marion & McCaslin, 1978). The fear probably is more pronounced in girls than in boys because females, looking at the intense relationship between the defective sibling and the mother, suspect that they too might be expected to do likewise if their family is affected. However, males appear to have been spared the responsibility of caring for the handicapped member of the family (Grossman, 1972).

Need for Truth in Communication

Lack of communication or misinformation between parents and normal siblings can lead to mixed feelings toward the handicapped child. The failure of parents to communicate openly and honestly with siblings about the nature of the handicap often leaves normal children with feelings of embarrassment and shame in social situations. Siblings may be embarrassed to reveal how uninformed they are about the handicap of their peer (Grossman, 1972). Many are ashamed to be seen in public with their handicapped brother or sister. Others cloak their embarrassment by not inviting their friends into their homes where they fear an explanation of the condition of the handicapped family member might be necessary. Older children especially can find it difficult to explain a handicapped sibling to a date (Cohen, 1963).

In every family with a handicapped child, the normal siblings have needs that must be met if they are to make the necessary adjustments for harmonious family relationships. Although research in normal sibling behavior is limited, some evidence (Grossman, 1972) indicates contrasts in lower-income and high-income family adaptations to a handicapped child. The most striking contrast is found in the primary impact of the handicapped child. In the upper-income family, the mother, because of her close contact with the children, subtly and clearly conveys her attitude toward the handicapped children. She can foster in the normal sibling an attitude of love, resentment, fear, or guilt toward the handicapped child. This is not the case with lower socioeconomic siblings, where parental reactions seemed to have little effect on their current thoughts and feelings about the handicapped member of the family (Grossman, 1972).

CONCERNS OF THE EXCEPTIONAL CHILD

Need for Truth in Communication

Just as parents want information and facts (Alexander & Clements, 1975), exceptional children have similar desires. Unable perhaps to express their wishes at an early age, they need to be dealt with in an honest and truthful fashion as they grow older and become more perceptive. For instance, children who must endure the scrutiny of numerous professionals (i.e., speech therapist, physician, physical therapist) have a right to know the facts about the nature of the handicap. As soon as they are able to understand and to benefit psychologically from an explanation, exceptional children should be given truthful information about how the exceptionality will affect their lives. This honesty and openness in communication should begin early with the handicapped child and should continue throughout his life span. It is particularly important that both entities that play such a vital role in the child's development (family and school) interact within the framework of P.L. 94-142 and the crisis producing periods (Hammer, 1972). That law was designed to facilitate communication among parents, teachers, and students. Parents have an opportunity to work with the exceptional child before he enters the schooling process. Upon entry into the formal school system, parents, teachers, and children should strive to become active participants in a communications network. This network should be constructed with the following need of the exceptional child in mind.

Need for Self-Actualization

Maslow (1954) conceptualized self-actualization as the ultimate need to be satisfied in his hierarchy of needs. Simply stated, self-actualization is interpreted as enabling all individuals to develop to the fullest of their potential. Public Law 94-142 was proposed to afford parents and schools additional opportunities to assist handicapped children to reach their maximum potential. For instance, the priorities assigned to severely and profoundly handicapped individuals under the law have given new hope to these children and their parents. Parents now are not obligated to consider their handicapped children as "vegetables" but can permit themselves the luxury of seeing a future for them.

SUMMARY

The handicapped child should emerge from the educational unit as a functional entity in society. Parents now are excited about the prospect that their exceptional children will receive an appropriate education in the least restrictive environment. They have no desire to discuss their child as an inanimate object. As a result of P.L. 94-142, some handicapped children will be educated with peers as much as possible. Others will be schooled in self-contained classrooms. Whatever the process, the handicapped child should be directed toward becoming a functional adult in society. This functional ability must become the goal of the parent-teacher-child relationship.

The birth of the exceptional child can have a traumatic effect on the family. Parents will pass through several stages of adjustments until they finally achieve a satisfactory level of acceptance. These adjustments are linked closely to critical periods in the lives of parents. As they pass through these critical times, they constantly seek to attain a positive state of mental health that will permit them to remain functional members of the family unit.

Other members of the family also are affected by the presence of the handicapped child. Siblings have varying reactions to their handicapped peers that give rise to needs that must be addressed to enable normal children to readjust to the altered family circle.

The exceptional child has needs that equal those of the normal sibling. This child not only experiences the developmental periods of normal youth but, in addition, seeks to adjust to the handicap within the family. Therefore, attitudes of parents and peers cannot be disregarded as facilitators or detriments to the adjustment of the handicapped individual in the family system.

Finally, the school has become a primary resource for the development of the exceptional child. Public Law 94-142 has thrust the special educator into a new and viable relationship with the parents and the family. This partnership has not adopted the "in loco parentis" doctrine of the prewar years. Nor has it succumbed to the adversary role of the 60s. Instead, special education, the teacher, and parents are breaking new ground as they work toward the goal of fulfillment (self-actualization) for the handicapped child.

Chapter 3

Roles for Helping Teachers in Special Education

One year after the passage of P.L. 94–142, a major challenge hurled at special educators was: "Professionals Are You Listening?" (*Closer Look,* Winter 1976). Teachers and other special education personnel were asked to take a fresh look at old roles. Parents were urged not to view special educators as awesome and inaccessible objects but as human beings with whom continuing dialogue was necessary and possible. Professionals were asked to acknowledge the equality that now existed between parents and special educators without any false barrier of status. In total special education, professionals and parents were expected to regard one another as equal partners and were thought to be entering a new atmosphere where the sharing of human problems was the number one concern.

In 1977 another slogan emerged: "What Does It Take to Make a Law Work?" (*Closer Look,* Winter-Spring 1977). Judging from the comments, parents indicated that they did not find the responsiveness from school personnel that they expected. Moreover, taking a more belligerent stance, parents now were exhorted to:

1. know the law
2. work with other parents
3. work with professionals
4. use the right to speak
5. stop pleading; education is a right
6. learn how to take part in planning conferences
7. remember: don't compromise—insist on full evaluation and clear goals.
8. be an active citizen (pp. 7–8).

Furthermore, feeling that there were "miles to go," parents were encouraged to keep fighting the status quo.

Finally, finding that confusion still was commonplace as special education teachers and parents grappled with their roles, parents were admonished to use their rights and to participate fully in the decision-making process. Consequently, they were expected to become involved in due process proceedings and to be full-fledged members of the educational planning team.

A NEW PARENT-TEACHER RELATIONSHIP

The passage of P.L. 94-142, the Education for All Handicapped Children Act of 1975, established a new relationship between parents and teachers. The act required that parents be considered allies in the education of their children and guaranteed all exceptional students the right to a free and appropriate education. While it is readily apparent that P.L. 94-142 demands a more sophisticated teacher approach to working with parents of exceptional children, it makes it clear that a sharing relationship must be established.

In the past, working with parents in a helping relationship probably was one of the teacher's least enjoyable tasks. This probably was due to the fact that teachers and parents tended to misplace the blame for the child's inability to learn. In these previous encounters the teacher might have felt that:

- the parents blamed the teacher for the child's problem
- the parental indictment of the teacher's techniques and interaction styles was overly harsh
- the parents wasted precious teacher time in useless conversation

On the other hand, parents might have perceived that:

- the teachers blamed the parents for the child's behavior
- the teachers were critical of parents who attempted to interfere with their management of the classroom
- the teachers were annoyed by parents' involvement in advisory committees and/or school curriculum changes

When these teacher-parent responses were viewed in the light of past relationships, infrequent joint contacts can be explained easily.

Today, P.L. 94-142 has changed dramatically the manner in which teachers must respond to the needs of parents with exceptional children. This new direction is chronicled ably by Alexander and Clements (1975) and Kelly (1973). Therefore, rather than review the historical trends of parental involvement, it can be said that the United States has moved from a position of limited parent involvement (Bijou & Sloan, 1966; Brown, 1969) to the present position of parents' extensive involvement in the educational programming of their children (Kroth, 1975; Grim, 1974). Initially, under P.L. 94-142, as teachers were re-negotiating their position with parents, most of the pressure upon educators was for even greater parent involvement in the curriculum planning for the child. Most teachers, working in the confines of the school planning period and/or in the insulation of the home, would have had little trouble creating Individualized Education Programs (IEPs). The dilemma underlying the law was the fact that teachers now not only were required to involve parents in educational planning but also were expected to work openly in committees with parents whose decisions concerning program accountability, child placement, and decision-making authority must be shared.

While most parents were eager to share in this new-found power, the dilemma facing teachers, new and experienced, was becoming manifested in the abdication of old roles. Barsch (1969) outlined the paradox that faced teachers in working with parents of handicapped children in earlier historical accounts. He noted that parents formerly assigned the educator the status of "specialist" or a positive role since they tended to believe that the endorsed classroom teacher had been "trained" in this area while they as parents were ill-equipped to deal with the child. On the other hand, he discovered that most teachers held a negative perception of parents and leaned toward control of their domain, the classroom. Therefore, he concluded that this culturally-oriented bias was at the root of many of the dilemmas faced by the teachers in their day-by-day operations.

However, the situation has changed considerably. Teachers no longer are held in awe by parents and their educational expertise is being challenged constantly by the general public through the media. There has been little that teachers could do to counteract the tide of blaming all societal ills on permissive open schools that are accused of having failed to teach the basics or on weak administrators who are said to have hired "radical," unprofessional teachers to mind the children. In this new day, teachers are seeking to counter the feeling that parents are to blame for the problems of their child. They are attempting to accomplish this by establishing the parents' coequal status. This is being done by letting parents know that their observations and viewpoints are important in developing a clear and concise picture of the child. This has meant that teachers not only must learn to work with parents who want to be allies but that educators also must deal with those who might want to abdicate all responsibility and involvement in the teacher-parent partnership.

SUCCESSFUL ROLES FOR TEACHERS

When the question of parent-teacher cooperation is viewed now, the following premise can be adopted: parent involvement means different things to different people. Most of today's professionals endorse the concept enthusiastically and often cite parent involvement as a needed link between the home and the school. Within this framework, some professionals view parents' involvement as counseling. Others think of this involvement as parent education or as teaching certain competencies to allow parents to continue school instruction in the home. All too frequently, educators conceive of parent involvement as merely a conference where information is exchanged and reported between coequals. Many other educators see their role as planners and convenors of parent group meetings. Professionals also regard themselves as referral agents, directing parents to community and other support agencies (Marion, 1979).

On the other hand, parents may perceive their involvement as teacher/learners being taught specified competencies by professionals. In turn, they are encouraged to teach specified skills to their children. They may see themselves as information seekers and conduits of that information to others. Sometimes they view their roles as advocates and agitate vigorously for changes in the educational plans of their children. Many other parents share the perspective that they are consultants to teachers and seek to maintain a coequal posture in the teacher/learner process (Marion, 1979).

In the final analysis, it does not matter what view is held. Today, both parties place great value in the concept. Therefore, whether parent involvement is viewed from the perspective of parent or educator, one thing is certain: it can be considered a permanent phenomenon.

Within these parameters, has P.L. 94-142 laid the burden of responsibility too heavily upon teachers? When all options are considered, the teacher does have the capabilities to work with parents within the framework of the act. However, to carry out the intent of the legislation the teacher will have to adopt three roles, becoming (a) an advocate, (b) an ombudsman, and (c) a case manager.

TEACHERS AS CASE MANAGERS

The term "management" has been identified most commonly with the world of business and industry. In the late 1960s, the business phrase "management by objectives", or MBO, became a catchall for educators, particularly administrative personnel such as superintendents and principals. Management also became a popular euphemism to replace the word "administration" in educational jargon as discussions regarding supervision responsibilities turned more and more to the "management team" concept. Furthermore, even teachers entertained the management phenomenon as teams of teachers instead of principals sometimes were appointed to supervise the operation of their schools. However, the majority of managerial or administrative responsibilities were thought to be associated with more well-known educational management types—superintendents and principals.

Management and administration are terms used synonymously to denote individuals who have the ability and/or authority to make decisions. Since decisions about children are made by all educators in systems and schools, administrators and teachers have tended to establish particular domains of control. Superintendents carry out the policies of the school board and are the chief administrative officers of the school district. Principals are assigned the roles of midlevel administrators on the "team" by the superintendent and are site managers (schools). Teachers traditionally have been thought of as managers or controllers of the classroom. Although control of the respective "turfs" has been established and agreed upon at each level, arbitrary decisions made by participants have caused conflict.

Adding to these disputes over territoriality and managerial prerogatives, special educators, administrators, and teachers have been given more stringent guidelines than those imposed upon educators working in mainstream education. Under P.L. 94-142, school districts are required to provide quality educational programs for handicapped children. Superintendents have allocated much of the leadership thrust to principals. Principals in turn have sought guidance from those most affected by the legislation—the teachers. This has been in keeping with the delegated managerial chain of command in schools.

Relationships also have changed between administrators (principals) and teachers, however, under P.L. 94-142. Most principals no longer have the luxury of declining or agreeing to participate in special education programs. Moreover, the law has structured the instructional means whereby education must take place. Under the act, instruction and related services are set forth in an IEP. The methods for obtaining the goals and objectives of the IEP are vested in the special education teacher. This unique instructional arrangement calls for the principal to depend more heavily upon the special teacher to assume more managerial obligations inside and outside the classroom. Special educators are expected to know the law under which they operate, to work with the internal systems at the site, and to coordinate the interaction of external systems (parents and other social service and health and medical agencies). These duties are sanctioned under P.L. 94-142 and are presumed to be manifested in an agreement (IEP) between parent and school. Any serious disagreement resulting from the contract calls for the participation of the special educator in still another capacity: giving expert testimony in cases requiring either external or internal adjudication.

Having been placed in such a demanding position through P.L. 94-142, special educators have been compelled to take an ecological view of management. They will seek to integrate the three environments in which the child will be found: the school, the home, and the community. Thus, they have become "catalytic" case managers. They are characterized by the way they interact as catalysts with parents and professionals within the parameters of the IEP. First, case manager special educators must have the ability to recognize differences that exist in the various publics with which they work. They must develop the capacity to vary their leadership styles according to the situation or to the demands of individuals. Second, case manager special educators who are catalytic leaders must be knowledgeable about P.L. 94-142 and realize that any actions on their part are governed by the law. Therefore, they must have a working understanding of the act and must be able to interpret it in everyday terminology for parents. Moreover they must be prepared to be patient until parents can develop an understanding of the law.

Developing Parents' Confidence

Having been patient until parents feel team oriented, the case manager special educators now can begin considering the task of imbuing parents with the desire to try harder and to develop confidence in their ability to work with the child. Case managers capitalize on the parents' desire to help and act as facilitators of the IEP. The case managers' role evolves into a coaching format. Their catalytic managerial style takes the form of helping parents to decide upon a plan and of answering the questions that arise from decisions about how the plan is to be carried out. Meetings must be held in an open atmosphere and case managers must assist in the decision-making process by working to:

1. get parents involved in the IEP process
2. prepare parents for their roles and responsibilities in the IEP process
3. teach parents how they can function as partners on the educational team
4. train parents for their role in the IEP meetings
5. help parents assess their child's educational progress
6. provide information to parents on due process and on the impact of recent laws and litigation upon the education of handicapped children
7. increase parental awareness about services available and how to obtain them
8. build communication skills to further the school-parent partnership

In carrying out any of these activities, case manager special educators must have a grasp of the guarantees of P.L. 94-142 and have the capacity to work within the organized plan (IEP) without feeling that their leadership prerogatives are being threatened. Thus, the catalytic special education case manager must take steps to make sure that parents are involved in IEP planning. Case managers should invoke in parents a feeling that their concerns about the child's placement, goals, and objectives will be given consideration equal to that given to professionals' opinions.

Realizing that parents are motivated by the self-satisfaction of seeing the child improve, special education case managers must take a variety of scheduling initiatives. When scheduling conferences, case managers are governed by the required regular meetings (annually), home visitations, or other regularly scheduled follow-up home activities. Regularly scheduled conferences are used to discuss the child's educational program, family involvement in home learning, and family needs. Home visitations are carried out to provide parents with skills, information, and support to assist them in meeting the needs of their children. Follow-up home activities are characterized by the educational activities that can be done at home with siblings and/or parents (i.e., puppet shows, rhythmic activities, flash card reading exercises).

The Role of Public Relations

Another case manager function with parents involves public relations. Successful special education case managers usually carry out a well-articulated public relations campaign. They use such means as a parents' handbook, newsletter, notes, and informal contacts to keep parents informed, to answer questions, and to reduce conflicts. Moreover, they attempt to use all these avenues to provide answers to the following questions:

1. Why does the program exist?
2. What is the source of funding?
3. What ages and types of children are served?
4. What are the program's beliefs toward the rights and needs of handicapped children?
5. What kinds of certification does the program provide?
6. Is information available about transportation, registration, health, safety, and other special considerations (parking, pickup regulations)?
7. Are parents allowed to visit the classrooms?
8. How are parents involved in decision making, program planning, and evaluation?

In addition to answering these questions, catalytic case managers must realize the importance of personalized contacts with parents. To meet this need, many special educators have been quick to program themselves to achieve maximum use of their most precious commodity—time. They program themselves to be prepared to greet the early elementary child and parent at mutually agreeable times. They are not caught dashing frantically around setting up the room and getting ready for the day. Realizing that most parents' schedules are not flexible, good case managers hasten to inform parents when schools are not in session or are dismissing early.

Successful case managers resist the negative tide that has enveloped some special educators. They do not avoid meaningful contact with parents. Instead, they assume that parents are concerned about their children and have read the various informational materials about their offspring. Thus, they use the informal occasions to give positive feedback. These special education teachers seize the opportunity to use pickup and arrival times to give impromptu positive messages to parents. They are equally careful to be brief and specific while reporting positively on the child's progress.

Attitudinal Changes in Educators

Understanding the need to build a cadre of more and better informed parents through a systematic approach to achieve these desired goals, case managers must take leadership responsibilities in working to effect an attitudinal change among fellow educators. Major leadership efforts in the area of public relations should be expended to sensitize colleagues to the needs of handicapped children and their families. Energy should be directed toward gaining a thoughtful first-hand acquaintance of the environment in which colleagues work and spend their time. Once this insight about others is gained, case managers should attempt to focus upon and meet their concerns through a comprehensive information exchange program. Case manager special educators become fact finders. They take the time to become thoroughly familiar with the working situation so that they can supply the information that can be used to dispel any myths surrounding the handicapped. They allocate ample time to gather the facts about expected problems so that attention can be given to appropriate planning and educational programming.

Successful case managers should set up appropriate times for efficient committee operations. Moreover, they must have an appreciation for efficient committee operation. Within this framework, case managers take care to ensure that all participants: (1) have an understanding of the limits of their committee responsibility in IEP planning and implementation, (2) have an appreciation of time in committee scheduling assignments and (3) are mindful of their responsibility in making periodic committee reports.

In working with colleagues, the staffing process offers one of the greatest opportunities for case managers to be catalytic leaders. Since the IEP is a plan of action, case manager special educators are looked upon as the persons who initiate the plan. Consequently, they are expected to:

1. explain to the committee the various special education options, possible modifications, and the strengths and weaknesses of each approach
2. stimulate the sharing of knowledge from other staff members who will participate in the placement decision
3. help make a professional judgment about the student's ability to complete the given curriculum, given specific modifications and supportive services

4. suggest ways mainstream educators and other professionals may gain additional information and skills necessary for work with handicapped students
5. suggest areas of internal and external support

As they continue to work within the IEP framework, case manager special education teachers strive to improve the plan by inspiring other professionals to do their best with the child. They must stimulate others by their performances and lead by example. They must adhere to the objectives of the plan and list detailed activities that place a premium upon helping the child reach the IEP goals. Case managers should not be discouraged easily, realizing that in some cases—the multihandicapped—results will not show up in the short term. Consequently, they should commit themselves to working for long-term results.

Developing Confidence

With both parents and coworkers, case managers must transmit a message of confidence in their ability to work together. Problems must be identified by all participants concerned with the child. Having identified the problem, case managers enlist the aid of the participants in a problem-solving approach, encouraging the participants to be creative about the child's problem and to brainstorm for ideas to bring about the desired improvement. Prompted by the actions of the catalytic case manager, colleagues and parents will be willing to enter into a working IEP arrangement.

Special education teachers have a special obligation under P.L. 94-142 when assessing their role as case managers. They must recognize that, basically, the planning and implementation of the IEP process is a study in communication. Reduced to its essentials, communication in this context is concerned with *who* says *what* to *whom* through which *channels* with what *effect* (Fusco, 1967). Thus, in taking any action concerning parents, special education case manager teachers should be propelled by the realization that parents are apprehensive about their new roles as equal partners. Basically, parents recognize that their total involvement in the educational planning and implementation of programs is a complex undertaking by school and family. Moreover, they are not yet consumed by feelings of overconfidence about their participation. In fact, the parents' confidence level about their participation probably ranges from little to none. These feelings leave many parents afraid and confused.

Case manager special educators must minimize parent misgivings and maximize parent involvement. Recognizing that parents and educators are establishing a new foundation for managing education, case managers must develop specific communication skills to build respect and trust with parents.

Attentive Listening

Case managers should strive to become empathetically aware of the feelings of parents toward their child.

> What the parents feel about their children's behavior, and how they express such feelings—these are important elements that require a constructive parent-teacher relationship (Kelly, 1973, p. 351).

Thus case manager special educators should seek to acquire the listening and attending skills so they can work with parents to:

1. identify the needs and concerns of parents as they relate to the needs of the child or youth
2. select appropriate strategies for responding to parental needs and concerns
3. improve upon or develop a positive working relationship between professional and parent
4. create additional chances for subsequent positive ripple effects on the child

By assuming an attentive listening posture, these special educators can assure the parents that their presence is important. They also will reduce the chances that parents will leave the conference or encounter dissatisfied with teachers. Since many meetings are charged with emotions, listening can be likened to courageous work (Rogers, 1961).

Case managers must work hard to get themselves in position to like many persons without placing conditions on acceptance. Those who cannot stomach the sight of the "low income" or "know it all" parent already have placed obstacles in the path of attentive listening. Attentive listening should be geared toward allowing parents to feel free to state their case without being judged. Special educators should convey the impression "I am listening to what you say with no 'ifs,' 'ands,' or 'buts'." (Rogers, 1961). Listening in this manner, case manager special educators can defuse emotionally laden situations by assuming a non-evaluative stance and listening with understanding. For instance, when parents say things are "great at home" but whose haggard, drawn appearance belies their words, listening case managers can move quickly to find out the problem behind the discrepancy and to understand the problem from the parents' point of view. Case manager special educators must put themselves in the parents' frame of reference so well that they can respond to and summarize their perceptions.

Responsive Feedback

Case managers must prepare to provide responsive feedback to parents within the context of their meetings or encounters. The interpersonal communication skills that facilitate immediate feedback can be identified as open-ended questioning, paraphrasing, giving illustrations, acknowledging previous comments, repeating previous comments, and sending nonverbal cues. These immediate feedback communication skills should be valued highly by case managers who wish to facilitate interactions between parents and professionals. If properly used, they can be applied by case manager special education teachers to:

1. be ego-supportive and nonthreatening to parents
2. help parents clarify their feelings and needs
3. serve as checks that parents and teachers understand each other
4. reduce the tension of volatile situations between parents and professionals
5. exhibit flexibility in working with parents and colleagues

Responsive feedbacks can be used by case managers to speak to the ego-supportive needs of parents. Case managers can use open-ended questions and acknowledgments of feelings to answer the parents' questions of: "Am I accepted?" or "Can I really trust this person?" Thus, case managers who are receptive do not make evaluative statements such as, "You're the child's parent and he is your responsibility" or "The child is not that hard to take care of." Instead, the educators will hear the parents' cry of "nobody ever helps" and will acknowledge their previous comments with a statement such as, "You're right, one can't be sure what the right answers are, and that can be very upsetting." Case managers who use the open-ended question technique are asking for parents' impressions and reactions. Thus, they ask, "Can you tell me more about it?" These response techniques can make parents feel adequate and accepted.

Responsive feedbacks also can help parents clarify their feelings and needs. As they seek to resolve the five issues just cited, case managers can use all of the responsive feedback tools as they attempt to answer the following questions:

1. Do parents and professionals trust one another?
2. What are the acceptable and unacceptable ways for parents and professionals to express different kinds of feelings in this setting?
3. Are expressions of feelings open and spontaneous?
4. How much variance is tolerated in individual styles of expressing feeling?
5. Is the importance of the expression of feelings accepted?
6. How much divergence of self-interest is tolerated?

Case manager special educators will have to use all available responsive feedback techniques to:

1. help parents and professionals to share feelings and ideas spontaneously

2. enable parents and professionals to discuss their own weaknesses and strengths
3. elicit from parents and professionals their honest feelings
4. report the effect of the way parents and professionals are reacting to each other's behavior
5. help parents and professionals express feelings and deal constructively with feeling content
6. accept expressions of feelings and encourage parents and professionals to express themselves in their own way

SUMMATIVE EXPLANATION

Up to this point, case manager special educators should have been involved in giving instant feedback to parents and other professionals in their discussions. This is necessary to ensure that a spirit of trust and respect is established among special educators, parents, and other professionals. Case managers must move past this position of instant exchange to continue promoting information exchanges and to clarify roles. Therefore, they should consider adopting the skill of summative explanation. The skill of summative explanation can be gauged by case manager special educators' ease in using concise summaries to give a brief, complete account of action at different intervals in the parent-professional encounters. To accomplish this objective, the case managers first should listen carefully to understand what parents and professional colleagues are saying so they can share their feelings. Then, when summative explanation is used, case managers speak directly and to the point. They report how others feel about the fact that they are being influenced. They offer their own views about how perceptions are being experienced by parents and professionals. They also clarify the meanings and interpretations of various individual perceptions. Finally, by summarizing, case manager special educators check their own perceptions against those of others to test for congruence.

The strength of the use of these skills in case management situations is evident if teachers recall and describe instances when someone helped them. Persons who helped them might have been following these principles and:

1. Made it clear that he/she was not "taking over" the problem—we had the responsibility for it and we had to do our own thinking about it.
2. Indicated in many ways that we were neither "stupid" or "unusual" because we had a problem.
3. Helped us see the values of working on the problem
4. Seemed to be aware of some reasons why we were having the difficulty but didn't tell us what was "wrong" with us.

5. Asked us valuable questions about the nature of the problem, why it occurred and what symptoms were evident.
6. As we talked further, helped us to set up criteria for testing our ideas about solutions (Jenkins, 1951, pp. 4–5).

In conclusion, then, teachers as case managers should do three things in their encounters:

1. allow parents to maintain their personal integrity and self-respect
2. give parents increased motivation to work on the problem
3. give parents help on methods of solving problems

As a result, parents gain greater confidence in themselves and increase their ability to cope in their lives with exceptional children. This outcome must be the priority of the case manager special educator.

SPECIAL EDUCATION TEACHERS AS ADVOCATES

One form of advocacy advanced for educator consideration has been voiced ably by Payne (1970). This perception of the advocacy role maintains that in order to effectively ameliorate the condition of individuals or groups made disadvantaged and relatively powerless by prejudice, injustice, and social institutions, it is necessary to actively espouse their interests and to contend with the institutions and practices that have caused their disadvantaged status or that are effectively preventing its remediation. Wolfensberger and Zauha (1973) proposed another model that stressed the universal desirable characteristics of the special educator advocate role. Their perspective held that:

1. the advocate must have a type of community stability which can sustain its relationship to the protégé.
2. the advocate must be willing to undergo training.
3. the advocate must understand the specific advocacy mission.
4. the advocate must have competence in whatever advocacy role or task he/she assumes.
5. the advocate needs to make a commitment to the mission.
6. the advocate should display "good moral character" as judged by the community after selecting his/her advocacy mission (p. 24).

Still others (McLoughlin, McLoughlin, & Stewart, 1979) have described the role of the advocate in behavioral terms. Distinguishing between internal and external advocacy, they clearly have shown a preference for the former concept. Instead of demonstrations, demands, negotiations, and legal action, they contended that internal advocacy as "a continuous and cooperative process between parents and teachers as partners in guaranteeing the rights of the handicapped child to appropriate services" was best suited for teachers of exceptional children.

However, viewed as a concept, the role of advocate must be given serious consideration by the special education teacher. While external advocacy might be frowned upon by educators in certain situations, internal advocacy also has its limitations and advantages. Perhaps the advocacy concept can be better fitted to the special educator if it is not seen from an internal/external focus but rather from an ecological vantage point. In this framework, special education teachers work within three systems to effect change for the child and to promote the parent-teacher partnership. Swap (1978), describing these three networks, called the first level the behavior setting and included in it the physical environment, program of activities, inhabitants, and location in time and space. Parents and children are components of the setting, influenced significantly by the expectations, constraints, and opportunities available in that setting.

Special educators also work at a second level in the ecological (advocacy) approach: child-environment and parent-environment situations that help them understand the behavior of the same child at home or school or the behaviors of children labeled handicapped and nonhandicapped in different settings.

Community and culture form what Swap termed the third level of influencing factors. Advocate special educators should pay heed to formal structures (educational, mental health, social welfare, legal, correctional, and religious systems) that affect the surroundings and programs for children of handicapped parents (Rhodes & Head, 1974). Advocates should have an understanding of the informal transmitters of cultural values (social networks, local newspapers, television programs). Finally, they should have an awareness of the physical characteristics (population density and housing patterns) that may affect the child's and parents' access to the service delivery system.

If the role of advocate special educators is conceptualized in this manner, the possibility of a debate over their internal and external advocacy is minimized. Special educators should be freed from a restraint to act either as an external or internal advocate and should work as parent-child advocates in an unfettered framework. Moreover, when this viewpoint is held, advocate special educators can claim a legal, theoretical, practical, and research-based identity (McLoughlin, McLoughlin, & Stewart, 1979). An ecological perception of advocacy can expand the capacity of the special educators to join in actions as external agents through their acquired knowledge that efforts to achieve parity for the parents often extend beyond the school walls.

Rights of Parents and of Teachers

In any assessment of the advocacy role, the family must be considered as a unit. Schools also cannot be expected to function in isolated existence apart from families. Thus special education advocates have the weight of P.L. 94-142 to assist them in whatever efforts they undertake on behalf of the child and parents. Although the act guarantees parents the right to due process, to non-discriminatory testing, to education in the least restrictive environment, to free access to the child's records, and to be involved in the development of the IEP, there have been wide variances in the way parents perceive these rights. Conversely, there often have been discrepancies in the way schools have communicated these guaranteed rights to parents. Parents frequently have felt abused and have looked for relief to the teachers as the first line of defense for help with their problems. Therefore, special education teachers should be well versed in the strengths of their position as well as in the problems implied in the ecological concept of advocacy.

Five major rationales have been proposed for parent advocacy by educators (McLoughlin, McLoughlin, & Stewart, 1979):

1. *Legal*: Public Law 94-142 has provided this base through its guarantees to parents. The rights granted to parents should become the foundation for parent-school interactions.
2. *Theory:* Knowledge is being accumulated that demonstrates the importance of parent involvement at all levels of educational programming.
3. *Research:* Investigative data are showing favorable results when parents interact on behalf of their children.
4. *Practical:* Special educators are finding out that parents lend credibility to programs. Community support is gained and chances for adversary positions between home and school are lessened.
5. *Moral and Ethical:* Special educators should be concerned that they have a responsibility to assure that parents are being treated fairly (pp. 52–53).

Thus it can be seen that the case for the special educator to function as an advocate is strong. However, these teachers should be forewarned of the problems that accompany advocacy actions. While Payne (1970) has applied them to the social worker, they can be perceived as being equally valid from an educator's point of view. He pointed out that problems arise from these areas:

1. Status: (a) Teachers are public employees and are dependent upon public support for their continued existence, (b) teachers are not hired to serve exclusively as advocates, and (c) the teachers will not automatically oppose every action that is inimical to parents.
2. Limits: Teachers are confronted with the problem of how far to progress in active involvement without transgressing appropriate professional behavior (pp. 14–16).

Therefore, in making a decision to assume the role of advocate, special educators who view the position only from an external or internal viewpoint will have serious problems attempting to reconcile the functions. Those who accept the internal advocacy model because it makes them "feel better" or fulfills a "don't rock the boat" stance have neglected their ethical and moral obligations to parents and children just as fully as educators who are unwilling to approach any issue without an antagonistic attitude or a confrontational action. Special educators who want to be effective advocates should project their images as three persons in their efforts to bring about change. Advocate special educators will be identified as "significant other" persons, "tender loving care" individuals, and "taking care of business" personnel. All of these image makers can be projected as vital to the composition of the advocate role for special educators.

Significant Other Persons

Significant others have been described in two ways:

1. parents, siblings, and close friends, since they made vital contributions to the development of the personalities of children and youth
2. persons whose effects have had a lasting influence on individuals' behavior and outlook on life (Hobbs & Blank, 1975).

Special education teachers have long ascribed to the second definition. Suffice it to say they have functioned as significant others in the lives of handicapped children for an appreciable time prior to P.L. 94-142. Several authors have chronicled this crucial function (Larsen, 1975; Hobbs, 1974; Morse, 1974; Dunn, 1968). Therefore, the coverage of significant others here is focused chiefly upon special educators' involvement with parents.

Tender Loving Care Individuals

Tender loving care individuals are most likely closely aligned to the Carl Rogers and Abraham Maslow schools of thought about human beings. Maslow (1954) offered a hierarchy-of-needs theory to explain human motivation. He saw people initially fulfilling basic needs and moving toward the highest need fulfillment of all—self-actualization. Rogers (1961) envisioned the "fully functioning" person as being an accepting person and understanding individual needs of others who were different. This capacity to accept others and to help them move toward self-actualization has been the trademark of tender loving care teacher advocates (Hamachek, 1971; McCandless, 1967).

Taking Care of Business Personnel

The taking care of business (TCB) educator is not given to allowing parents to participate in destructive compensatory behavior. Rather these teacher advocates engage parents in activities:

1. that allow them to select satisfying and useful endeavors which reflect their strengths and weaknesses
2. that stimulate them to express their ambitions in concrete effort
3. that help them to appreciate their positive attributes rather than worry about their negative qualities (Hamachek, 1971).

By incorporating all of these traits into the role of advocates, special education teachers have an opportunity to articulate effectively the position of parents when they are caught in crisis situations. Moreover, they are exempted from operating with a deficit parent model since all of these positions assume that special education advocates are according parents coequal status.

CRISIS PERIODS FOR PARENTS

Parents of exceptional children experience certain crisis periods in their lives. Many of these crises are associated with schooling when special educators are working with parents and have been occurring earlier in the children's lives since the passage of P.L. 94-142. This legislation has afforded special education teachers additional chances to advocate on behalf of parents.

One of the stressful periods occurs when the diagnosis has confirmed that the parents indeed do have a handicapped child. For perhaps the first time, parents now seek information about the nature of the handicap, wonder about the future for their child, and begin to raise questions about the educational opportunities available. Special education advocates have a responsibility to fill this void for parents.

One opportunity for advocacy is afforded when parents request information about the nature of the handicap and the educational prognosis for the child. Advocate special educators not only should fill the knowledge gap for parents but also assist in meeting their affective needs. Teacher advocates may have the foresight of being the only professionals with a positive outlook about the handicap. Their insight and knowledge of infant-parent programs is a plus in parent-teacher relationships. Advocates who provide infant-parent program information may find that their efforts have a balancing effect to the parents' initial feelings of loss. Working with parents, advocates can form some hypotheses about the preschool program for the child. At these times, educators can be considered significant others, tender loving care individuals, and taking care of business personnel.

Advocate educators are depended upon when medical, economic, psychological, and professional problems tend to overwhelm parents. Consequently, advocates should not allow parents to give up the dream for their child. Rather, they should expend most of their energy on assisting parents to adapt their dreams to a realistic focus. Much of the special educators' efforts should be geared toward helping parents to achieve a better self-image of themselves as persons and to establish a relationship whereby parents are willing to exchange information about the educational future of the child. Special educators should be alerted that the medical, psychological, professional, and financial problems may be outside of their problem-solving areas. Thus, they must enlist the support of social service agencies if these burdens threaten the well-being of the family. The presence of the advocate special educator is a steadying influence on the parent-teacher relationship as they work together in the referral process. These efforts by teachers are aimed toward alleviating the pressures of the environment or changing the delivery system. Again, significant other, tender loving care, and taking care of business advocates can make positive changes in the lives of parents.

As the child approaches the age for preschool activities, special education teachers often are called upon by parents in search of early childhood programs. The parents might be seeking information about P.L. 94-142 as it affects their children. This point of inquiry can be viewed as another opportunity for the advocate educator to act as a significant other, tender loving care, and taking care of business person. Special educators should not be rushed into making assumptions that parents are knowledgeable about P.L. 94-142 and its guarantees when initial inquiries are made. Advocates may have to pursue the parents' right to such information aggressively. In fulfilling this obligation, special education personnel may have to take the initiative in informing parents of their rights under the law. Some advocates undertake this task in individual conferences upon referrals from other parents with children in school. Others may meet the demand when parents form groups for exchanging information.

DEMYSTIFYING THE LAW

Regardless of the setting, advocate special educators must attempt to demystify the law and to make parents intelligent consumers of information. The advocates do not categorize information for parents. For example, certain kinds of information are not reserved exclusively for professionals, with other types of information considered all right for parents to know (Munsey, 1973). Advocate special educators must not use language that parents cannot understand. They must put aside educational jargon and hold discussions in lay language that parents can understand (Marion, 1979). They can be considered significant other, tender loving care, and taking care of business individuals since the evidence seems to indicate that in the order of importance to the well-being of children, teachers are regarded as second only to parents (Hobbs, 1975) or as the person parents turn to most (Torrie, 1973) when interacting with the formal system of schooling. Hence, parents are pleased to learn that P.L. 94-142 does provide incentive grants to states that wish to engage in preschool programs. Parents always are relieved to know that other parents are sharing like experiences. Consequently, information about parent groups or associations generally is well received.

Again, during this crisis state, advocate teachers must learn that they can continue to function as educational therapists in promoting the mental health of parents of exceptional children. In addition to dispensing and exchanging information, advocates often work to free parents from a "deficit" image relationship with schools. Special educators seek to avoid abusing the concept of significant other as it relates to the "expert" status conferred upon them by some parents (Barsch, 1969). These same advocates are not offended when other parents appear equally knowledgeable and request that they be granted equal partnership. Consequently, with both kinds of parents (compliant or demanding), special education advocates seek to address the level of need as determined by Maslow's (1954) hierarchy of needs.

Perhaps one of the most opportune times for the special educator to demonstrate the ecological approach to advocacy is presented when the child is preparing to move from preschool to the regular school program. Not only do advocates deal with environmental change, they also face parent involvement in program planning that might include restructuring the educational and support systems. For instance, special education teacher advocates face a myriad of tasks when they seek relief for parents of low socioeconomic level whose financial problems lead to distress and whose child is noticeably unattended. The advocates must help parents to obtain financial relief and to feel good about themselves. For these parents, advocacy efforts might be aimed toward gaining their participation in home-school activities and encouraging their acceptance into parent groups. Additional advocacy energies might be needed to help parents to seek relief from guilt reactions that might be perpetuated through abusive encounters with other parents and adults. The advocate special educator's role modeling as an understanding adult can help parents move into the belonging stage and eventually toward self-actualization.

However, the advocacy role is not limited to the uninformed or ill-educated public. Advocate special educators often are sought out by the more informed and well-educated parents. The advocacy function can be useful when parents and schools disagree over the proposed support systems for the child. In this situation, special education teacher advocates are not trying to ostracize parents, to quote school regulations, or to become impatient and to block communication. Rather, they are attempting to:

1. keep the lines of communication open
2. regard criticisms or rejections as directed toward the system, not to themselves
3. continue to suggest and explore workable alternatives with parents
4. remain calm and continue to work on the problem

Advocates who follow these guidelines can work through any of the parental crisis periods and through subsequent family stressful situations precipitated by the child's age and level of schooling.

The effects of this approach and the use of the guidelines can be mirrored in future advocacy actions by special educators. Crisis periods of adolescence, vocational preparation, and young adulthood then can be treated with a sensitivity while not minimizing the parents' urgency for action. Moreover, as students mature toward puberty and become candidates for vocational training, the time demands on special education teachers to advocate for parents will escalate. At the secondary level, parents increasingly are concerned and frustrated about the lack of total programmatic efforts for adolescents, the rising number of vocational mismatches, and the inability of teenagers to function effectively in society. All of these perceived needs have contributed to parental desires for advocacy efforts by special educators on their behalf.

PROBLEMS IN SECONDARY PROGRAMMING

Advocate special educators who want to work effectively with parents of exceptional adolescents should be forewarned that secondary programming is in a state of flux. Generally, it has been characterized by three kinds of educational programming. The first focuses upon the maintenance of the status quo. This type of program for exceptional adolescents is patterned after regular mainstream school routines and offers the regular fare of academic courses without much variety to meet the special needs of the exceptional child. The second type emphasizes modification of the regular program. This kind of program focuses upon regular academic subjects with some modifications and with some vocational preparation. The third kind opts for total alternatives to traditional adolescent programming, favoring the teaching of functional (everyday living prevocational) and work skills within the environmental framework in which the student is found (Wiederholt, 1980).

Key Assumptions Underlying Choices

When advocate special educators are faced with these educational choices and with anxious parents, they should be prepared to work from the following three assumptions:

1. Parents care equally about their teenagers as does the school—or more so.
2. Parents have a right to know about and to be involved in their adolescent's education.
3. Parents can become effective teachers.

From these assumptions special educators can acknowledge the right of the parents to take an active role in the education of the adolescent. Moreover, advocates should attempt to influence the behavior of adolescent and parents by providing the latter with activities and opportunities that are purposeful and satisfying learning experiences for the teenager. Advocates should encourage parents to model attitudes and habits appropriate to adult life skills.

Within this framework, advocate special educators work with the parent in choosing appropriate programs. Essential decisions concerning career development, vocational and academic needs, and functional living skills are given appropriate attention. For instance, when choosing the type of program, special education advocates are not governed by expediency or must choose the alternative that requires less energy and time or that costs less. Thus, advocate educators are not characterized by attributes that tend to be prejudiced toward school goals and are not equally reflective of parental concerns. Special education teacher advocates must be prepared *not* to:

- communicate pity toward the parents

- romanticize the needs of the children and youth

- keep parents in a dependent position

- seek to relieve the lot of the parent without altering the root causes of injustice

- allow fragmentation of services to occur (pp. 309–310) (Bikler, 1976).

Rather, when making program choices, special education advocates should perceive their role as:

- seeking to identify the conditions that make the parent dependent

- trying to understand the parents' feelings, experiences, and needs through their accounts

- expressing anger, not pity, toward the conditions that have dehumanized the parent

- accepting the disdain and criticism of those agencies and people whom they question (p. 310) (Bikler, 1976).

In attacking the problem of appropriate program choice, special education teacher advocates should be concerned that parents are involved in what will take place when the school assumes responsibility for the education and well-being of the teenager. By the same token, advocate educators should communicate to parents that the adolescent's best interests are served by close cooperation with the school. Whether the final choice of program is finalized as regular, modified, or alternative, special educator advocates face situational, curricular, and socioemotional problems when working with parents of exceptional adolescents.

Situational problems are prompted by the four dimensional environments of education in which adolescents interact—regular education, special education, vocational education, and vocational rehabilitation—all of which are related to the development of the teenager. Advocate special educators must work with parents to effect the right balance of these programs. While P.L. 94-142 calls for education in the least restrictive environment, it also requires that vocational education not be ignored in IEP planning. Section 504 of the Rehabilitation Act of 1973, charges employers with the responsibility of assuring handicapped persons an equal opportunity in the job marketplace. Finally, vocational rehabilitation legislation instructs rehabilitation specialists concerning the services they can provide to disabled young adults.

Choosing from Among Viable Options

With such a myriad of programs to be considered, special education teacher advocates face the dilemma of assisting parents to choose viable options. Choices must be made between (1) regular or traditional, (2) modified, or (3) alternatives. Whatever the situation, special education teachers should alert parents to the realities of the program. Thus advocates should inform parents about the traditional methods of educating adolescents, focusing on explanations of self-contained, resource room, and other traditional instructional arrangements. Advantages and disadvantages of each should be explored. Evidence that severity of the handicap has influenced self-contained placement should be presented. Additional information that reveals that normalization may be occurring in such situations should be discussed. A traditional program of part-time normalization with the exceptional child's normal peers in the resource room may have to be discussed. In this arrangement, supportive and other integrative services are used to enable the student to function on a regular or part-time basis in traditional classrooms.

Advocates who favor this type of traditional programming would be likely to convey to parents that what has been done traditionally in educational programming for adolescents is good enough to be continued. These special educators would be considered advocates of the status quo type of programs. Their curricula would tend to follow the predetermined programs of regular or traditional education. They view the self-contained, resource room, and regular classrooms as desirable habitats for the socioemotional growth of adolescents.

Special education teacher advocates who support a modified program approach with parents believe that existing programs need to be made appropriate for today's adolescents. Consequently, they do not disagree with past programs but strive to get curricular modifications from the predetermined course of study. While arguing for curricular modification, these advocates stress individual differences and ask for accommodations to these differences. The adolescents' socioemotional development is linked to their adjustment to the systems—home, school, and community.

Lastly, special education advocates work with parents under the belief that viable alternatives to traditional or modified programming should be considered. Advocates who are proponents of this method of educational programming go beyond seeking improvements in past programs. Instead, they are determined to work with parents to find new programmatic arrangements that fit the new lifestyles demanded of students in their generation. When this rationale predominates, the curriculum is decided upon jointly by parents, students, and educators, and guidance is made a vital part of the instructional program. Students are accorded major responsibility for their learning experiences. Socioemotional growth is linked to the development of responsibility, personal fulfillment, and freedom of choice.

Roles for Special Educator Advocates

Since parents value highly the opinions of teachers (Hobbs, 1975; Torrie, 1973), special education advocates who support these views of programs for adolescents can be considered significant other, tender loving care, and taking care of business individuals. The taking care of business advocate might work with parents to bring about change by:

- writing letters to set up a formal recordkeeping system of attempts to acquire services for handicapped persons
- establishing alternative model programs to existing traditional systems

- creating communication networks for community education
- attempting to simplify service delivery systems that tend to confuse parents
- working with other service delivery professionals to improve services to parents and adolescents

Likewise, special educator tender loving care individuals may be found advocating for:

- neglected adolescents whose parents have the resources to provide for them but are unwilling to do so
- indigent parents who are unable to provide the resources, skills, and knowledge needed by their teenagers
- adolescents and parents who are unable to receive the necessary support and assistance from other teachers and professionals to which they are entitled

Finally, significant other special education advocates are committed to the following principles:

- ensuring that parents are aware of the importance of the written and spoken language in educational planning and implementation for their teenagers
- striving with parents to create learning environments that will meet the socioemotional needs of adolescents
- deciding with parents and adolescents what curriculum is related to the skills and knowledge that will enable the youth to function as a competent adult in society

In conclusion, it can be said that the advocacy role has universal, humanistic, and ecological appeal for the special educator. Special education proponents have encouraged education for *all* children and youth, hence its universal approach. Special education has attempted to follow Maslow's hierarchy-of-need approach, thus offering a humanistic appeal. Recently special education has recognized, through the "least restrictive environment" requirement, the significance of fostering learning in various settings. Therefore, special education can be called ecological in its approach to formal schooling.

Special educators seeking to answer the question of how to support parents can try a new role within the parameters outlined here. This role can be fulfilled through advocacy.

SPECIAL EDUCATION TEACHER AS OMBUDSMAN

The ombudsman concept is a newcomer to the American scene. Its inception can be traced back to Finland and Sweden in 1713. There, the institution of ombudsman became synonymous with the protection of citizens' rights and interests. In the United States, the concept was introduced by Congressman Henry Reuss of Wisconsin, who sought unsuccessfully to establish a federal ombudsman office in 1966 (Payne, 1970).

Since the ombudsman idea is so new, some definitions of the term should be examined. One was advanced by Rowat (1968):

> The ombudsman is an officer . . . who investigates complaints from citizens that they have been unfairly dealt with by government departments and who, if he finds that a complaint is justified, seeks a remedy (p. 7).

Another explanation of the concept was offered by Rosenthal (1964):

> The ombudsman is a law officer, appointed . . . for the task of supervising the activities of certain categories of public service and of public authorities. His main concern is with the rights and liberties of the citizens. The supervision of the activities under his control has . . . the observance of the laws as its primary objective, not the general suitability of decisions (p. 227).

While these two definitions have been drawn from reputable sources, the phenomenon of ombudsman has undergone some changes in its application in the United States. Rowat (1968) commented upon these modifications:

> In the United States, the ombudsman idea has recently become so popular that the word "ombudsman" is now being used to describe any new complaint-handling or appeal machinery (p. 35).

Another author who recognized that a transformation was taking place was Anderson (1968):

> Strictly speaking, the word "Ombudsman" should be used in English only with the range of meaning which (Rowat) carefully defines. It may be, however, that we will follow the Swedish example and develop a vast array of ombudsmen. If so, we should follow (Rowat's) advice . . . and distinguish other applications—as the Swedes do—by

the use of modifiers: campus ombudsman, corporate ombudsman, etc. (p. 3).

While these definitions of ombudsman are useful, they cannot be applied universally to the teaching profession. Payne (1970) thoroughly examined the concept for certain essential characteristics that might be considered by educators. He discussed the commonalities of the ombudsman concept under the following attributes:

1. One essential characteristic of the ombudsman concept is that *the ombudsman is external to the system he investigates* . . . Thus, while the ombudsman is external to the agencies he checks on, he is part of the larger public administrative system. This "within-but-external-to" status is rather distinctive and is essential to the traditional ombudsman concept.

2. Closely related to the first concept is the tradition that *the ombudsman is impartial in his investigation.* Thus, an important feature of the ombudsman's office . . . is that he can and does defend and uphold the bureaucracy against unjustified criticism . . . For this reason the successful ombudsman is not viewed by the bureaucrat as an inherent enemy, rather he is seen by the bureaucrat as well as by the citizen complainant as an impartial, neutral and objective investigator . . . the accomplishment of this feat is an essential characteristic of a successful ombudsman.

3. The third necessary feature of the concept . . . is that *the ombudsman's only real power is his prestige and the related force of public opinion.* None of the established systems allows the ombudsman to reverse a decision, he can only investigate decisions and call to the attention of the public officials concerned any fault in a bureaucrat's decision or service.

4. The fourth essential characteristic of the ombudsman concept is that *the ombudsman's responsibility does not include solving all the problems between citizens and the state.* . . . The ombudsman's function is to investigate and to encourage the amelioration of any injustice suffered by a citizen as a result of the actions of public administrative officials . . . This does not include helping the claimant to deal with or to escape the onerous consequences of a fairly made administrative decision; the ombudsman's responsibility to an individual complainant stops when he has determined that there is no error of omission or commission by the public official.

5. The fifth essential characteristic of the ombudsman concept is that *the ombudsman can and does make policy recommendations as well as case recommendations.* . . . More often, perhaps, than the

high level, policy making administrator, the ombudsman is made aware of the imperfections in programs and policies as they affect individuals and he can make the policy makers aware of the deficiencies he perceives (pp. 5–7).

Most special educators probably have some reservations about attempting to fulfill the function of ombudsman upon cursory examination of the role. However, the positive attributes of the role should not be overlooked too hastily. In the first instance, special educators can be viewed as external to the system in which they operate. Special education teachers who are desirous of functioning as ombudsmen should be sensitized to the fact that in the minds of many, they and their area of special education are thought of as external to the system. This perception can be viewed from a positive or negative aspect. When perceived from a negative viewpoint, several hypotheses have been advanced to cast special education in a negative light. First, it has been argued that special education is a labeling agency that relegates those of lesser ability to the permanent role of second-class citizenship (Dunn, 1968; Hobbs, 1975; Hurley, 1969). Second, it has been charged that special education has not operated in the best interests of minorities (Dunn, 1968; Jones, 1972; Marion, 1979). Finally, it has been stated that special education has fostered an isolationist climate between mainstreaming and special education (Gihool, 1976; Abeson, 1973).

Alternative, Promotional, Cooperative

Some proponents with a positive perception of special education have argued that it has maintained an alternative approach for children and youth with special needs (Deno, 1973; Reynolds, 1973). Others have insisted that special education has been largely responsible for promoting the cause of the handicapped for a better quality of life (Cruickshank, 1967; Kirk, 1963). Still others have taken pride in creating a closer working relationship with other contributors to mainstream education (Gallagher, 1974; Hobbs, 1975; Morse, 1969).

Regardless of the viewpoint, special educators who accept the challenge of ombudsmanship seek either (1) to improve the negative opinion held by others and/or (2) to reinforce the positive viewpoints held by supportive individuals and groups.

Thus, the special educator ombudsman should not be surprised that some parents of mainstream education children and youth assumed that the special education children are getting all the money and those in the mainstream are "suffering" because all the federal funds are being earmarked for the handicapped.

As the first line of defense, the special education ombudsman should be prepared to hear the parents out, to present factual information, and to discuss the complaint in a rational manner. The ombudsman should not give merely scant attention to the complaint of parents who feel that children with special needs are usurping all of the regular classroom teacher's time. These parents earnestly feel that the mainstream students are suffering from what they regard as lack of attention.

Special educators as ombudsmen have the obligation of defining their roles as regular education consultants to parents and of presenting evidence that shows the advantages of normalization. In keeping with the theme of normalization, ombudsmen should conceptualize the continuum-of-services delivery model to the extent that they are comfortable in explaining instructional patterns to parents. An understanding of the Reynolds or Deno continuum-of-services model is an asset for special educators who would function as ombudsmen.

Another plus can be counted when the objectivity of the special educator is equated with the subjectivity of parents in the grievance process. Special teachers must understand P.L. 94-142 and its guarantees of due process concerning the parents' rights to be informed of any change in the child's program, to disagree, to appeal, and to be granted a hearing before an impartial hearing officer. Ombudsmen should not be lulled into complacency by a feeling that once P.L. 94-142 was enacted it would precipitate equitable and dignified service to all recipients. On the contrary, ombudsman special education teachers must evaluate the proposed delivery system to determine not only that the proposed educational and supportive services are of proper quality but also that they are appropriate for the child.

Special educator ombudsmen, by virtue of the coequal status assigned to teachers through P.L. 94-142, can bring about an equalizing relationship between the schools and the parents. Thus, to many parents the special education teacher ombudsman will be seen as *the* person to whom they turn to resolve school problems (Torrie, 1973). Furthermore, even when school-home problems escalate to the grievance stage, ombudsmen should have a measure of involvement. Many parents, because they tend to trust teachers, still have a level of confidence sharing with special education teacher ombudsmen that does not exist at other levels in the school establishment. This characteristic of "within-but-external-to" status that is attached to special educator ombudsmen has allowed teachers to stand apart from the administrative structure. Therefore, parents have viewed special education teachers as being with them and as members of the disenfranchised group in education apart from the "downtown" administration.

Impartiality a Vital Tradition

Related to the "with-but-external-to" concept is the second factor—the tradition that ombudsmen are impartial in any investigation. Special education ombudsman teachers should not have a problem in fulfilling this function. They can be guided by P.L. 94-142. Within the parameters of the IEP, ombudsmen must maintain a posture of openness and accessibility to any and all complainant parents. However, these ombudsmen must project an air of neutrality during their discussions. This should not be construed to mean that special education ombudsmen convey to parents that future discussion is futile, nor should parents perceive that the complaint will not be investigated and that an answer will not be forthcoming.

Rather, special education ombudsmen should be primed with the understanding that many complaints will be unfounded or based upon incomplete information. In such cases, they should be understanding of the situation surrounding the parents' complaint. The ombudsman should project an image of an aggressive investigator. For example, if the complaint involves a misunderstanding of the IEP agreement on annual goals for the child, special education teacher ombudsmen will have checked recorded minutes of the IEP meeting against what was written in a letter to the parents. Acting in this fashion, the ombudsmen can determine whether the parents' complaint is justified. If the complaint is proved rational and just upon investigation, the ombudsman must take steps to rectify the situation or to provide a remedy.

Conversely, if the special educator ombudsmen find the charges are without foundation, they need have no hesitation in defending the school and involved educators against unjust and undue criticism. Thus, as long as ombudsmen are viewed as understanding and nonthreatening persons, they need have little fear of alienating the bureaucracy. Instead, they will be viewed as able defenders of the establishment as well as neutral and objective investigators.

Special educator ombudsmen should be forewarned that this image is hard to cultivate with parents and with the system. Schools often are looked upon with suspicion by parents who frown upon the permissive atmosphere that they contend surrounds today's education. If education seems unable to exhibit the resiliency to correct many societal ills, blame often is affixed to teachers and schools.

The insensitivity or lack of knowledge of administrators to the needs of special children and youth can be linked to the negative image conveyed by schools. Lack of parental understanding about P.L. 94-142 and dependence upon hearsay have contributed to the difficulty of establishing a proper ombudsman climate between home and school. Teachers who do not understand the importance of the ombudsman role have not sought actively to establish their position as nonthreatening impartial listeners and friends.

To achieve the ombudsman image of impartiality, special education teachers must present a picture of persons who are not reluctant to investigate a complaint. They should have little hesitation in defending the school when evidence substantiates the rightness of its position. Working in this fashion, the special education ombudsmen will not be seen as dragon slayers of the schools. Neither will parents see them as protectors of the status quo.

Prestige and Public Opinion

The third concept guiding the ombudsman special educators is the recognition that the real power of the position is vested in the prestige of the office and the related force of public opinion. Schools and teachers generally have been accorded a place of respect second only to family in importance in the lives of children (Hobbs, 1975). Torrie (1973) has seconded this importance of teachers in the lives of handicapped children. With this prestige should be coupled the force of public opinion. The 1970s was called an age of revolution for children and youth with special needs (Brodinsky, 1973).

Special educator ombudsmen are accorded national respect due to the passage of P.L. 94-142. Nationwide public opinion urging equal educational opportunities for handicapped children gave impetus to the act and to its earlier companion, Section 504 of the Rehabilitation Act of 1973. Ombudsman special education should be community oriented and should be concerned that the prestige of the position be used in a constructive fashion.

Special education teacher ombudsmen should be prepared to work openly with the media, community-based organizations that serve handicapped students, colleagues, and students. These professionals should work to make parents aware of their strengths and their limitations so the parents will be fully informed about P.L. 94-142 and their rights and responsibilities under the law. Ombudsmen should share with parents what professional responsibilities and obligations are expected of professionals under the act. By building this position of respect and trust, the ombudsman educators can call attention to the fact that their position often becomes one of investigating and pointing out discrepancies in services or faults in decisions. In this fashion, the final decision sometimes must be made as an IEP team ruling. However, the ombudsmen's views will carry considerable weight because of the expertise the special educators bring to the situation.

As an example, P.L. 94-142 called for an annual IEP for every student in special education. The IEP planning process is carried out through a team approach involving teachers, administrators, evaluators, parents or guardians, and the student when appropriate. When agreement has been reached on the child's level of functioning, goals and objectives, educational and support services, evaluation procedures, and time spent with peers, the plan can be signed by all parties and placed into operation. If disagreement arises about the progress of the child or youth toward achieving the stated goals, ombudsman special education teachers can be contacted by parents about the advisability of goal modification. Upon receipt of the parents' request, the ombudsmen seek a meeting of the IEP committee to study the inquiry.

Ombudsman special teachers move toward fulfillment of this characteristic of the concept. They do not attempt to reverse the goal decision alone but demonstrate their ability to call the parents' serious concern to the attention of the team. The team has less reluctance to address the problem when it has been analyzed by a respected colleague.

The fourth quality attached to the ombudsman special education teacher concept is the fact that these individuals cannot solve all of the problems between school and home. One problem inherent in the concept is that teachers are expected to solve all of the issues brought before them. In special education, this expectation has caused many setbacks. Special education was created to serve students who had special needs beyond those of the normal, average, or regular pupil (Cruickshank, 1967). However, special education lost its sense of purpose in the decades following its inception, according to its critics (Dunn, 1968; Hurley, 1969; Jones, 1972). It then became a haven for culturally different and socially maladjusted pupils (*Children Out of School*, 1974; Marion, 1979). It became a dumping ground for pupils of regular teachers who might be tempted to say to special educators: "I've got one just for you."

In defense of special educators, it can be said that they attempted to provide an alternative for students who were unwanted in other curriculums. Another common note was the fact that these children wanted to be in special education rather than in regular education (Nondiscriminatory Testing Conference). Still another reason for pupils' being in special education was the expertise that parents perceived these teachers to possess to work with their children (Barsch, 1969).

Ombudsman special educators should realize that they cannot solve every complaint by parents. They do have a responsibility to investigate every complaint for its legitimacy, but if they judge that there has not been an error of omission or commission, they should feel justified in rejecting it.

To illustrate the point, the actions of ombudsman special education teachers are governed by P.L. 94-142. If parents and the IEP team have agreed that placement of an educable mentally retarded (EMR) pupil in a resource room is fitting for the child, then that assignment can be instituted. Parents might have second thoughts—a change of heart—after agreeing to the placement. In their appeal to the teacher, instead of considering what is best for the child, the parents are caught up in their own feelings of lack of self-esteem. They are arguing for a change for their benefit, rather than what has been a successful placement and learning experience for the student. At the risk of losing friendship, ombudsman special educators consider the evidence that went into the placement decision. Concurrently special educators will wear another hat (advocate) to work with the strong emotional feelings that parents may be harboring.

The Ability To Influence Policy

The final characteristic of ombudsman special educators lies in their ability to affect policy. Perhaps more than any other teachers, those in special education have been projected into situations where they can make administrators aware of imperfections in programs. Public Law 94-142 guarantees the delivery of educational and support services. Ombudsman special educators are cast in a unique position to point out service delivery discrepancies. They often function as intermediaries between parents who need services and organizations that offer the services. At other times they have had input into legislation affecting abused children, mental health, and juvenile delinquency.

In each of these categories, special education teachers have access to the experience and records of students. Drawing upon these experiences and the breadth of their knowledge, special educators can fulfill a vital function. They can be asked to supply testimony without breaking confidence with students or parents or to present case studies for community groups and legislative task forces. These public-minded groups might be interested in legislation that affects the quality of life of handicapped individuals.

Whenever special education teachers have a desire to function within this concept of the ombudsman, they should be guided by the following criteria:

1. They should have an appreciation of the law and the legal foundation for the special education program.
2. They should have an understanding of the nature of the school system and the site in which they work.
3. They should have some expertise in certain areas (i.e., mental retardation, generic, crippled, and other health impaired).

In the case of the first requirement, ombudsmen must have a knowledge of P.L. 94-142 so that they can discuss and interpret it in lay terms with parents and other professionals. The second criterion is closely related to the first and to the need for the ombudsmen to understand the administrative structure of the school system and the administrative unit in which they work. Special education teachers should have gained some insights into the district's philosophy and commitment to special education. They should seek to ascertain whether building administrators will follow a line of minimum adherence to P.L. 94-142 or are interested in going beyond the intent of the law. These questions should have been resolved before special educators take on the ombudsman role.

Finally, special educators should display some expertise in working with the handicapped population. Possession of this expertise enhances the role of ombudsman and can gain additional respect for the special educator. Competent special teachers who demonstrate a capacity to work successfully with exceptional children and youth are appreciated by even the most skeptical parents (*Closer Look*, p. 4).

In conclusion, when reviewing the characteristics essential to the role of ombudsman, a case can be made for special educators to incorporate the concept into their teaching styles. Teachers should not expect to become miracle work-ers, nor should they be put in the position of being all things to all people. Public Law 94-142 mandated the services that can be provided and created an opportunity for parents and professionals to work together as coequals. The concept of special education teacher as ombudsman has the potential to make the task less stressful as parents and professionals endeavor to meet the chal-lenge.

Chapter 4

Involving Parents of Mentally Retarded Children

Very clearly, mental retardation is a problem we cannot ignore. It directly affects some six million retarded Americans, almost as directly involves millions more in their immediate families, and in the long run touches us all.

President's Committee on
Mental Retardation, 1976

If there has been an exceptional condition that has truly touched the lives of many people, it has been mental retardation. From birth, parents are concerned that their child be normal and healthy. For most, this can be translated as average intelligence. Parents whose children are presented after delivery always are relieved to hear the words, "You have a healthy baby." Unfortunately, not all parents are blessed with these words. Instead, many parents have heard "You have a Down's syndrome child" or "Your child is retarded." Upon hearing these words most parents are thrown into a state of shock, confusion, anxiety, and pain.

Parents are subjected to these emotions because of the loss they feel has occurred. Before they have seen the child, someone who obviously has a great deal of intelligence (the physician) has just told them (who the doctor assumes also are intelligent) that the child is low in intelligence. Immediately the parents are confused. Mental retardation has different meanings to parents, depending upon their familiarity with the concept. Some may have an image of the "funny looking kid" with hanging tongue and folded eyelids. Others, more versed in the literature, may have questions about the degree of retardation—minimal or severe. Still others may have a flashback of a mentally ill child confused with the true picture of their retarded infant. Regardless of the circumstances, the situation surrounding the birth of a mentally retarded child is surrounded by confusion and anxiety.

The controversy that follows the birth of a mentally defective child has its roots in the strong feelings that arise within parents. It should be remembered that two of the crisis periods in the lives of parents of handicapped children involve (1) the birth and (2) the subsequent diagnosis of the handicap (Barraga, 1963). It is during these periods that the feelings of denial, ambivalence, anger, mourning, chronic sorrow, rejection, and guilt are likely to consume parents.

For those with a retarded child, the feelings can be justified. Consider what has happened to the parents' narcissistic desire to attain immortality. With so much ego at stake, human beings have within them the basic impulse to deny the imperfect. They can have ambivalent feelings, such as the urge to destroy the imperfect child, or can be filled with love for their infant. However, parents can be expected to experience a reasonable amount of guilt because of these love-hate feelings. Moreover, the sorrow reaction leading to mourning can be understood better when viewed from the perspective of parents overwhelmed by the thought of a lifelong burden.

Discussion of these reactions during crisis periods should include the nature of mental retardation. Different levels of retardation must be recognized. The terms educable, trainable, or severely/profoundly retarded often are defined in IQ or mental age terms for the purposes of educational placement and programs. Since these definitions are important to the involvement of parents, they are used as a basis for this discussion. Inasmuch as the slow learners or borderline learners (IQ of 70 to 85) are now removed from special education classes, the three categories mentioned above will be considered. Included are the educable (IQ of 50 to 70 or 75), trainable (IQ of 30 or 35 to 50 or 55), and severely/ profoundly (IQ of below 25 or 30) mentally retarded (Kirk & Gallagher, 1979). Each one of these classifications can evoke the entire range of emotions attributed to parents of exceptional children. However, the intensity of these feelings during each of the crisis periods can be evaluated by examining studies that have recorded the efforts of parents seeking to reconcile family and school differences and to work with the mentally retarded child.

Initially, the premise must be accepted that at birth and upon diagnosis, parents of mentally retarded children give expression to all the emotions discussed earlier. Parents can be expected to feel sorrow, guilt, ambivalence, denial, anger, and other similar attitudes. However, differences of intensity among parents of children in categorically distinct retarded groups must be recognized. For instance, parents of educable mentally retarded infants have a full share of all of the feelings of trainable and severely retarded adults. However, problem differences can be noted. The educable mentally retarded child may not have distinguishable physical characteristics at birth, so the developmental delays that parents and professionals observe are written off in the hope that the child will catch up.

Professionals and parents are allied in this conclusion in many instances since society is unforgiving to the individual who labels falsely. This is especially true when children are very young, ages 1 and 2, and adults are hoping that developmental delays may have been occasioned by factors other than retardation. However, around the age of 3, parents must face the fact that something may be different about their child. Whereas they previously found comfort in "individual differences," they now are fearful that these differences will set their child apart from peers. These fears can escalate among parents who plan to send their youngsters to preschool or who now receive the diagnosis from a reputable source.

Among the first group, the fears are heightened because they usher in the third crisis period for parents. This period is characterized by their apprehension about their child's attending school. They now face the reality that their child may act differently from the other pupils. They are fearful that special treatment and consideration will make the child conspicuous among his classmates. Moreover, doubts that their child will be accepted by professionals and peers might be gnawing at their minds.

Combined with these fears, parents have a great desire for more information about school expectations and the ability of their youngster to survive in the school environment. The latter has great relevance to parents of educable mentally retarded students since P.L. 94-142 gives priority to the severely and profoundly handicapped and to students not previously being served. Today's parents of mildly (educable) retarded students are disturbed over the fact that many school districts have oversubscribed to a misinterpretation of P.L. 94-142. They have expressed their displeasure that local school districts have concentrated all their efforts on the severely and profoundly handicapped to the exclusion of the educable retarded (Marion, 1978; Meyen, 1979). Much more on this debate will be heard in the 1980s.

SCHOOLS AND EMRs

The notion that attending school is important is inbred in U.S. society. This idea is accorded high priority by statute (compulsory education in most states) and state funding for public education. Special education has provided equal schooling opportunities to special needs students under P.L. 94-142. If so formalized and systematized, why has special education been called the "greatest labeling factory in the world?" (Hurley, 1969).

Parents who seek to enroll their children in preschool or school have supplied some of the answers. Barsch (1969) identified these parents as those who arrived at the school door without the knowledge that their child had a handicap. Schools then became the first identifier to tell the family that the child was exceptional. Parents of the educable mentally retarded (EMR) had one primary child care system tell them that another child caretaker system had produced a defective person. Instead of being happy to deliver their child over to the school system, parents now had apprehensions about the separation. The prospect of school, preschool, or kindergarten became less appealing. Typical questions asked of schools during this period include:

- What academic skills will the child be able to master?

- What occupations can the child expect to enter?
- Will the child be self-supporting?
- Will the child be able to live a normal adult life?

TEACHER-PARENT RELATIONSHIPS

The bond of the teacher-parent helping relationship is formed as teachers attempt to assist parents in finding answers to these questions. Teachers must realize that many parents are at crisis periods one and two. Since parents still are struggling with the feelings arising from the child's handicap, much of the teacher's work will be ego-supportive (Keel, 1976; Dalton & Epstein, 1963). Therefore, teachers should be acutely aware that the child is now functioning in an environment that is alien to the parents. They should not be surprised to find that parents may resist special education placement for their child. Thus, teachers may have parents who return time and time again with the same questions concerning schoolwork and the child's ability to perform the required tasks. Teachers should remember that parents are being confronted with the realization that schools have asked them to face the truth—they have a retarded child. The fact is documented by a first-rate child care institution—the school—and cannot be wished away.

Another realization teachers must face is in assisting and identifying realistic levels of functioning for the handicapped child as opposed to normal pupils. This task can tax the teachers' capacity for several reasons. First, P.L. 94-142 stresses educating students in the least restrictive environment. This requires schools to recognize that, as often as possible, handicapped students must be educated together with their nonhandicapped peers. Several of the instructional arrangements designed by schools to meet this demand have led special and regular educators to negotiate new, mutual working arrangements. Special education teachers thus begin to fulfill a consultant role to regular educators. Second, since P.L. 94-142 requires an Individualized Education Program (IEP), both regular and special teachers should be involved in the planning. Working together, they will have the self-actualization of the student as their prime objective. Third, these two groups must involve the parent as a partner during the planning and implementation of the IEP. Instructional arrangements such as these give special educators a large measure of responsibility within the totality of the IEP process and assure them of numerous parent contacts.

Teachers have one responsibility. Parents often are caught up in the deep feelings that they are experiencing because of the presence of the handicapped child. Special educators have a specific obligation not only to bring some objectivity to the positively charged situations but also to help parents reach a level of acceptance in any negative phase in which they may find themselves.

The entry and attendance of the exceptional child in school has been referred to as the third major crisis in the lives of parents with handicapped youngsters (Hammer, 1972). Although other crisis situations of eventful proportions occur during ensuing school years, parents' fourth major stressful period is associated with the onset of the age of puberty in exceptional youth. Parents raise questions about the ability of their children to handle the academics, to absorb sex education, and to begin the process of preparing for a job. At this stage, parents are at a different stance in their development. Having lived with a handicap for a long while, they may be accused of being apathetic at times. Teachers, in turn, may be regarded as unsympathetic to the parents' suffering. Other parents may have a feeling of betrayal toward the concept of least restrictive environment. Having grown accustomed to self-contained classrooms, they have strong doubts about the seeming about-face of the mainstreaming doctrine. Helping to raise their anxiety level have been the conflicting debates in which they see teachers engaging over mainstreaming. Perhaps many have feelings similar to those of the mother of a 14-year-old:

> I've fought the mainstreaming battle also. I've disagreed with educators, professionals, parents, etc. If my child were put into a class— at preschool age or earlier—maybe it would work if the schools, teachers, "normal" children's parents and all other "extra curriculum" teachers were educated to the "needs" of the handicapped child and to the proper functioning of the special education teachers (*Exceptional Parent,* October 1978, p. 3).

Parent-teacher relationships can be strained during another crisis period as parents watch with anxiety as their handicapped adolescents develop physically. They might have equal perplexities about the ability of the EMR teenagers to handle the confusing feelings that envelop them as they view their maturing bodies, unable to comprehend all of the changes going on within and without themselves. In earlier times, with sex education taboo in schools, parents could suppress sex drives and accompanying questions. In today's society, EMR teenagers have the option of learning the truth about their bodies in schools or of picking up a lot of "falsehoods in the sheets." During this stage, many parents of EMR adolescents have been reluctant to face the challenge of sex education.

Subsequent to the puberty stage, parents' fifth crisis period is characterized by the arrival of EMR teenagers at the point in their lives where they must begin preparation for a vocation. For years, the youths' chances of entering vocational classes in schools were dim. In 1968, it was found that vocational education had done a poor job of preparing the handicapped for the world of work (President's Advisory Committee on Technical Vocational Education, 1968). Six years later the picture had not changed drastically. Even the outlook for the 1980s is not too encouraging. National Institute of Education sponsored reports challenge the concept that vocational education reduces the number of dropouts and is an effective tool in alleviating poverty. It is even suggested that it lowers aspirations and discourages postsecondary educational pursuits. These findings sound dire warnings for EMR adolescents seeking to overcome a legacy of high dropout rates and low aspirational levels.

However, of the many categories of handicapped youth seeking to be served by vocational education, EMRs fared better than any other group. Of a number of secondary schools surveyed in 1976, EMR adolescents were involved in 57 percent of the vocational education programs (TEA Survey of Secondary Programs). A 1979 survey report of six states tends to show a downward trend although results were labeled "mixed." One state with 66 percent of its schools reporting indicated that they did not have a job placement program. In another, 25 percent of the students indicated that it was a problem for them in vocational education classes and 33 percent said they faced problems in nonvocational education classes (Allen & Gorth, 1979).

The final crisis period that involves schools—entrance into adulthood—has been extended through P.L. 94-142. The act gives exceptional youth the opportunity to pursue a public education until the age of 21. This extension of educational rights affects schools as they seek to educate these students for a better quality of life as exceptional adults. Schools now face the challenge of preparing these young adults for leisure time activities and for lifelong learning experiences. Special educators henceforth must focus their attention upon a full continuum of services for a mentally able adult evaluated at the 9- to 13-year-old range, rather than to rivet their attention upon a vast array of preventive measures at an early age.

INVOLVING PARENTS OF EMR CHILDREN

Involving parents of educable mentally retarded in special education is defined in this discussion as affecting teachers working within the framework of P.L. 94-142. Within these parameters and schools, teachers now are obligated to work with parents of exceptional individuals from age 3 through 21.* That being the case, schools must be ready to shoulder primary responsibility for becoming the diagnostic, screening, and prescriptive agents of educational programs for children. Regular teachers are most likely to have taken on the function of referring the child to special education. However, ombudsman special education teachers should be prepared to handle the major share of the counseling responsibility. In the pre-elementary and early elementary years, teachers must be ego-

---

* These age limitations are exercised with the full realization that some states have implemented statutes that exceed the age limits of P.L. 94-142, or that some changes in national policy in the future may alter present age limits. This posture is applied in each succeeding chapter.

supportive to the parents. To achieve this the teachers should be prepared to be good listeners. If ombudsman special educators have the courage to listen to what parents tell them, if they have understood what personal meaning the child's handicap has to the parent, if they have sensed the emotional factor that affects the parents, then teachers will have removed one of the largest blocks to personal communication (Rogers, 1961).

Such an approach has the potential of being a good avenue of communication with parents. This has great therapeutic value to parents who have a need for understanding when the child's disability is diagnosed. A nonjudgmental, empathetic listening approach can be initiated by ombudsman teachers without waiting for parents to talk or with a minimum of cooperation from them. This approach can be used by teachers to help parents deal with the defensive mechanisms that characterize their reactions to the handicapped child. Advocate teachers can use the listening approach to help parents drop these barriers of defensiveness (guilt, grief, and mourning) as they find out that the teachers' only intent is to understand and not to judge.

Lessening of Tensions

Advocate special educators must have the ability to listen and not to evaluate. They must have the courage to perform this task with parents. After all, they are working with parents who perhaps are shopping around for a cure, or are attempting to obtain appropriate educational services. Therefore, advocate teachers take a risk that they might be misunderstood as they seek to place themselves in others' frame of reference. Tensions run high when parents are encountered while undergoing the first two crises. When emotions are strongest, teachers have the most difficult time establishing good communication, yet they listen and summarize these feelings for parents. When teachers operate in this fashion, they lessen the tension between themselves and the parents.

Lessening of tension can be facilitated by placing the discussion of the handicapped child within the context of family adjustments or priorities. Special educators can resolve dissonances that may arise concerning the child's potential by attempting to determine "where does the family hurt the most?" By responding in this manner, ombudsman special educators can avoid the possibility that goals for the child will be approved externally. They will not have conveyed to parents that "we know what is best" for the child. Instead, the special educators will have allowed the parents to find their own way, resulting in their ability to make use of help and resources.

Care must be taken by the special educators to steer clear of imposing personal ethics upon parents. Parents must not be burdened or prejudged by a prevailing philosophy that gives high priority to a middle-class ethic associated with a struggle for high achievement. Nor should they be afflicted with a fear that special educators are contemplating a takeover or removal of the child from the potentially nurturant family circle. Therefore, teachers' responses to ''shopping'' parents who are concerned about conflicting information should be phrased, ''That must be very confusing'' or ''I might feel very angry about that if I were you.'' Similarly, replies could be made to the parent who accuses special educators of not understanding because they have never had a handicapped child. Ombudsman special educators should not be afraid to acknowledge these facts by responding, ''It's true I won't always know what you're going through'' or ''You feel that I don't know how things are with you.'' These admissions of humanism have the effect of letting parents know that they are understood and enhance teachers' influence with the parent.

In working with parents in the IEP process, the ability to listen will prove invaluable to special education helping teachers. The educators must be sure that the parents feel understood and accepted as individuals. In turn, the parents most likely will become less defensive and more open to suggestions concerning the educational plan. Special educators can assist parents in their helping-person roles of advocates, ombudsmen, and case managers. In the expansion of these roles, teachers must make certain that they are perceived as a source of help and that parents have had the chance to express their differences.

The Dual Involvement Role

For parents of EMR children, teachers should adopt three involvement roles during the elementary years. As a part of this function, the advocacy ombudsman and case manager aspects should be maintained. Teachers, together with parents, must be strong advocates of the EMR child's rights. Formerly labeled ''slow learner,'' this student has posed a threat to the concept of mainstreaming.

Regular teachers have not viewed the integration of EMR students favorably. Larsen (1975) reported on a study that showed regular educators initially expressed optimism about integrating EMR students into their classrooms. At the end of the school year, this optimism had disappeared and had been replaced by a feeling that it would be difficult to integrate EMR students without a large variety of specific methods and materials. Another finding of interest was that special educators contributed to the perpetuation of a ''mystique'' concerning handicapped students. Additional evidence of a similar nature was noted by Gickling and Theobald (1975). They found that there were grave disparities not only between the perceptions of special educators and regular educators but also among regular educators themselves toward mainstreaming. Thirty percent of special educators indicated that they believed regular classroom teachers felt imposed upon when required to help special education students, whereas nearly 50 percent of the regular educators voiced a similar sense of imposition. Less than 15 percent of the elementary teachers felt that they had the skills to help exceptional children. Regular teachers agreed unanimously that they would try mainstreaming if they were given assistance in the form of *services* and *time* to work with special education personnel.

Secondary regular education teachers also voiced opposition to the mainstreaming of EMR children. One study (Flynn, Gacka, & Sundean, 1978) stated that 58 percent of regular teachers felt that they were inadequate to teach mainstreamed EMR students. Rumble (1978) offered additional evidence that the majority of regular educators without prior contact with handicapped persons were reluctant to teach such pupils. These educators ranked EMR students fifth behind orthopedically handicapped, nonhandicapped, deaf/hard of hearing, and learning disabled for preferences in their willingness to work with exceptional pupils. Of all the reasons advanced by secondary teachers to substantiate why mainstreaming was impractical, the need for modified or individualized curriculums headed the list.

With elementary and secondary regular teachers exhibiting such disparities in their thinking about EMR children, special education teachers have a two-fold mission: they must work with parents, and they must continue to be ego-supportive. These teachers must realize that parents will need their understanding as they face the uncertainties of regular class placement for their EMR child. Parents can be expected to voice anxieties over the treatment they expect regular teachers to extend their children.

Mainstreaming: Are Children and Schools Ready?

These anxieties most likely will be expressed in the form of two questions: (1) Is my child ready for mainstreaming? and (2) Is the school ready for meeting the needs of a handicapped child in a mainstream setting?

Special educators must approach each question openly and honestly in their roles as advocates, ombudsmen, and case managers. As ombudsmen they should be prepared to listen to the confusion over the first question caused by the misunderstandings engendered by the interchangeable use of the terms "mainstreaming" and "least restrictive environment." Advocate special education teachers then have the responsibility of establishing the fact for parents that P.L. 94-142 is not mainstreaming legislation. They should explain that mainstreaming as a term does not appear in the law. Least restrictive environment as a term does appear, and its significance should be emphasized. Parents should be informed that the least restrictive environment provision requires each placement decision to be made on the basis of each individual child's needs. Ombudsman special educators should assure parents that decisions to include the exceptional child in regular class programming will be documented in the Individualized Education Program. They can extend additional guarantees as they point out that the IEP is a joint agreement between parent and school on behalf of the exceptional child.

Special education teachers have another opportunity to expand their role with parents. It will be calming to parents to learn that the ombudsman special educators will be involved in the negotiations on their children's access into programs. Case manager special education teachers will be extremely helpful if they are prepared to speak to the program options (music, art, physical education) for students. Parents then will have more information upon which to make decisions.

When seeking to answer the second question regarding the readiness of the school, special educators again must face up to the possibility that staff members and colleagues will hold varying opinions concerning handicapped students. Therefore, they are obligated to take the position of ombudsmen. For some colleagues, mainstreaming has the connotation that "they are all coming back into the regular classroom." Others may harbor concerns about the "other 30 children." Ombudsman special educators must be sensitive to these concerns and communicate the range of feelings that exist in the school environment. However, their efforts should not be limited to sharing information. They should shoulder a responsibility to assure school acceptance of exceptional children. Advocate special education teachers should work with fellow teachers, administrators, and other interested individuals to arouse community interest in the welfare of exceptional children and to destroy any myths that may have surfaced concerning their abilities. They should have an active role in the PTA, teacher organizations, and community affairs. Advocates should honor requests for speechmakers and for television and radio spots. Although many of these activities might be considered external to the school, they add validity to special education teachers' claims as advocates, ombudsmen, and case managers.

Creation of Parent Groups

Sometimes parents can be helped with these anxieties by the formation of parent groups. Teacher-case managers should assist parents in creating the groups and to help guide the discussions into areas of their needs. Special educators should have specific reasons for forming a parents' group. By proceeding in this fashion, they are assuring that the interaction among group members will be meaningful. Thus, groups might be organized around legislation, services to children, or the support of research and special projects. Special educators could work with parents to obtain results such as these:

- development of respite care service

- development of a home curriculum for children and youth

- establishment of public information service to familiarize the public with the exceptionality and program needs

- completion of a directory of available services
- investigation of adult and community care schemas

The advocate special educator should earnestly pursue a consensus by parents upon goals. Goal seeking must be accorded a priority since many projects are time-consuming and incapable of being acquired through individual efforts. Therefore, the advocate teacher should strive for a division of labor concept. As case managers, special educators also can assist group members to study and resolve situations. In this manner, special educators will be assured that parent members will share the problem and that the work will be spread among them.

Finally, parents can be helped only when the helping special education teacher recognizes where they stand in the stages of acceptance and on Maslow's (1954) hierarchy of needs. Maslow postulated a needs theory that began with basic physiological needs and was consummated in a need for self-actualization. In between these feelings are needs of safety, belonging, and esteem. Parents should be engaged in meaningful exchanges that allow special educators to determine their level of need. For example, parents of the elementary EMR who are operating at a basic level of needs with a concern for food and shelter cannot be expected to give immediate attention to the mention of a home-school program. Likewise, parents concerned about the stigma attached to the EMR level and about belonging are not likely to listen attentively to the merits of special class placement. Special educators will be forced by circumstances to function as case managers, advocates, and ombudsmen. As a case manager in the first example, special educators should assemble the facts of the situation to ascertain what kinds of services will be required to satisfy parents' needs. The educators must make sure that these are incorporated into the lesson plan. Acting as advocates, special educators must obtain services for the parents or see that they are provided. Thus, getting the home heated might have the effect of forming a lasting parent-teacher partnership (Barsch, 1969).

The Shift to Secondary Schools

Because of the emphasis on elementary special education, attention only recently has shifted to the needs of secondary exceptional pupils. Elementary EMR parents may not experience the feelings of isolation that are common to their secondary counterparts. This lack of attention by schools to the needs of secondary exceptional pupils has been reflected in feelings of alienation on the part of parents. Special educators should be prepared to meet apathy, hostility, and suspicion upon encountering parents of exceptional adolescents. Teacher advocates will not be offended by these outward manifestations of alienation; rather, they will seek ways to lessen the skepticism that parents may feel. Thus, they will encourage parents to look at all the alternatives of placement and ask them to consider the negatives and positives of each placement (McLoughlin, McLoughlin, and Stewart, 1979).

In addition to the ego-supportive function, teachers must bring other skills into the consulting agreements that they arrange between parents and regular classroom teachers. First, they should become an advocate with the parent on behalf of the EMR to make certain that regular educators become involved in the Individualized Education Program (IEP). If 38 percent of regular educators and 29 percent of special educators (Gickling and Theobald, 1976) indicated a lack of frequent contact on behalf of special education students, the helping special educator must work actively to bring parents and regular teachers into close contact. This effort to improve communication will have more lasting impact if both parents and regular educators are in possession of important facts. As advocates, special educators must make sure that regular educators and parents have a clear picture of the EMR child. Helping teachers should present developmental information that will be of assistance in filling in the gaps for parents and regular teachers.

While presenting such information, special educators should listen carefully to ascertain the anxieties of each party. When these anxieties arise, helping teachers have the option of becoming ombudsmen to negotiate differences that may develop concerning the capacity of the EMR pupil to handle the proposed IEP and to gain needed supportive and educational services to fulfill the requirements of the IEP.

In the ombudsman role, special educators must exercise the full range of communication skills. By listening, helping special education teachers can build a bridge of trust among themselves, parents, and regular educators. Having listened, ombudsman-special educators can negotiate the demands of each party. In the eyes of regular educators and parents, the special educator must maintain an air of impartiality. Any distrust displayed by either party should be talked through and mediated.

As the member of the IEP team with expertise in working with exceptional children, the helping special education teacher must shift into the role of case manager to assure that the delivery of service methodology will meet the child's needs. Therefore, ombudsman special educators will present, or have presented, information that will delineate the child's present level of function. Following this disclosure of information, ombudsman special education teachers should work with an IEP team to:

1. arrive at goals and objectives for the child or youth
2. agree upon ways to determine the individual's progress
3. prescribe the kinds of help or services that the individual will receive
4. show when the services will be provided
5. show the amount of time the exceptional pupil will spend with peers in regular class situations.

One of the real dangers to successful programming lies in the different perspectives that each member of the team brings to the meeting (McMillan, Jones, & Meyers, 1976). For instance, parents may enter the meeting with divided loyalties toward the concepts of resource room and mainstreaming. The administrator (or that executive's representative) may hold a positive outlook toward the concepts. Such a favorable position may be due to the administrative efficiency of resource room scheduling. On the other hand, regular teachers may paint a bleak picture of the concepts. They may be more concerned about handling classroom teaching loads because of what they perceive as an added burden—the handicapped child. The special education ombudsman's efforts should be directed toward having each individual suspend judgment and toward allowing each team member to consider the benefits of the program to the child. Therefore, instead of a breakdown in communication, the helping special educator will have made giant strides in reconciling any distortions in perceptions that may have been held by those involved.

The Case Manager Function

The final role for helping special educators is the case manager function. As case managers, special educators have the responsibility to help parents and regular educators with the mechanics of the IEP. They will be looked to for guidance on what is to be done with the EMR youth. Regular educators will expect special educators to give them "helpful hints for daily living" that can be implemented in their classrooms. The "in their classroom" approach is the important component. Regular classroom teachers cannot be expected to implement strategies that require gadgetry or extreme modifications that are time-consuming. For example, the special educator may have overhead projectors and reading machines and an aide in the classroom for assistance with the 10 to 12 students. The regular teacher may not have the luxury of these mechanical and human aids with a class of 30 students. It is highly unlikely that this teacher will feel compelled to attempt suggestions by the special educator that require the use of extra machines and people.

Parents can be expected to participate only when they are coequal members in IEP planning and implementation. They then can be depended upon to see that contracts are fulfilled, to participate in behavior modification techniques and practices, and to work with children at home. As case managers with older children, the helping special educators can assist parents as they focus upon the unique problems of community housing, vocational placement, and leisure time activities. Parents and families must be assisted to live *with* rather than *for* their children and the teachers must have the skills to advocate or mediate for appropriate educational and vocational preparation programs. However, parents of EMR children have a difficult time balancing the wish for independence versus the need for protection. This ambivalence is created in part by the fear that the schools have not prepared their child for independent living and in part by their reluctance to expose their teenager to the outside world. The latter fears are well documented. Lax (1974) presented evidence that more than 60 percent of retarded youths spent their time watching television following graduation from high school. Another study showed that the health needs of the mentally retarded had not been well served (Maternal and Child Health Service, 1972). It also has been established that the mental health services for the mentally retarded are not of sufficient magnitude to serve these persons adequately (President's Commission on Mental Health, 1978).

Independent Living a Key Goal

The wish for their EMR adolescents to acquire independent living skills has long permeated parents' thinking. They have expressed their feelings in different ways but they all have wished for the same goal. However, parents of EMR adolescents before the passage of P.L. 94-142 were overheard saying: "I hope my child dies before me or who will look after my child if I am no longer here?" (Meyen, 1967; Marion, 1975). Statements such as these characterized the frustration that parents felt between their expressed desires and their unfulfilled needs. Many parents have expressed a desire to see their EMR teenagers participate in community life in as normal a fashion as possible. Some would have preferred a purely independent status (i.e., employed, married, etc.). Others favored community-living arrangements (semisheltered environment). Very few would favor institutionalized living.

These expressed feelings have been constant in the crisis periods that accentuate the lives of parents of exceptional children and youth. Crisis stages occur when the EMR teenager nears the age to obtain vocational training and when the EMR adolescent becomes a school leaver. In the past (before P.L. 94-142), educators had no mandate other than parental wishes to work actively to prepare EMR adolescents for careers, independent living, and the world of work. This situation was altered with P.L. 94-142 since the IEP requires all components of student programs to be adjusted together with the amount of time spent with peers.

With only parental wishes as motivators, many schools were lax in secondary programming until the mid-70s. However, programming for the adolescent now has increased. This has been coupled with an emphasis on career/vocational programming. Such a thrust has caused parents of EMR youths to harbor hopes that their children will have something other than residential living in an institution or household confinement as their future.

To prepare adolescent EMRs for independent living, advocate educators should follow the curriculum listed here to assure that the student at the early adolescent level will be proficient in (TEA):

1. utilization of academic skills
2. development of responsibilities
    a. in home management
    b. of citizenship
3. development of awareness and understanding of
    a. job opportunities in the community
    b. skill and training necessary for jobs
    c. ways to obtain jobs
    d. individual limitations and potential
4. acquisition of
    a. satisfactory relationships
    b. fundamental vocational skills
    c. recreational and leisure time activities (1970, p. 48).

These activities are designed to prepare students for the next level of activities that assist teenagers in the (TEA):

1. acquisition of increased skills in
    a. the utilization of basic academic skills in life situations
    b. management of the home
    c. participation in work and recreational groups
    d. working relationships with other employees
2. development of
    a. aptitudes and interests in vocations
    b. self-confidence, dependability, and work tolerance by participation in school work experience
3. development of awareness and understanding of
    a. qualities necessary to hold a job
    b. various vocations
    c. responsibility toward self, the family, a job, and the community
    d. a need to prepare for a vocation
    e. vocational potential and limitation
    f. differences in employers (1970, p. 62).

As special educators help adolescents master these skills, they assist them to ready themselves for independent living. Possession of prevocational and vocational skills gives EMR teenagers and their parents options other than home TV recreation and living. Obtaining and maintaining employment also can contribute to good mental health (Braginsky & Braginsky, 1975). The education and adjustment training of the EMR adolescent will not have been completed until the teenager has taken part in activities designed to assist him (TEA):

1. in adjustment to
   a. personal and social relationships
   b. work experience
2. in the acquisition of skills needed
   a. for a specific job
   b. to become a productive employee
   c. for daily living
      • in the home
      • on the job
      • during leisure hours
3. in the acquisition of experience in job preference
4. in the evaluation of self in relation to requirements of the job (1970, p. 79).

Special educators who have worked with the parents and EMR adolescent through these sequences of preparation will have attempted to fulfill their responsibilities as advocates, ombudsmen, and case managers.

The Scope of Responsibilities

As case managers, the special educators' first responsibility is to develop an empathetic understanding of the parents' feelings and attitudes. Together, parents and case managers must study the EMR adolescent's abilities, limitations, degree of motivation, problems inherent in the environment, and the design of personality patterns. Parents and case manager special educators should set behavioral and educational goals that are in agreement with the adolescent's needs and abilities. Next, advocate special educators should work with parents and youth in planning to meet these goals. Following schemas outlined earlier in this chapter, the advocate special educators then will collaborate with parents to devise and implement plans for the development and growth of the EMR adolescent. Advocate special educators will give way to ombudsman special educator roles at times in the process. Special educator ombudsmen should encourage parents to be realistic in their expectation for the retardate and in making feasible choices and plans in areas such as recreation, vocations, and interests.

In the case of vocations, data have shown that parents of EMR youth have strong justification for their criticism. The reviews on vocational education for mentally retarded have been mixed. Two national reports (Vocational Education, 1968; Report to the Congress, 1974) have given low marks to vocational education on its involvement of handicapped persons in its programs. However, follow-up studies of EMRs by other agencies have yielded different results. They have shown that retarded workers can experience work success (Tigard, 1951; Charles, 1966; Kidd, Cross, & Higginbotham, 1967; Neuhaus, 1967). On the other hand, parents who are worried about preparation and employment do not have to choose sides. Their concern is centered on the fact that their children not be vocationally mismatched and not be prepared for dead-end employment.

Special educators will have to function as case managers, ombudsmen, and advocates to see that these concerns are met. First, the case manager special educators should survey the community to ascertain prevailing attitudes toward EMRs and to determine what jobs are available for them. With this information, advocate special educators work with parents to prepare the EMR adolescent by giving instruction in (TEA):

1. learning to obtain and hold a job
2. becoming a more productive employee
3. maintaining acceptable behavior patterns
   a. on the job
   b. at home
   c. during leisure hours
4. acquiring an opportunity for developing
   a. truthfulness
   b. honesty
   c. reliability
   d. concern for others (1970, p. 103).

Teachers who share these concerns should be understanding of the anxieties that undermine the confidence of these parents. As case managers, helping teachers must minimize the danger that the parents will feel overwhelmed by the enormity of the task of obtaining educational services for their youth. Helping teachers also must build bridges among several areas of education to achieve the maximum results.

The educational program of the EMR adolescent can have ramifications for areas other than special education. Vocational education, physical education, and vocational rehabilitation have been found to be most underrepresented in programs for handicapped adolescents. This has been especially true for vocational and physical education programs (Hayes & Higgins, 1978). Special educators normally negotiate access to these programs for their students wherever possible. The passage of P.L. 94-142 guaranteed exceptional adolescents access to these education programs.

However, the guarantees have not minimized the skills that the ombudsman must bring to the IEP meeting where joint decisions about the adolescent's program must be made. Therefore, the ombudsman special educator must be prepared to mediate conflicts that arise over curricular modifications and to make suggestions that will allow colleagues from other disciplines to involve students in meaningful activities. Physical educators may need a list of activities they might use with retarded teenagers without risk of injury. Vocational educators may be relieved to discover that retardates can handle certain machines with limited supervision or with adapted safety guards. The parents must be satisfied that physical education and recreation, vocational education, and vocational rehabilitation are represented adequately in the youth's IEP. Professionals must be accorded respect for their positions but must be mindful of the rights and status of parents as coequals.

As case managers, helping teachers are responsible for advocating for the full array of services and programs for the EMR adolescent. Parents must be included in the planning and implementation of these services. Special educators must not be dismayed if all parties cannot agree on all components of the IEP. Conflict can be expected when persons representing different viewpoints are presenting from their vantage points.

Helping teachers must listen and make sure that each participant feels understood (Rogers, 1961). Therefore, special educators will be obliged to shift to the ombudsman position to mediate any differences of opinion (Payne, 1970). The helping persons should have the foresight to recognize that the parent will arrive at some decisions from an affective perspective. Viewpoints expressed by professionals can be expected to be based on cognitive perceptions. Again, the helping teachers must be prepared to use the communication skills of verbal restatements and exploratory questioning to make sure that parents understand exactly what is being said and to avoid misunderstanding or misinterpretations. In the process, the special education teachers will be perceived as a source of help. Moreover, they are seen in a positive light and parents have the feeling that they respect their capacity for decision making. Parents then can be expected to feel freer to explore their perceptions, feelings, and assumptions.

When this happens, the helping persons will have alleviated some tensions that the parents may be feeling about the EMR youth and about the protectiveness extended over the adolescent. The special educators probably have eliminated much of the suspicion and mistrust that parents may have felt after being surrounded by so many school people.

In conclusion, it can be said that EMRs and their parents are a distinct category in special education that has touched the lives of many persons. Families with EMRs are touched profoundly and are never the same; families without EMRs more often than not will have to acknowledge the presence of an EMR individual in the school or in the neighborhood.

THE TRAINABLE MENTALLY RETARDED (TMRs)

The trainable mentally retarded child (TMR) can be differentiated from the educable mentally retarded child (EMR) in several respects:

1. The TMR child is lower on the IQ scale.
2. TMRs can be expected to achieve the capability of caring for their personal and physical needs, of performing routine tasks, and of carrying out simple directions.
3. TMRs may have to work in sheltered situations, but could have the capability of developing work skills for gainful employment.
4. TMRs probably will need assistance in certain situations from other adults to make decisions and to participate in community activities.

The experience of parents of TMR children will be different from that of parents of EMR children. Chief among these differences are the time when the defect is recognized, the TMRs' characteristics, and the parents' expectations and immediate objectives for the TMR.

One of the most distinguishing characteristics in the teacher-parent relationship is the fact that the TMR handicap—severe retardation—is easily recognizable and is clearly visible. The child with Down's syndrome (mongolism), one of the most commonly seen handicapping conditions, and other TMRs have the obvious distinction that they are physically different. Moreover, the crisis periods that engulf the families of TMRs begin at birth since the defect can be diagnosed earlier because of its recognizable symptoms.

In the crisis period following the birth of the TMR child, intrafamily and interfamily problems begin to appear. These pressures may be self-induced, family caused, or financially determined. In the case of the former, such everyday problems as "How can I teach my child to eat?" or "How do I toilet train him?" may seem such heavy burdens that parents are unable to cope.

Family problems can be precipitated if one spouse feels that the other is not giving sufficient time to the help and care of the TMR youngster, or may be based on family pride and a desire to "hide away" the child. These problems may be linked to the perception that parents see the TMR child as a lifelong burden. Under these pressures, parents formerly found it easy to feel that institutionalization was the answer to the best quality of life for them and for the TMR. Today, however, parents no longer are convinced that institutionalization is necessarily the best solution. Numerous studies (Goldfarb, 1954; Dennis, 1960; Freud & Dann, 1951) all attested to the fact that institutionalized children suffered ill effects from the lack of socialization with other humans. Parents of TMRs often make the decision not to institutionalize purely on the basis of human kindness and are not apprised of the problems they face in rearing a defective child in the home. These parents not only need understanding during this time of decision, but also need the facts concerning the child's outlook.

Involving Parents of TMRs with Teachers

If parents make the decision to institutionalize the child, it should be remembered that the teacher-parent relationship is not ended. Recipients of TMRs, mostly state schools and hospitals, have educational systems and are governed by P.L. 94-142. Therefore, parents must be informed of their rights and responsibilities under the law (Midwest Regional Resource Center, 1978). For these parents, the source of greatest help can be helping special education teachers. In former years the greatest complaint by teachers was the fact that they didn't see the parents. Today, that cry still can be heard but it has been muted as many parents follow a course of "normalization" or approximation of normal living conditions. The effect of this decision can be seen in the fact that large numbers of TMRs now are living in sheltered community homes or are spending some time at home with the family.

It should not be assumed that all parents willingly accept the edicts of P.L. 94-142. Just as mainstreaming has affected the manner in which public schools deliver services to pupils, so also has the law affected institutionalized children. Some parents will not have developed a state of readiness to cope with the practice of normalization. An AMD article raised the specter of harm that can be done to the family when the system either cannot or will not make accommodations for the TMR child. It pointed out these possible ramifications:

1. TMR children may not be accepted back into the family;
2. family, public, and political pressures may force the retreat of the TMR child back into institutional living; and
3. consequently the institutional concept will become more firmly entrenched (Gottlieb & Corman, 1975, pp. 72–80).

These developments demonstrate that helping teachers must be both ego-supportive and case managers for parents. Therefore, during the child's early institutionalized years, the helping teacher will have to assume the position of a nonthreatening and responsible listener for the parents. This factor must be stressed since parents either are not likely to be frequent visitors or are likely to visit as often as possible. Listening is an important part of the working relationship with parents in either case. In the first instance, listening should be given high priority because of the limited access that the helping teacher will have to the parent. Parents in the latter group should be accorded this respect since their visits are likely to be prompted by feelings of remorse, overprotectiveness, guilt, or relief, or may be considered necessary to keep them current with their child's development.

Therefore, the case manager teacher should reassure parents that their feelings and concerns are being attended to and are important in any decisions that affect the child. To show this empathy, the helping teacher should be attentive and should not dominate the dialogue. Parents caught up in this situation dwell not only on the problems of the institutionalized child but also upon intrafamilial relationships. Helping teachers should be cognizant of the fact that they might be seeing parents who are:

1. still struggling to resolve their feelings about the placement of the child
2. still attempting to justify to family members the cause of the defect
3. still trying to work out family roles in the aftermath of the birth, entry into the family circle, and the subsequent placement
4. still reacting to community attitudes about the defect

The helping teacher should be sensitive to these needs and should work with the parents to help them alleviate these feelings. Parents appreciate the nonjudgmental listener who can respond reflectively to their needs. Ombudsman teachers should be watchful for opportunities to communicate positive information to parents that will encourage future contacts with them. Parents who are ambivalent in their feelings cannot be expected to absorb negative reporting about the child and not use these factors as an excuse to stop their visits.

The Skill of Reporting to Parents

Reporting information is another skill important to success with parents. This skill should not be downplayed by helping teachers. Many parents have been won or lost in discussions with professionals. The tone of voice, the optimism of the speaker, and the credibility of the teacher definitely have an impact upon the parents (Zander, 1961; Lippitt, 1965). Ombudsman teachers should be reminded that they are agents for change when they work with parents. Therefore, they have a responsibility to help parents to think of their child as an individual and not as a lifelong penance. The helping teacher should be acutely aware that reporting can be an anxiety-provoking situation for parents. Most parents who visit infrequently are prepared to hear the worst about the child and generally have resigned themselves to their situation. Frequently, they are thirsting to hear good tidings about their child. Helping persons can do much to restore human dignity if they can share some small achievement or improvement with parents. Recognition by the professional that parents desperately want to see and hear an understanding individual who will not judge them can be an important step in building bridges of mutual trust and respect.

Reporting should not be considered only as an account of the child's limitations or good qualities. Professionals who truly wish to be helpful should examine their own limitations, feelings, and attitudes before seeking to assist parents. The fact that the helpful teacher has to share information with another adult can be either an enlightening or a frightening experience. Sometimes teachers report what they think parents want to hear. Others make inadequate responses because they have not been able to deal with the emotions expressed by parents of defective children. This kind of reporting and attending to parents can lead only to a nonproductive session. In other words, much of the discomfort of professionals with their own and the parents' feelings will arise because interpersonal feelings precipitated a struggle for control between two parties (Wallen, 1972).

Reporting has another focus: the helping teacher should assist the parents to explore reality situations so that reality-oriented decisions can be made (Trexler, 1976). A helping attitude in an accepting teacher who understands his limitations or feelings is destined to build an atmosphere of cooperation.

Buttressed by this feeling, the helping teacher and parent begin to help one another in the educational process. When teacher and parent communicate in this manner, they point the way to a mutual exploration of potential solutions. With this open-minded approach, teachers can increase their opportunities to understand the parents' feelings and can spare themselves the agony of responding inadequately to those concerns.

'Every Day, Every Time' Solutions Infeasible

Advocate teachers should be wary of responding with solutions each time they visit with parents. Rather, they should spend a great deal of time working to lower parents' resistance to continued contact so as to help them achieve fuller self-actualization (Maslow, 1954) and to give them a more realistic evaluation of the child's needs. As can be deduced, these tasks are weighted with problems. The "every day, every time" solution-oriented professional will not earn the respect of these parents. Faced with a long-term institutional commitment, the helping teacher must be tuned in to the full range of the parents' emotions.

While reflecting these feelings, helping persons must have an understanding of the problems—familial, financial, educational, emotional—so they can lend support in a professional manner. Faced by anxious parents, the truly helping teacher must not be offended by their insistence upon a solution. On the contrary, the advocate special educator should be determined to use this opportunity to clarify discrepancies in the parents' perceptions of the problem. Perhaps parents are saying one thing but in reality are perceiving the problem at another level. Helping teachers assist parents when they pose carefully phrased questions and comments that point out the discrepancies (Trexler, 1976).

Operating in this fashion, the helping person can assist the parents to recognize and clarify their discrepancies by relaying information back to them. For example, the special educator may see what appear to be attractive, intelligent, and conscientious parents who may give the impression of self-assurance and competence. Inside themselves, these parents are living with despair and anger. The ombudsman educator may have an opportunity to get those feelings out where they can be worked with. In the final analysis, the parents could have accepted the fact that the child will be institutionalized. However, they still may be angered at the long procession of doctors and professionals they encountered through the years before the decision to institutionalize the child.

The advocate teacher should move parents toward discovering potential alternatives for dealing with problems. Exploration of alternatives in an open and acceptant atmosphere can promote a receptive climate that permits parents to talk out their problems, needs, and conflicts. Parents in such a working relationship can reduce their need to withhold their worries. Helping teachers, secure in the relationship, work to help parents deal not only with their concerns about the exceptional child but also to create a broader base for coexistence between institutionalization and normalization.

Involving Parents of TMRs in the School

Schooling tends to start earlier and to continue longer for TMR children since the passage of P.L. 94-142. Where TMRs formerly were confined to institutions, the act emphasizes their education in public schools, deinstitutionalization, community provisions, and normalization (Kirk & Gallagher, 1979). In taking note of these developments, schools are involving parents of TMRs to demonstrate their intent to comply with the doctrine of coequality in the child's educational programming. If the contact begins at school, the helping teacher can expect to be greeted by parents who:

1. have lived with the child's handicap for some time
2. have been functioning at various levels of acceptance with the child
3. have a suspicion that things will be different for the TMR child in school
4. have all the worries of normal parents plus the knowledge that the TMR child is limited mentally

In past years these parents were made painfully aware that the school existed as a center of learning and that their children were seriously deterred from full participation in its functions (Abseson, 1974). The helping teacher must be prepared to offer ego-supportive counseling to parents. These teachers should concentrate their efforts on relieving parental anxieties, suggesting alternatives on child-rearing practices, assisting parents to increase potential solutions to their problems, and changing their negative attitudes and behaviors.

Many parents of TMR children, having experienced feelings of hopelessness, ambivalence, and resignation related to their child, are beset by feelings of inadequacy. Many schools still are struggling in the early stages for fuller implementation of P.L. 94-142 for TMRs. Ombudsman helping teachers, by becoming attentive listeners, obtain an estimation of the parents' level of acceptance of the handicapping condition. Many parents do have a satisfactory level of acceptance but others have not been able to face the limitations imposed by the handicap. As teachers listen, they should attempt to determine whether parents are concerned with the following education-related questions:

1. Should educators emphasize the full development of the child's personality and help him become a happy, contented person? or
2. Should educators direct their main efforts toward stimulating and motivating the child to greater achievement?

Where the previous literature reflected doubt as to the ability of schools and parents to achieve both of these objectives, P.L. 94-142 requires the coequals to meet the challenge. In this vein, parents often voice concerns about their child's curriculum. Special educators should work with them to individualize the program and to assist the TMR child to develop physical and sensorimotor skills that will enable him to use his body and senses effectively. Parents and special education teachers should develop a variety of skills with the child:

1. *Physical competencies*: Gross and fine motor, visual, auditory, tactile, taste discrimination, olfactory discrimination, and sensorimotor skills
2. *Person and social:* Self-help, self-care, mental, acceptable social behavior, communication, and language skills
3. *Vocational:* Attitudes, number concepts, and environmental awareness

Facing the Challenge

The advocate teacher should listen to determine the parents' readiness to commit themselves to the challenge of helping the child with school and home adjustment difficulties. A relationship of trust can evolve into increased parent involvement in the process of education, thus affording TMR children additional options for achievement. Higher levels of success can be expected when parents and teachers resolve their discrepancies regarding the child's potential. Helping teachers should be sure not to appear silent and unresponsive and must be aware that parents may have apprehensions about talking if the helping persons do not give indications of understanding, support, and interest.

While responding to parents, the ombudsman should have an open mind and never engage in argumentation. Although the ombudsman may be presenting factual information, parents sometimes feel they have to defend themselves against the truth and reject suggestions that they find impossible. The mere presentation of clinical diagnosis and recommendation has not always been sufficient nor perhaps what parents were seeking (Sheimo, 1951). Helping teachers must continue to maintain an open mind when this occurs. If holding up reality results in parental denial, counterargument will have minimal effect. Rather, the ombudsman should reflect the denial back to the parent together with a statement of the reality.

For instance, a young TMR may be behaving as a "holy terror" at home. The child has a feeling of safety in his home surroundings. However, at school in alien territory, the child has a calm demeanor. Parents might deny the existence of this behavior for fear of being thought of as bad parents. At this juncture in the session, helping teachers should attempt to gain additional insight into the parents' true feelings. They should accept the fact that parents may not be able emotionally to deal with facts that cause them pain. Parents may need help to marshal their remaining strength to sustain themselves as human beings. Realizing this, helping persons have the capacity to withdraw into acceptant listening, to assist parents in getting in touch with their feelings. They can promote discussion by responding only to what the parents really are saying and by encouraging expression of feeling (Jones, 1968). The ombudsman thus should attempt to reflect the emotions being expressed to enable the parents' feelings to surface.

While working with parents in need of supportive counseling, helping teachers should be guided by the following principles:

1. They are not trying to restructure the personality of the parents.
2. They are aware of their own strengths and limitations.
3. They are avoiding any effort to minimize the parents' problems.
4. They are not presenting themselves as the "expert" or "therapist in residence" on the problem.

The special education teacher functioning under these guidelines will have little trouble being perceived as a "helping person" in ego situations with parents.

Schools do not always find parents at ego-supportive levels. Helping persons often are confronted by parents who seek assistance as the handicapped child develops self-help or other functional skills. Many other parents, while admitting child development is important, have numerous concerns about school adjustment problems. Case manager teachers not only must be ego-supportive but also must assist parents in formulating and implementing the IEP. The parents' need for assistance does not lessen in this instance. On the contrary, when the parents in early or later years of schooling seek assistance, helping persons should attempt to establish a basic attitude between parents and themselves.

Using a Questioning Posture

When parents come for help, the helping persons put into practice "unconditional positive regard" (Rogers, 1957). To effect this practice, instead of focusing on the question, "How would I solve this problem?" the case manager asks, "How can I help this parent to try to solve the problem?" The helping teacher must remember that it is a problem for these particular parents and that it exists because of misinformation, confused thinking, inappropriate attitudes, or misinterpreted impressions.

In this case, the special educators will be forced to serve as ombudsmen, advocates, and case managers. If the problem involves misinformation about the educational program and IEP, case managers should spend time with the parents to interpret terms and the law and to talk about program modifications. As advocates, special educators would work to change parents' aspirational levels for the TMR child. Many parents have mistaken notions about the capacity of the child to be a functional individual in society. Advocate special educators must provide parents with an accurate assessment of the child's ability. Therefore, teacher and parental observations, formal assessment instruments, and informal assessment by other knowledgeable professionals all will be used by the advocate special educator to assure the proper data are collected and used according to the agreed-upon plan.

The 'Why' of Doing Things

Finally, ombudsman special educators should emphasize "why" things are being done in certain ways. These educators also could solicit input from parents to assure the "why" is emphasized strongly. These questions should be addressed to parents (Turnbull, 1978):

- What skills would you like your child to learn?
- Are there concerns about your child's functioning at home that could be addressed by work at school?
- What aspects of your child's behavior do you believe need to be improved?
- What do you believe to be your child's strengths and weaknesses?
- What methods have you found to be effective in rewarding and punishing your child?
- To what extent does your child interact with children in the neighborhood?

- What are your feelings about providing opportunities for your child to interact with nonhandicapped children? (p. 462).

Working together with the parents, the ombudsman turned case manager special educator must strive to take the surprises out of the development of the IEP. Teachers who are not helping persons have trouble with this approach. It has its drawbacks even for those who prefer to use the method. Suppose parents request assistance in learning to teach self-help skills. Often teachers have been more than ready to tell them how to handle the situation rather than remembering that others may not be able to adopt the educators' methods effectively. Helping teachers are not bound by this traditional method. Rather, they ask, "Why does the parent need help in parenting skills?" and "How can we assist them to select or develop skills they can use?"

How about the parent whose child has just arrived and is new to the school this year? The advocate teachers are appreciated if they recognize that parents want to know about P.L. 94-142 and its regulations that apply to the child's IEP. Helping teachers must assume major responsibility for imparting information about P.L. 94-142 (Midwest Regional Resource Center, 1978; *Closer Look*, 1978). Many times parents seeking help about the law have information at hand; their difficulties arise because they cannot get it together into a format that will help them. Helping teachers should assist parents to discover their role of coequal in the relationship.

As case managers, the helping teachers work with the parents in a variety of ways. Recognizing that they are not legal specialists, helping teachers use their knowledge to make parents intelligent consumers of the law. Being part of the system, helping teachers have the option of being either advocate or ombudsman. If the parents' needs are additional services, the helping teachers may have to advocate for those resources. Perhaps there has been disagreement over the interpretation of P.L. 94-142 when applied to the child's IEP; in this case, the helping persons might have to assume the role of ombudsmen and mediate the stressful situation.

Helping teachers may be confronted by parents who are anxious because they feel the professional does not know the child well enough to make sound recommendations about his educational program. Since P.L. 94-142 requires parents and teachers to work closely in implementing the IEP, special education helping teachers should seek ways to involve parents in the establishment of a more effective information-gathering and feedback system. In this effort, helping persons should be committed to the coequal doctrine. This commitment can be exercised through communicating to parents what is expected of them, that their views will be respected, and that their input will contribute to responsible decision making and programming.

These concerns surface during the early crisis periods, upon entry into school, and in the early school years. They will vanish or recede during succeeding school years. Each successive crisis period has the effect of resurrecting old fears that haunted parents from the birth of the child. For example, the onset of puberty, vocational preparation stages, and school leaving all are crisis periods. Taken in sequence, the anxieties of parents can be analyzed and the helping attributes of teachers can be outlined.

Puberty: A Trying Time for All

Puberty has been noted as a trying time for adolescents and parents (Cole & Hall, 1970). Emotionally, physically, and socially the teenager undergoes dramatic changes. Curriculum and configurations of school are geared to reflect these changes. Families must exhibit flexibility and adjust to the teenager. The community expects to see the mischievous child transformed into a responsible young adult. Viewing these anticipations are parents of TMRs. Their previous fears are resurrected and age-old familiar questions are raised. Do the schools have a program for my child? or, Will my child be able to marry and have children? These are two of parents' most common inquiries.

The helping persons again should adopt an ego-supportive posture and become case managers, advocates, and ombudsmen. If schools do not have programs, the helping persons must become advocates or ombudsmen. This help might have to be implemented at various levels of acceptance. In one case, working with an affiliate of the National Association for Retarded Citizens, a helping teacher acted as advocate for a TMR program. This person was not afraid of sitting in at school board meetings, had no qualms about assisting parents to go around the heads of school sites, and sided openly with these parents when disputes arose over school locations (*Austin American-Statesman*, 1967). Another teacher helping in a different way chose the ombudsman route. Realizing that this was not as sophisticated a situation as in the first instance, this helping person acted as ombudsman to mediate the dispute. Encouraging exchanges of information between school and home, this teacher succeeded in changing the attitudes of two sets of parents toward their TMR youths' dating (Marion, 1976).

In each of these situations, helping teachers functioned as case managers. Being attentive, listening, and providing empathetic responses, they were able to communicate to parents that they were not giving them an immediate solution. Using appropriate questions and nonthreatening inquiry, the helping teachers mirror their acceptance of the problem without evaluating the parents or branding them as failures. As they worked through the problem, the helping persons pointed out to parents that it was in their interests to seek the best answer. Finally, helping teachers always had respect for the parents' personal integrity and ability to make decisions.

Vocational Preparation Problems

Problems of vocational preparation present helping teachers with enormous discrepancies. At this level, most teenagers are beginning to acquire a limited specific vocational skill. The helping teacher must work with adults to set realistic goals while not plateauing the youngster. This posture is consistent with Maslow's (1954) hierarchy of needs. Based on this philosophy, the helping person must exchange information with parents, advocate for placement in vocational education classes, and mediate disputes between curriculum areas.

Helping teachers should be responsive to the wish of parents that their children reach their potential. However, helping persons may have differing views on that potential. Parents may have the perspective of the three Rs or may set unrealistic academic goals for their teenager. Helping persons should have little trouble discerning these concerns. Parents whose youngster has suffered the pains of the "dummy room" label may suffer from a lack of direction. These parents are gratified to find a sympathetic listener. By being attentive, helping persons can suggest that parents might follow a course that will produce a functional young adult. The curriculum of the Adult Performance Level (APL) competency-based diploma plan (Marion, 1978) could meet this desire of parents and youths.

Vocational programs can be suggested. The helping teachers should be willing to advocate entry of some TMR students into regular vocational programs, although they might well have reservations about entry for all such pupils. Vocational educators have expressed a desire for curriculum modification before enrollment of handicapped persons in their programs (Fair, 1976; Preston, 1975; Allan & Gorth, 1979). This endorsement of vocational education by helping teachers probably will have to be mediated at the ARD (Admission, Review, or Dismissal) meeting or screening team session. Both parents and vocational educators are likely to have reservations to share about the entry of the TMR youth into the program. Helping persons will have to reconcile these differences in the best interests of the youth. Sometimes sheltered workshop situations or vocational programs for handicapped youths are the least restrictive alternatives.

School leavers through attrition or graduation have long been a concern of educators (Brown, 1975; Dvoky, 1969; Passow, 1976). Parents of TMR youth fear that the world of unemployment awaits their children. However, they should be counseled against despair. P.L. 94-142 gives them new hope. The emergence of new educational programs required by the law plus the extended length of time spent in school by the handicapped should result in renewed vigor by helping persons. They should seek to change community attitudes toward the handicapped. Case manager teachers should conduct community surveys to determine prospective employers and possible job sites. The development of work-study and sheltered workshop sites on and off campus are necessary developmental stages for young adolescents. By working with parents to develop pre-vocational skills, helping persons can be assured that TMR youths are reaching their full potential.

The mentally retarded population of the United States is recorded as .25 or .50 percent who are trainable and .50 to 1 percent who can be classified as educable mentally retarded (Kirk & Gallagher, 1979). Working with parents of mentally retarded children always has been a challenging task to professionals and still is considered an important portion of their responsibility. The education division of a professional organization devoted to serving the mentally handi-capped holds this opinion (American Association on Mental Deficiency, 1975). Almost 36 percent (35.6) of professionals responding on behalf of the Education Division of the American Association on Mental Deficiency felt that counseling was an area that required strengthening and ranked first as a knowledge need. Parent involvement and parent education ranked third as an important need perceived by professionals in the educational field. Such endorsements have made the case.

Chapter 5

Counseling Parents of Learning Disabled Children

From a teacher:

> I am teaching remedial reading to students in grades 1–5. Some of my students have been diagnosed as having dyslexia. I know very little about dyslexia and even less about remedial work to help them. Would you please send me any available information that I might use to help my students? Thank you for your time and trouble.

From a parent:

> Our eye doctor discovered our son has dyslexia two years ago.
> His teachers seem to refuse to accept the fact that he needs a little more help than the "A" student. He is eleven years of age.

and

> I have recently heard that a new state law is expected to become effective in the near future, which will no longer qualify children with minimal brain dysfunction for special education.
> My nine year old daughter is presently receiving one hour and fifteen minutes of special education each day. She was examined by a qualified pediatrician in December 1977 and diagnosed as showing "soft neurological signs" and MBD.
> I have heard from several sources that a diagnosis of MBD or MBI will no longer qualify a child for special education in the 79/80 school year.

I am very concerned about this and would appreciate any further information you can give me.

*Texas Association for Learning
Disabilities, 1978*

These letters portray vividly the condition of the fastest growing subset of special education: the learning disabled (LDs). Not only has this subset experienced rapid growth but the category of learning disabilities has encountered unusual turmoil both within and without the field of special education.

The complexity of problems presented by learning disabled children continues to perplex teachers, parents, and other professionals. The crux of the problem is characterized both by the type of professionals who comprise the field and by the different kinds of disabilities that are covered by the term ''learning disability.'' Learning disabilities is a professional designation. The field consists, for the most part, of educators, physicians, and psychologists concerned with a population of individuals who evidence specific deficits in their learning performance, yet who are sensorily intact and intellectually normal by psychometric standards (Wiederholt, 1975). For reasons implicit in the definition, then, the field has been defined from the viewpoint of the practicing professional toward the child.

Wiederholt (1978)* has ably chronicled the history of the field from many perspectives. He found that educators, physicians, and psychologists had been concerned about learning disabled persons since the early nineteenth century. History has shown that while the basic premise and issues in the field have remained remarkably consistent, the semantics and trappings have changed periodically. For example, the terminology used prior to 1963 tended to be medically-oriented. Therefore, the terms brain damage, brain injured, cerebral disorders, neurological impairments, or dyslexia were used to describe the handicap. During the foundation phase (1800–1930), physicians had a major role in investigating the etiology of specific learning disorders and classifying and categorizing the different types. Goldstein (1942) and Strauss and Lehtinen (1947) made important contributions during this period.

During the transition phase (1930–1960), psychologists and educators tried to translate theory into practice. Charles Osgood and Joseph Wepman developed models to explain the process of communication through speech. Wepman later developed the Language Modalities Test for Aphasia (Wepman & Jones, 1961). Kirk, McCarthy, and Kirk followed with the development of the Illinois Test of Psycholinguistic Abilities (ITPA). Samuel Kirk, Anna Gillingham, Marion Monroe, and others began to develop tests and programs for students with written

---

* Much of the history that follows (1900–1973) has been adapted from Wiederholt's chronology of the field. Specifically, see *Teaching the Learning Disabled Adolescent* by Mann, Goodman, & Wiederholt, Houghton Mifflin Company, Boston, 1978, Chapter 1, pp. 10–8.

language disorders. Still other professionals such as Raymond Barsch, William Cruickshank, and Newell Kephart were concerned with perceptual motor assessment and program development (Mann, Goodman, & Wiederholt, 1978).

Learning disabilities as a field was organized formally April 6, 1963. Samuel Kirk gave definition to the field while speaking at a conference sponsored by the Fund for Perceptually Handicapped Children, Inc. He said:

> Recently I have used the term ''learning disabilities'' to describe a group of children who have disorders in development in language, speech, reading, and associated communication skills needed for social interaction. In this group I do not include children who have sensory handicaps such as blindness or deafness, because we have methods of managing and training the deaf and the blind. I also exclude from this group children who have generalized mental retardation (p. 3).

This speech marked the beginning of the third phase. It was called the integration period and lasted from 1963 to 1973.

Kirk's speech was effective in two ways: (1) it served as a catalyst to provoke interest in the field and (2) it isolated the characteristics of the population to be served under the ''learning disabilities'' category.

In 1966, a national task force under the direction of Clements (1966) and funded by the National Society for Crippled Children and Adults and by the National Institute of Neurological Diseases and Blindness, Public Health Service, U.S. Department of Health, Education and Welfare examined the problems of terminology and identification in the field of learning disabilities. It listed the ten most cited characteristics of learning disabled children. In order of frequency they were:

> (1) hyperactivity; (2) perceptual-motor impairments; (3) emotional liability; (4) general coordination deficits; (5) disorders of attention (short attention span, distractibility, perseveration); (6) impulsivity; (7) disorders of memory and thinking; (8) specific learning disabilities: (a) reading (b) arithmetic (c) writing (d) spelling; (9) disorders of speech and hearing; (10) equivocal neurological signs and electroencephalographic irregularities (p. 13).

However, it took until 1968 for another national group to issue a formal definition of learning disabled children. In that year the National Advisory Committee on Handicapped Children released a report that said:

> Children with special learning disabilities exhibit a disorder in one or more of the basic psychological processes involved in understanding or in using spoken or written language. These may be manifested in

disorders of listening, thinking, talking, reading, writing, spelling, or arithmetic. They include conditions which have been referred to as perceptual handicaps, brain injury, minimal brain dysfunctions, dyslexia, developmental aphasia, etc. They do not include learning problems due primarily to visual, hearing, or motor handicaps, to mental retardation, emotional disturbance, or to environmental disadvantage (p. 14).

The final period (1973 to present) is labeled the reaction/action phase by the author. During this period special educators of learning disabled children have been preoccupied with four issues that were stated clearly by Larsen (1978):

1. determining the true parameters of the learning disabilities field;
2. monitoring the proliferation of tests and materials presumed relevant to viable educational practice;
3. insuring that learning disabled students are provided instructional opportunities in accordance with their educational needs and civil rights; and
4. determining professional standards necessary for competent and ethical practice (p. 7).

When examined individually, Wiederholt's (1978) contention that issues generally have remained unchanged has validity.

First, special educators still are concerned about what children should be included in the learning disabilities subset. Another problem is raised by the fact that regular educators tend to label underachieving students as learning disabled and to use the label as a dumping ground for all students who misbehave or underachieve in schools (Larsen, 1978). Wiederholt (1978) and Hammill (1978) agree with this concern and generally take a position similar to Larsen's. These modern-day advocates have argued for exclusion of populations that could be better served by other specialists (reading and mathematics) and have fought any new criteria that would seek to expand the definition advanced by the National Advisory Committee on Handicapped Children in 1968.

Second, the proliferation of tests and materials in the field of learning disabilities has become a major concern. Larsen (1978) lamented the fact that the sudden growth of the learning disabilities category had given rise to the proliferation of numerous tests that purported to "diagnose" and "remediate." Wiederholt (1978) expressed concern over the same issue. To alleviate possible quackery or misguided intervention in the field, these educators suggested several cautions or indications that could be used to determine questionable tests and materials. Larsen (1978) suggested that special educators look for these indications of pretense:

1. promise of quick and easy "cures";
2. elaborate use of "clinical" descriptions or testimonials attesting to effectiveness;
3. absence of research, validity, or efficacy of the test or material; and
4. claims that the device in question is better than others found on the market (p. 9).

Wiederholt (1978) echoed the concern but from the standpoint of listing the shortcomings. He said:

1. Some tests are poorly constructed with regard to item selection, resulting in low reliability and poor validity.
2. Often these devices are poorly normed or the reliability of the devices is undetermined for problem learners.
3. In many cases the grade or age equivalents are not normed low enough to provide a specific score for the learning disabled adolescent.
4. Many tests rely heavily on reading and therefore are unsuitable for use with many learning disabled students.

Thus, the thrust for better tests and material has continued into the action/reaction phase.

Third, the issue of guaranteeing that the learning disabled student is provided equal educational opportunities still is being fought. It has been felt that many state agencies and local districts have been too inflexible in their attitudes toward program development for the learning disabled. Thus, LD professionals have reason to fear that the intent of P.L. 94-142 has been blunted. Instead of focusing on the severely impaired learning disabled student, most school systems have adopted the resource room concept. This has allowed them to focus on students with universally mildly handicapped underachieving conditions to the exclusion of those who are truly learning disabled.

The tendency to mainstream learning disabled students via the resource room arrangement has overshadowed the needs of the moderately to severely involved students. While the resource room service model combined with consultation with the regular classroom educator has been found appropriate at the elementary school level, it has encountered problems in the secondary schools. These problems can be traced to the conflict in the goals of the elementary and secondary curriculums, to the differential preparation of elementary and secondary teachers, and to different class configurations in elementary and secondary schools. As a result, educational alternatives for moderately and more severely impaired learning disabled students are circumscribed seriously. This same constriction of roles for special educators has hampered the development of programs for learning disabled adolescents. Thus, special education programs have failed to serve these youths adequately (Larsen, 1978; Weiderholt, 1978; Deshler, 1978).

The last issue that has called for action by educators has been the development and maintenance of professional standards. The field of special education has been in existence for only a little over a century and a half. However, it has enjoyed phenomenal growth since its inception. With this growth, professionals have felt a need to establish guidelines for the preparation of practitioners and to develop a code of ethics governing professionals in the field. Learning disabilities can be considered a latecomer to the field (1963). The Division for Children with Learning Disabilities (DCLD) has developed a code of ethics that can be used as guidelines for professionals. DCLD, the national organization for professional educators specializing in learning disorders, also has adopted standards of competencies needed by professionals who work with learning disabled students *(DCLD Newsletter,* 1976, p. 4).

From the professional's vantage point, the field of learning disabilities can be summarized in the words of Steve Larsen (1978), the tenth president of DCLD:

> To summarize, the field of learning disabilities finds itself at a point in time where significant and pervasive advancements may be obtained if appropriate actions are taken. Basic to any modifications of the current situation is the realization that the educator is the central person in planning, conducting, and/or coordinating the overall diagnostic and remedial efforts employed with the learning disabled individual (1978, p. 11).

PARENTS OF LEARNING DISABLED CHILDREN

If professionals have lived through the growth pains of the field, how have parents survived the differences in the state of the art? Parents of learning disabled children also have lived through the changing times in special education. Their children have been placed inappropriately, considered mentally retarded or emotionally disturbed, or described as hyperactive or dumb. Throughout all these changes, these parents have persevered. This tenacity was rewarded after Samuel Kirk's 1963 speech cited earlier. Following that speech the Association for Children with Learning Disabilities was formed, primarily to provide a forum for parents of learning disabled children. The influence of this parent group and its state affiliates is well documented. A survey of national programs by Clark and Richards (1968) showed that more than half (53 percent) of the states stated initially that parental pressure was the basic impetus for starting programs in learning disabilities. In the 1980s all states have educational programs for LD populations (Larsen, 1980).

Another special case can be made for parents of learning disabled children. McCarthy and McCarthy (1969) advanced this thesis on behalf of these parents.

They hypothesized that parents of cerebral palsied children were among the first to form peer groups. They were followed by parents of the mentally retarded, the emotionally disturbed, and then learning disabilities. It seems that parents of cerebral palsied children had powerful motivators to spur them into action. Half of all cerebral palsied children have degrees of retardation, approximately 70 percent have speech problems, many have associated visual and/or auditory handicaps, and all have brain and motoric problems. These multiples of handicapping emotions mobilized parents into action. Thus, the evolving characteristics theory of handicaps that motivated the formation of later parent groups have been less dramatic. Retardation is less dramatic than cerebral palsy, emotional disturbance is less dramatic than mental retardation, and learning disabilities are less dramatic than emotional disturbance. So following the dramatic theory hierarchy proposed by the McCarthys, parents of the learning disabled did not fare well until the passage of P.L. 94-142.

However, while parents of learning disabled children may have been late in forming their parent groups, they were active in promoting rights for handicapped individuals in the 1970s. They are showing little signs of lessening their efforts in the 1980s. Issues that commanded the attention of parents of learning disabled children include:

- the number of children assigned to the category of learning disabled in special education
- the preparation of special and regular educational personnel who will work with these children
- the instructional placement of the children
- the issue of free and appropriate education in the least restrictive environment
- labeling and its effects

CONCERNS OF PARENTS OF LDCs

Parents of learning disabled children (LDCs) are perplexed by several of the issues that beset special educators who work with these students. For example, these parents have strong feelings about the labeling process. They also have watched large numbers of children, mild and underachieving, being pushed toward the category of LD in schools. Parents of LD children are left wondering about the intent of school systems to comply with P.L. 94-142. They have the feeling that Larsen (1978) was right in his assessment that schools were using the LD subset as a catchall for the mild to moderate underachiever. Meanwhile, schools have continued to expand LD programming (Deshler, 1978).

Parents of LD students are concerned about the preparation of educators who work with their children. They have witnessed the many professional influences such as food additives, deficient environments, or neurological disorders that have dominated the field. While acknowledging these influences, parents are frustrated and confused when they see special education learning disabilities specialists working as tutors and reading teachers or assisting all underachievers in the regular classroom. They would rather have the talents of these professionals used with their LD children, especially the more moderately and severely impaired students. Another issue of teacher preparation that puzzles LD parents is the regular educators' lack of knowledge about LD children. Since P.L. 94-142 has made special education a national priority, parents of LD youngsters are questioning the commitment of teachers in one school district who referred 40 percent of children for suspected learning disabilities (Larsen, 1978).

Such behavior on the part of regular educators so infuriated a mother of an LD child in a Texas school district that she led the fight to get State Board of Education approval that *all* elementary and secondary teachers preparing to obtain teacher certification in Texas must have knowledge and skills relating to the education of exceptional/handicapped pupils, including the concept of least restrictive alternatives; characteristics and learning differences; informal assessment and instructional techniques; and processes of admission, review, and dismissal in Individualized Education Programs (Marion, 1978).

Placement of LD children has long occupied the attention of their parents. In all LD children, intelligence essentially is normal. The contrast between their normal and subnormal behavior and abilities has caused parents to feel great frustration. This chameleon type of behavior has been called a "touch of honey" (McCarthy & McCarthy, 1969). This "touch of honey" phenomenon is characterized by an absence of deformity in physical appearance and the presence of average or above average academic ability in some areas in the child. The frustrated parent entertains false hope that the LD child's erratic behavior will disappear and that academic performance will improve. Such a syndrome has caused parents to long for a cure for the educational, medical, or psychological treatment that will enable the youngster to "become completely normal." Some parents feel it was these very elusive characteristics of learning disabilities that made it easy for educators to deny the existence of this handicap and contributed to its absence in special education until 1963.

Another issue that creates a great deal of anxiety among parents is the concept of mainstreaming. Already concerned about the lack of placement or misplacement of their children, the preparation of teachers, and the labeling process, these parents have come to question the concept of mainstreaming that offers them only one alternative—the resource room. They are especially confused and angered by local school districts that have decided learning disabled pupils are children exhibiting universally mild academic problems that can be handled the most efficient and economic way by periodic trips to the resource room, with the balance of the school day spent in the regular classroom. It has been precisely this kind of dilemma that has caused parents to conceptualize mainstreaming in the following manner:

> A fourth grade class has 24 pupils. Three of the students are classified learning disabled. One of the LD students has been retained a year and is functioning at a third grade level in math and is physically large for his age. A second LD pupil is performing at grade level in math but reads at a pre-school level. The third LD youngster is at grade level in reading but is at a first grade level in math. Another youngster labeled mildly retarded has been retained twice and has second grade math and reading skills (Cawley et al, 1979, p. 28).

Watching their students in this regular classroom, it has appeared to parents of learning disabled children that their youngsters have been assigned automatically to a resource room, have been mainstreamed, or have been assigned to a helping teacher (Larsen, 1978). In their minds, parents of the LD children in this class are assured that their youngsters will not receive the attention they need to achieve success academically.

INVOLVING PARENTS OF PRESCHOOL LDs

> A particularly crucial function . . . is that of guidance or treatment of parents. . . .They have a right and a responsibility to participate closely in the planning for [the child's] care. . . . Some parents have experienced profound difficulties in caring for their . . . child, owing to the nature of the child's condition, to their own subjective difficulties, or as usually the case, to a combination of the two (Kelman, 1956, p. 46).

The challenge of working with parents of preschool learning disabled children from that perspective can be approached through an examination of the crisis periods in the lives of parents of exceptional children that were discussed more fully in Chapter 3.

The first crisis often comes at birth or on suspicion of the handicap. Generally the latter factor has been predominant, since the majority of learning disabled children do not exhibit telltale signs of handicapping conditions at birth. Thus, the child's early behavior in school or in the home often has been the initial warning to parents that something is wrong. Parents of a preschooler can be heard describing their youngsters in these terms:

"He's constantly on the go"

"He's easily upset"

"She has a terrible temper"

Although such statements could describe children in general, the feelings attached to them by parents of potential LD children are laden with emotional overtones. Parents who suspect a handicap are worried, troubled, and bewildered. Some experience troubled feelings because they fear the schools might not condone the erratic actions of their children. Others are bewildered because they have seen their children act like other normally developing youngsters in so many other daily situations. Still other parents are worried because they harbor the feeling that their child might not be all right and might have to be labeled as "deviant." Thus, the "touch of honey" syndrome is introduced early into parents' daily routine.

In times like these, the special educator has the opportunity to be helpful to the parent and/or to the regular educator. If the child is participating in preschool or kindergarten activities, the helping special educator can encourage the parents to seek an early diagnosis and also show an understanding of their reluctance to seek such assistance. Helping educators should be tolerant of parents' feelings about early identification and diagnosis. Early diagnosis and prevention have gained wide acceptance and approval in medical and psychological circles but they only recently have enjoyed the same status in special education. More specifically, it took the passage of P.L. 94-142 to establish the field of learning disorders firmly as a legitimate entity among handicapping/exceptional conditions in children (Larsen, 1978).

Having watched what the stigma of labeling has done to children in the areas of emotional disturbance and mental retardation, parents of LDs can be excused if they are not ready to embrace wholeheartedly the designation of "at risk" for their youngsters. Helping teachers should be understanding of the anxiety that envelops these parents, who ask themselves: "What if the diagnosis shows mental retardation?" "Will my child be diagnosed and then recommended for mentally retarded or emotionally disturbed classes?" Although P.L. 94-142 has made such subjective judgments a thing of the past, many parents have long memories, and past inequalities of treatment are not forgotten easily. Helping special educators must work with parents to minimize these fears and exchange information with them. Lack of knowledge about the exceptionality of LD can cause much of the anxiety parents feel.

Helping teachers should be concerned that parents not be overcome by the many forms of LD. Realizing that even professionals have had difficulty in ascertaining all of the LD groupings, helping professionals should be sensitized to accept the parents' confusion. To ease this crisis, the helping persons should listen for the confusion in the parents' verbal and written communications, analyze it, and respond in a manner that will clarify LD classifications. Their responses can be framed to meet the parents' individual needs. Perhaps the parents want more information concerning the disability. Special teachers can take the initiative and advocate that additional information be provided to parents. However, it may be decided by the professionals interacting in the case that the special educator functioning in the role of ombudsman may be better able to communicate the nature of the disorder to the parents.

The parents may be fearful that confirmation of the diagnosis actually will persuade the child to act "a certain way all the time"—retarded or disturbed. Many parents are not prepared to have their child pay this high cost of being deviant (Sagarin, 1976). After all, parents have had their "touch of honey" and are not willing to relinquish this hope for normalcy for the harsh reality of a diagnosis. They could have a healthier state of mind if they denied the child's condition and hoped for the best. In this instance special education teachers can be helpful in the denial process by acting as sounding boards so that parents can reflect upon the reasons for their statements. Helping teachers can be instigators of a healthier approach to an understanding of the problem by listening, reflecting, and making nonjudgmental responses that accurately restate the parents' beliefs. Parents can be assured, however, that under P.L. 94-142 their rights and those of their children will be protected.

In summation, the outcome of the special educators' work at this level should have produced parents who are willing to have their child undergo diagnosis. The special teachers have been supportive and understanding, have provided information, and have made suggestions when asked for them. The final decision, however, has had to be made by the parents.

Learning To Cope with the Diagnosis

If parents have consented to the diagnosis and if the diagnosis of LD is confirmed, the parents confront another crisis. Some are unable to accept the diagnosis that their child is learning disabled or they may have second thoughts concerning the diagnosis. Having watched the child in the protected environment of the home, the parents might have reservations about accepting the school's confirmations and recommendations. Parents' anxiety concerning early identification and diagnosis can cause them to fight against the acceptance of the finding. Old fears about labeling can materialize. Parents have been known to cite the child's highest levels of performance as proof that he is not retarded or disturbed. In doing so, they often conveniently neglect to mention other areas in which the child is functioning poorly (Krupp & Schwartzberg, 1963).

This rationalization and denial of the child's condition is not surprising to the alert special education helping teacher. Having heard the parents recite example after example to disprove the diagnosis and the recommended courses of action, the special educators do not attempt to prevent them from shopping around by arguing with them. Rather, the teachers will have the sensitivity to forego lecturing parents, to show them how expensive searching for a cure can be, or to inform them that they have gotten the best information that money can buy. Realizing that parents might be helped by the act of shopping around, the teachers are accepting and understanding, demonstrating support by allowing parents to return again and again with the same questions until they become more knowledgeable about the child's learning disability.

It should be noted that ombudsman special educators are careful to show impartial attitudes toward parents during their shopping ventures. If they observe that shopping has therapeutic value, they should encourage parents to get a second opinion. However, special teachers should be reminded that while some shopping is therapeutic, parents caught up in their emotions can become engrossed in futile searching. Advocate special educators have responsibility to assist parents to overcome the desire to pursue an extended search when accompanying symptoms of grief and depression appear to be chronic. Not only should special educators have an open-door policy, they also should move more aggressively to involve parents in discussions that may offer the educators an opportunity to suggest actions other than shopping during this period of protest actions. Special educators, realizing the trust that parents have in them (Carter, 1974), should move aggressively to mirror the frustration that parents undoubtedly are experiencing. On each succeeding visit, they should feed back parental disclaimers of the child's exceptionality until parents are better able to accept evidence of the handicap. If advocates fail to accomplish this goal, they then should be understanding enough of parents' feelings to refer them for additional professional help to avoid endangering their mental health.

During this period, one of the dilemmas parents face is, "What do I tell my friends?" Special education teachers can be helpful in explaining to parents in lay language the nature of the learning disability. Professionals often use the words dyslexia and aphasia without the accompanying sensitivity to the parents' desire for a clearer definition of their meanings.

Professionals' failure to relate the learning disabled condition specifically to the child and to describe expected behavior patterns often leaves parents feeling less than coequals. Parents will be accorded respect by helping teachers who exhibit compromising or nonpaternalistic behavior. By so doing, the educators assure parents that they should not feel too intimidated to ask questions or to seek to clarify the diagnosis.

The end result of this parent-teacher interaction should leave the parents intelligent consumers of information. Using this information to explain the learning disability to friends is important to parents. Parents who are dubious about the diagnosis will have been helped to overcome any guilt they might have felt when discussing their child's learning disability with others.

The Problem of Others' Reactions

This "others' reaction," as it is called (Weber, 1974), has serious implication for parents and special education teachers. The teachers should understand this feeling without assessing blame. If the parents already have blamed themselves, or feel guilty about what and how to tell others, any show of unrewarding behavior on the part of the teachers will convince the parents that they were at fault for the condition. Special educators should help parents reduce any guilt they might feel by listening to their complaints without condemning them through silence. It is of the utmost importance that helping teachers not become the accusers by silent consent, but become active participants by asking questions designed to clear up parents' discrepancies regarding their perception of the handling of the diagnosis.

Up to this point, the discussion of the learning disabled child has been carried on within the framework of the preschooler, with emphasis on identification and diagnosis as a positive approach to working with exceptional children. Special education teachers should be cautioned that not everyone is prone to view diagnosis and identification as prevention in such a positive perspective when the problem is considered an educational issue. Keogh and Becker (1973) have stated the case well. They have indicated that educators are hypothesizing when they seek to identify preschool and kindergarten youngsters as learning disabled. In other words, the atypical conditions of learning disabilities and failure and school have not yet developed. The educator's concern is that the atypical conditions will develop. However, if young children have not been exposed to a grade level reading program, they cannot be classified as failures. Therefore, special education preschool helping teachers must recognize the inherent danger in joining in the prediction or hypothesis of a learning problem. They should be aware of the possibility that predicting learning problems has a built-in expectancy phenomenon. When children are identified as high risk in the early years, there is a danger that a set of expectancies, anxieties, and differentiated treatment patterns can be fashioned into a negative self-fulfilling prophecy by teachers (Larsen, 1975). These effects must be considered by special educators seeking to assist parents who are fearful that they have a learning disabled child.

To be successful in working with parents of preschool children with the potential for learning disabilities, special educators should have a firm commitment to early identification. They should be convinced that it is critical to the well-being of the child. Therefore, they should be prepared to follow these guidelines (Keogh & Becker, 1973) when hypothesizing with parents:

1. specification of outcome
2. recognition of children's abilities and competencies that might be used to maximize success experiences
3. inclusion of task and situation
4. assessment of school behavior
5. identification and remediation

The preschool special educator who follows these guidelines should feel a great deal more comfortable when working with parents and when advocating early diagnosis of children with the potential for learning disabilities.

INVOLVING PARENTS OF ELEMENTARY AGE LDCs

> Early diagnosis is desirable when it leads to prevention, early treatment or constructive counseling; it is irrelevant if it is purely academic and does not change the course of events; it is harmful if, in balance, child or family reap more disadvantages than benefits (Wolfensberger, 1965, p. 65).

These words regarding the mentally retarded are equally valid concerning the learning disabled child. In the case of the latter, the plea has been made for early identification and diagnosis of preschool youngsters. Despite some of the negative effects associated with premature prediction, the positive results of improved functioning on the part of the child are convincing arguments in support of its continued use in early childhood educational programs.

Elementary school programs for the learning disabled have made extensive use of the diagnostic-prescriptive approach in educational programming. However, the majority of the remedial efforts were directed toward individual instruction in a small classroom setting (Hansen, 1970). Perhaps this process was instrumental in the schools' thinking that promoted the concept of the LD specialist as tutor, reading teacher, or teacher's aide. The stress on remedial reading and/or related compensatory educational attempts may have facilitated equating learning disabled pupils with the unmotivated and poorly taught underachievers, the environmentally deprived, or the dull-normal (Larsen, 1978). The process could have been precipitated by the lack of attention given the roles and responsibilities of the LD special educator by the professionals themselves.

The problems of role definition and program misdirection in elementary schools probably relate more closely to the confusion in the field of LD than to any other factor. The field of learning disabilities is characterized by a wide spectrum of educational characteristics that do not lend themselves to a convenient classification and categorization system. Cruickshank (1977) stated that "there are absolutely no adequate data of either an epidemiological or demographic nature to provide a base for adequate programming" (p. 61). Larsen (1978) noted that a common frame of reference for understanding and intervening with the LD pupil has not developed. He observed that until 1975 and the passage of P.L. 94-142, LD was not recognized as a legitimate entity in special education.

The years 1963 to 1975 covered an era when schools and families went about the business of attempting to educate young learning disabled pupils. However, if parents of elementary LD pupils expected Samuel Kirk's attempt at a definition to open the doors to a full education for their children, they were mistaken. Instead, parents watched as their children continued to be identified mistakenly as emotionally disturbed or mentally retarded by regular educators. LD professionals became involved in the issues of definition and characteristics. From the standpoint of the professional educator, Larsen (1978) made the following point:

> However, it is important to note that while issues such as dietary treatments, "deviant" home environments, articulatory disorders, and neurophysiological retraining may have some relevance to learning disabilities in general, they are largely tangential to the primary characteristics and behaviors that have caused the pupil actually to be labelled as learning disabled (p. 6).

This statement basically created the paradox that exists to date between LD specialists and parents. Barsch (1969) first recognized the paradox and stated:

> Most parents . . . regard their child's teacher as being well trained for the job. They automatically assign their child's teacher the prestige of "specialist." . . . This produces an interesting paradox. The teacher has been influenced to regard the parent negatively while the parent has been influenced to regard the teacher positively (p. 9).

The paradox has special meaning to parents of elementary LD children. If there is a bias in education, it has been more pervasive at the elementary level (Marion, 1978). Schools at this level have been called child care centers. Teachers and curricula have been labeled child centered. Even parents have seemed to acquiesce in this phenomenon in education. They have made their presence felt in elementary Parent-Teacher Association meetings by sheer force of numbers. Elementary years, then, have become the Mecca of parental efforts. Special education generally has followed the lead of regular education. Emphasis and effort have been placed on the elementary grades. Growth of LD programs at this level has been rapid. Deshler (1978) commented on the growth of programs during the span from 1963 to 1975:

> During the past ten years educational programs for children identified as learning disabled have evolved as major educational options at the elementary level. The rate of growth has far exceeded similar special education alternatives for other groups of handicapped children (p. 2).

If LD programs have been increasing rapidly at the elementary school level and have been directed toward the appropriate age groups, what is the paradox and why does it exist between parents and educators?

Behind the Paradox

The paradox can be tied to the belief held by many teachers of LD pupils that their educational role is superior to the emotional needs and wishes of the parent. Parents, however, consider the needs of the child in a holistic sense. In this sense, educators' tangential concerns are of major concern to parents. All too frequently special educators for elementary learning disabled children went about the business of diagnosis and remediation with no concern for the expressed feelings of the parents of the pupils. Thus, LD teachers were more prone to zero in on educational aspects of the problem and to leave the counseling to experts. In the meantime physicians, optometrists, and social workers developed programs designed to lessen the effects of the learning disability. The professional educator was assigned the role of the specialist who carried out the prescriptions of other professionals in the school setting. In other words, "the extremely crucial and pervasive role of the educator was largely diminished and underplayed when compared to other supposedly more expert professional disciplines" (Larsen, 1978).

Parents had a different perspective of the LD teacher's role. They were not content with the efforts of physicians, optometrists, and social workers. They saw physicians and optometrists working from a medical model. This model was mostly diagnostic, with little time for counseling and even less for instruction. While social workers supposedly were offering counseling for parents, much of their effort centered on the referral process since their preparation in working with the handicapped population was limited. After listening to parents, they facilitated the movement of LD parents back to these same specialists for remediation. This impeded the role that LD teachers played in the helping process. The major effort of the process was being handled by professionals whose training was geared to the deficit model—learning disability was a pathological agent. As Barsch (1976) stated:

> In the early days of the movement, definitions as well as interpretations were slanted toward delineation of various pathological agents which could be held etiologically accountable for a learner's present state of difficulty (p. 13).

However, parents viewed these professional decisions unfavorably. They wanted more from the special educator than a piecemeal approach ordered by a professional who saw them only occasionally. Parents viewed the special educator as the person who should be working with them and their children as the expert to educate, counsel, and assist them in remediating the problem. It was this difference in outlook that produced the paradox between LD special education teachers and parents.

Just as Barsch (1969) recognized this dilemma between LD educators and parents, he also was one of the first to recommend a remedy to resolve the paradox. In *The Parent Teacher Partnership* (1969), he advocated a closer, helping relationship with parents from a positive viewpoint. This model would be based upon a mutual cosharing of experiences and responsibilities between parents and teachers of LD children.

Many LD teachers in the early stages took on the challenge of working with parents. However, many continued to bypass the dilemma until P.L. 94-142 took effect in 1975. This forced those early elementary LD teachers who had taken refuge in the "carry out the prescription" approach to try another way. The act attempted to resolve the paradox by guaranteeing a coequal status for parents and making the basic assumption that educators were willing to work with parents.

Bewildered parents of elementary age LD children soon learned that it no longer was feasible to expect other professionals to provide leadership in determining the methods by which their students could be served. The initiation of the Individualized Education Program seemed to them to clarify the role of the teacher of LD children. Thus, under P.L. 94-142, LD teacher roles became more prominent but also more demanding. The act gave the schools primary responsibility for the well-being of the LD child outside the family, and established the role of the LD educator as a primary caregiver. The LD teacher now has become a front-line advocate ombudsman and case manager for the LD child and parent.

Facing Two Types of Parents

The teacher of elementary learning disabled children should be prepared to face two types of parents. The first group is composed of adults who have been made aware of the handicapping condition through preschool screening methods. The second group has enrolled children in regular kindergarten or first grade in anticipation of a regular grade sequence pattern. Sensitive kindergarten and first grade teachers were the first to note inefficiencies of learning and to initiate referral processes to provide appropriate placement for the child (Barsch, 1969).

Regardless of the placement sequence, both groups of parents need a sensitive, helping special education LD teacher. Parents in the first group (preschool screened) enter the regular school program with the expectation that it will have continuity with preschool efforts and that their input will be welcomed. At present, these parents are in the minority of adults with LD children. Teachers of these learning disabled children should be willing to accept parents who have experienced the trauma of the diagnosis and are prepared to seek participation as full-fledged members of the instructional team. Eager to improve and to assist, the special education helping teacher faces the possibility of a meeting with well-educated parents from a middle to upper income bracket who have taken the time to read and to study the symptoms of the condition (Marion, 1979). However, the special educator should not be lulled into false complacency when encountering these parents. Chances are excellent that these parents have been consumed by the same feelings of bewilderment and confusion as the others as they struggle with the uncertainty of the meaning of a special child. These parents also probably have experienced the "touch of honey" syndrome. Fortified now with the preschool experiences behind them, these parents arrive at the public school door for a continuation of the therapeutic efforts that have characterized the child's early days.

The task of special education helping teachers has been either helped or hindered by the preschool experiences. If the former have been positive, the chances of encountering parents who are disposed to show a positive attitude toward schools is enhanced. In this instance the parents anticipate special education for their children, but may be found at different stages of acceptance regarding the exceptionality. The special educators must not be dismayed if parents still question the diagnosis, still search for a cure, and still hope for the miraculous recovery. These stressful situations occur often in meetings between the early elementary special educator teachers and parents. Teachers hope that at this stage parents are farther advanced on Maslow's (1954) hierarchy so they jointly can work out an IEP for the child in a less emotional atmosphere. Many parents, however, still are struggling. Some have problems of self-esteem. Others attempt to fight feelings of estrangement or isolation. Wherever these parents are located along the continuum of emotions, the helping teacher must have the patience to listen and to accept their feelings and to assist them toward self-actualization.

When faced with these situations, helping special educators have the responsibility to hear the parents out. Most assuredly, armed with objective facts, the special educators must keep the parent in touch with reality. However, many parents are caught up in the mistaken belief that food additives, drug therapy, vitamin insufficiencies, or florescent lighting are the guilty culprits in their child's learning disability. The uncertainty over the diagnosis may cloud the learning disability prediction. The net effect may result in confused and bewildered parents who are looking to the helping special educator for the cure-all prescription. Special teachers should be careful not to try to impress the parents with the foolishness of their beliefs. Rather, the teachers should be listening to discern the parents' concerns. As they listen to the feelings that may be causing the discrepancies, helping teachers can provide constant feedback to the parents through repetition of important feelings. Hearing these feelings has the effect of a sounding board for parents who otherwise might not have been aware of their level of acceptance of the child's condition.

From Advocate to Ombudsman

Helping teachers should remember that their primary efforts at this point should be directed toward building an atmosphere of trust and mutual respect with the parents. Mindful of this function, teacher helpers assume the role of advocates for the child. Rather than admonishing parents for their searches, special teachers seek to communicate the children's unique characteristics and learning problems. Helping persons must not dismiss parents' feelings or relegate them to a second-class position. They must not engage in argumentation concerning the relative merits of drug, food additives, or genetic predispositions toward dyslexia. Helping teachers acknowledge these concerns but also orchestrate the child's educational plan as case managers. As such, helping teachers listen, ever alert for parental thinking and wishes that may produce discrepancies in the IEP planning.

At times helping teachers must assume the role of ombudsmen to ameliorate the feelings that result in frustration for the parents. Professional opinion may prescribe drugs for a hyperactive youngster. Parents may be frustrated and worried because of what they perceive as a possible addiction to the drug and because of the possible effect of the medication on school performance. Helping teachers must deal first with the emotions being expressed by parents. By listening empathetically, helping teachers should be prepared to offer parents guidelines for observing their child. Parents should be encouraged to ask the following questions:

1. Does the child finish what he starts—chores, games, projects?
2. Does the child play cooperatively?
3. Is the child flexible about sudden plan changes or situations?
4. Is the child impulsive and takes risks without thinking?
5. Does the child procrastinate and dawdle a lot?
6. Does the child "fool around" at mealtime rather than eat?
7. Does the child get "over stimulated" or lose control when angered or excited? (Fowlie, 1973, p. 354).

If the responses are in the positive, parents can be expected to display additional anxiety, to become increasingly concerned about the ill effects of the drugs, and to bring their concerns to special educators as a sounding board on what to do. Even if the questions are answered in the negative, special educators should be prepared to continue to buttress parents who might need to be reassured that they are doing the right thing.

Special educators should assure parents that they, too, will be vigilant and concerned about the child's welfare and functional ability in school. Thus, they will be volunteering to observe the child's classroom behavior. Helping teachers will observe the child's ability to function in school and ask themselves these questions:

1. Does the child work in spurts slowly and often not finish the assigned work?
2. Is the child's handwriting illegible and messy?
3. Does the child initiate or become involved in most of the classroom incidents?
4. Do little noises of the other classmates disturb or distract the child?
5. Does the child have a poor or fluctuating memory?
6. Does the child have a loud voice and use it at inappropriate times?
7. Is the child impulsive in work? (Fowlie, 1973, p. 352).

Parents and teachers who can answer these questions in the negative have reason to believe that the prescribed drug is working effectively and helping the child to function properly in the education setting. Parents and teachers who respond in the affirmative probably harbor doubts about the effectiveness of the dosages. They also may be concerned about attention and concentration and/or other evidences of academic and performance problems that affect the child's ability to function in school.

Working together, special educators and parents agree to do two things by design: (1) The helping educator acknowledges the parents' right to be concerned. Helping persons respect the ambivalence parents may feel. (2) Special educators are attuned to the fact that parents might fear that the child cannot function without medication but are equally terrified about possible addiction.

Helping special educators acting as ombudsmen between parents and physicians can empathize with parents to ameliorate differences between the two sides and to act as advocates for inclusion or exclusion of elements in the child's program based on factual observation. In either instance, case manager special educators work with parents to draw up or to implement an educational plan that will record in the IEP either the parents' favor or disfavor of drug use.

Demoting Pathological Origination

One of the biggest obstacles in working with parents of learning disabled children has been the emphasis upon LD as of pathological origination. Barsch (1976) indicated the chronology of agents: first, it was family breakdown, then metabolic disturbances, next vitamin deficiencies, followed by food allergies, and finally the emphasis on dyslexia. However, the problems of the majority of learning disabled children are not rooted in pathology. Thus, parents continue to be concerned when their children fail to learn. Successful learning has eagerly been sought by parents for their exceptional LD children at the elementary level.

However, these parents should not be compelled to seek out educational alternatives.

The learning disabilities helping person should join with parents as an advocate to insist that the necessary school resources be allocated to prevent or to minimize failure. This role should be apparent to the LD educators and to the parents. Helping special educators are uniquely qualified to cope with the needs of this population. Therefore, when considering the IEP and its programmatic and supportive components, LD helping persons must be primed to advance the placement of the pupil in the most advantageous learning environment. Realizing that parents of LD students already are fearful about the benefits of mainstreaming, they should be dedicated to the task of ensuring effective programming. While supporting the posture that mainstreaming is a viable alternative, they also should acknowledge to parents that the field *is* exemplified by severe academic underachievement, often accompanied by language disorders.

In instances where resource room arrangements or consultation with regular teachers are dictated or in cases of severe learning difficulties, the role of LD teachers must be extended beyond that of advocate. Certainly advocacy for program and placement is to be desired and advocacy for resources should be promoted. LD helping persons should be advocates for parents who are seeking services. However, the more crucial roles for the helping teachers may be those of ombudsmen and case managers for the parents.

Clearly, LD helping teachers are pointedly aware that they must assist parents a great deal in the area of the affective (feeling) domain. Helping teachers always must recognize parents ''in pain'' and respond to their pleas for guidance. However, the majority of the parents' concerns, while cloaked in feelings and emotions, are focused on the inability of the children to achieve academically. Thus, teachers describe youngsters in these terms:

''The child is easily distracted even by minor noises or movements in the classroom.''

''The child's overall IQ is in the above-average range but he scores below average in math.''

''The child talks slowly and is hard to understand.''

Parents can be heard discussing the same children in the following phrases:

''The teacher says the child is unteachable because he will not pay attention in class.''

''The child does pretty well with most of the subjects, but can't learn to do math.''

''The child twists words or stutters.''

Parents and teachers thus view the same problems from different educational perspectives. The basic issue is whether the two principal child caretakers can resolve their differences in order to remediate the problem.

For instance, the parents could be concerned over the child's inability to read, and the inability to read might be linked to an impairment in visual perception. Parents might constantly ask the universal question: "What can I do to help my child?"

In response, the special education helping teachers have the opportunity to establish rapport with parents. They should attempt to keep the lines of communication open by exchanging information with parents in a nonthreatening manner. First, any exchange of information must be at the parents' level. Some parents will have to be communicated with in lay language. Others have the sophistication to understand the problem when defined in more professional terms. Second, helping teachers should make suggestions for strengthening the child's visual modality. These suggestions should be given with the understanding that they not only will help the child's reading problem and enhance his self-concept but also will do much to increase the parents' self-esteem. The teachers' suggestions for home-school cooperation should be inexpensive and should not be so specialized that parents cannot perform them with their children. Teachers can suggest the following ideas to parents:

1. *To increase visual discrimination and a left-to-right progression across the page*
   a. Ask the child to circle the letters of the alphabet in sequential order. Begin with the letter "a" and end with "z." Use a magazine or newspaper article. Letters (g, v, and z) appearing infrequently (not after three lines) can be written in by parent or child. An alphabet should be available to the child who does not know the alphabet in sequential order.
   b. Ask the child to circle every "b," capital and small letter, in the article or paragraph. This exercise is especially helpful for the child who cannot distinguish "b's" from "d's." Next have him make small b's into capital B's with a red pencil.
2. *To increase visual memory*
   a. Select a word from the article and write it in manuscript on a card or sheet of paper. Then ask the child to locate the word in the magazine or newspaper and underline it from left to right.
   b. Point to a 3 letter word in the magazine and ask the child to write it from memory. Let him see the word to determine the correctness of his answer.
3. *To encourage the child's interest in words and reading*
   a. Ask the child to look through the magazine and cut out all of the words in headlines that he recognizes. Have him paste the words on a sheet of paper for reading to his parents.

b. Have the child locate all the scary, happy, or action words in an article. If the child can't read, parents can read sentences and the child can indicate when he recognizes a word from the designated category (De Genaro, 1973, pp. 102–105).

In these examples, the LD teacher will work with parents interested in helping their children develop reading skills. Similar parent-school programs in mathematics or other academic areas could be offered. Most elementary parents would be gratified that they would not have to play it by ear. Life at home would be improved, with parents becoming coequals in the educational program. Children who have been subjected to failure and have poor self-esteem will have an opportunity to continue at home with the successes started and achieved at school. Parents are pleased and their children are satisfying to them. The special education helping teacher will have assisted by acting as case manager, advocate, and ombudsman in the process.

INVOLVING PARENTS OF LD ADOLESCENTS

As children identified as learning disabled in the elementary grades have progressed through the programs provided them, it has become apparent that the impact of their learning ability disabilities has not been substantially altered and that, consequently, they enter secondary schools still hampered by their disability (Deshler, 1978, p. 2).

This quote was made by a leader (Deshler, 1978) in the field of learning disabilities, but parents of LD adolescents have known this fact for a long time. They have lived with the effects of the educational system on the adolescent for years. Their youths have been objects of ridicule and accused of not trying hard enough when in reality they are making the best effort possible. Unsuccessful academic attempts sometimes have resulted in juvenile delinquency. At other times, attempts to correct educational and social inadequacies have so threatened LD adolescents that they have retreated into withdrawal. In a minority of instances, parents have watched their teenagers become creative, productive, and/or develop survival skills in spite of their handicap.

Concerns of Parents of LD Adolescents

For most of these parents, the problem generally has been one of long duration and only in rare cases of recent vintage. However, schools still label a high percentage (5 to 10 percent and sometimes as high as 40 percent) as learning disabled. This can be attributed to unclear perceptions of what constitutes an LD pupil or to administrative expediency (Larsen, 1978). Whatever the reason, parents are measuring the amount of services available at the secondary levels against the growing number of young children being labeled. When they have considered the amount of money appropriated and the artificially imposed population ceiling in special education (2 percent), they become even more threatened by the likelihood of reduced services. Parents are afraid that hastily conceived programs to correct long-time academic problems in reading, mathematics, or language will be inadequate for preparing the adolescent to function effectively in the world of work.

Another parental concern is the fascination of secondary schools with the concept of mainstreaming. Wiederholt (1978) stressed the pitfalls of wholesale adaptation of the elementary models of resource room and consultation with the regular teacher. Different curriculum problems, larger and constantly changing student populations, and different types of teacher training all contribute to the unmet needs of parents who wish to see a student-centered rather than a subject-centered curriculum at the secondary level. Parents fear that students with less severe conditions will fall through the cracks while more severely disabled students will be thrust into learning situations that are not the required least restrictive environment alternatives.

Parents also are bewildered by the lack of programs that focus on the social and emotional development of LD teenagers. One of the frequent criticisms of secondary school programming is that it traditionally has centered on the academics to the exclusion of career/vocational and social/emotional needs of students. Parents see these deficits as caused by schools' failure to provide assistance in programs or curricula that would help the adolescents develop the kind of personality that would not turn people off or would enable well-adjusted youths to develop job-seeking and job-holding skills in society. They are asking schools to return more acceptable individuals to a more acceptable society (Seigel, 1974).

Parents are concerned over what they perceive as an inadequate supply of trained personnel to work with LD adolescents. They are well acquainted with the high dropout rate of handicapped adolescents (double that of nonhandicapped students) (Brolin, 1976). Parents have a firsthand knowledge of the underemployment and unemployment figures (Martin, 1972). They have been made personally familiar with the lack of academic progress of secondary students (Barsch, 1969: Deshler, 1978; Larsen, 1978; Wiederholt, 1978). Based on these results, parents complain about the lack of success of schools in working with LD adolescents.

CONCERNS OF SECONDARY LD EDUCATORS

A major concern of secondary LD educators who work with adolescents is that of definition. Secondary educators have not been immune from the struggle to maintain the purity of the population they serve. Larsen (1978) emphasized the importance of the problem and listed it as one of the primary issues facing LD educators. Hammill (1978), Deshler (1978), and Wiederholt (1975) also noted that concern for this problem warranted consideration by professionals in light of LD adolescents' lack of academic achievement.

Another concern of secondary professionals in the LD area is the issue of territorial rights (Wiederholt, 1975). Teachers of LD teenagers have been caught up in the mainstreaming favoritism of schools that tends to obscure any other educational arrangements (Larsen, 1978). Even though the term mainstreaming has given way to least restrictive environment, many school systems cling to the resource room or consultation with regular teacher as the major instructional arrangement.

Another concern of secondary LD teachers centers on instruction and assessment. Wiederholt (1978) bemoaned the fact that secondary special education had tended to follow the dictates of regular secondary education in its approach to LD adolescents. Larsen (1978) decried the programming of public school systems that underutilized the talents of LD specialists as tutors, reading teachers, or aides. Both criticized the wholesale adoption of commercial assessment instruments by school systems without consideration of their reliability and/or validity. They were joined in this criticism by other leaders in the field (Hammill, 1975; Hammill & Larsen, 1974; Newcomer & Hammill, 1976).

Still another important concern is teacher preparation. Although secondary schools have been under attack for several years, it took P.L. 94-142 to accelerate programs in secondary special education (McNutt & Heller, 1978). When programs were initiated, they tended to follow the traditional patterns of secondary schools. This approach often was to the detriment of LD adolescents (Wiederholt, Mann & Goodman, 1978). However, Deshler (1979) observed that while general education should not dictate decisions for the handicapped, special educators should have an awareness of what is occurring with their counterparts to become productive decision makers. Teacher training programs for secondary LD personnel are affected by the actions and feelings of their counterparts who teach the larger proportion of children in the regular curriculum. At present, despite P.L. 94-142, not many secondary teacher preparation programs or public school secondary programs have been established.

WORKING WITH PARENTS OF LD ADOLESCENTS

The special education teacher who seeks to help parents of LD adolescents does not have an easy task. Helping teacher responsibilities are extensive, as defined by the Council for Exceptional Children and its Division for Children with Learning Disabilities. The teachers are expected to carry out the following duties:

1. establish and maintain rapport with parents
2. develop and maintain channels of communication with parents with regard to their child's social, physical, and academic progress
3. effectively conduct parent conferences
4. develop and supervise instructional programs using parents as intervention agents
5. plan and conduct efficient parent meetings
6. understand and follow due process proceedings with regard to assessment, placement, and programming of a student
7. involve parents in a meaningful way in the development of the student's IEP
8. assist parents in developing realistic expectations for their child and/or adolescent in academic and occupational areas
9. direct parents to community and governmental agencies, volunteer and non-profit groups and parent organizations which provide supportive services to learning disabled students.

While these competencies were designed for LD teachers at all levels, they are included here to show the complexity of the tasks when working with parents of secondary LD adolescents. The individual competencies can be grouped under four general headings: (1) consulting and counseling with parents and students; (2) planning, implementing, monitoring, and evaluating the educational program; (3) selecting appropriate teaching strategies and curricula; and (4) establishing effective communication and working relationships with other professionals and educators. The consulting and counseling designation is used here to emphasize the importance of these parent-professional competency requirements. Several examples illustrate its dominance.

The IEP Meeting

One of the main concerns of parents of LD adolescents is centered on planning, implementing, monitoring, and evaluating the IEP. Parents at IEP meetings often have contrasting attitudes about the student from those of the teacher. Speaking of parents' and teachers' contrasting attitudes, Barsch (1969) explained:

In spite of the fact that the teacher and parent meet on the common ground of interest in the child's development, there is an initial barrier to communication which exists between them. . . . It would be nice to assume that their common interest would serve to unify their perceptions but there is no reason why their encounter should automatically produce harmony and understanding (pp. 12–13).

Helping teachers must be prepared to transcend these differences in attitudes that can produce barriers to communication. Sometimes these barriers are formed as parents become preconditioned by the youths' performances in the privacy of the home. The teenagers' erratic behavior has left the parents docile, resigned, or even apathetic. Helping special educators must resist the temptation to write off the parents as uncaring. They must work hard to build a climate of trust and respect. Helping teachers who have acquired the communication skills of interviewing, listening, and reporting find themselves in an advantaged position when attempting to communicate with these parents. The educators must be more directive with parents and force the interaction with the use of open-ended questions that will require parents to examine their feelings before responding. However, the questioning and reporting functions must be worded carefully so as not to threaten the parent. Helping persons should be advocating and reporting the strengths of the child since any further diminishment of the youngster's ability is liable to erode the parent-teacher relationship. First and foremost, teachers must remember that they are advocating for the child.

Parents may have been preconditioned by the schools and bounced from teacher to counselor to psychologist to specialist year after year. This is an old story with parents of LD adolescents. Something was not quite right with the youth, they were told. The adolescent had been kept back in school, or it had been subtly suggested that the youth would be served better if he were institutionalized. In this type of case, helping teachers face hostile, angry parents who are demanding services for their youth.

In either case, helping teachers will have to work with these parents to make sure that they understand P.L. 94-142 and its guarantees. In this, they will be taking on the role of advocate with parents. As advocates, they can help obtain the needed services. Working within the confines of the IEP has advantages for both the parents and special educators. By focusing upon needed services, helping teachers can help parents give full range to their feelings. By asking pointed questions such as "Have you been attended to by school personnel?" or "You seem to have had a difficult time obtaining services," helping teachers can remove emotional roadblocks that might have hindered further discussion.

Before embarking upon the IEP, parents and special education helping teachers should share assessment data that have been gathered to obtain an accurate picture of where the adolescent is functioning. Although most special educators will have the services of an educational diagnostician or psychologist for test interpretation, the teachers should be prepared to hear parents' request that they review the student's file to "make sure the child is where he is supposed to be."

Educational Planning a Major IEP Issue

The one concern that transcends all others in IEP planning for adolescents is educational planning. Parents still are grappling with the problems of underachievement. They have trouble understanding how an adolescent can memorize an entire TV show with the teenage idols and still have a problem in school. As one father said:

> We have a 13-year-old son. The school psychologist is suggesting that we take him out of all academic classes and put him into something strictly vocational. I just don't know if I'm ready to close the door on him yet (Harrington, 1978, p. 245).

These and similar comments are heard often by special educators working with parents of LD adolescents. The educators should work with the parents to develop the best intervention plan. Programs with remediatory, compensatory, and alternative curriculum focuses should be reviewed. If the LD adolescent has deficits primarily in the areas of reading, spelling, and mathematics, educators and parents should work toward remediation, leading to at least minimal competencies in these areas. Parents and special educators will have to agree that, in terms of this student, the least restrictive environment is the resource room and that the LD adolescent should be mainstreamed.

If the intervention strategy is to be compensatory programming, nontraditional methods should be used. LD students are taught to compensate for a deficiency by relying on aids. For instance, a multimedia approach may be used in teaching reading. The teenagers are introduced to tutors, taped materials, and audiovisual aids. A two-pronged approach is used as modifications are sought by the use of different instructional variables and in the learning style of the student. Again, this approach has mainstreaming as its focus and parents and special educators must agree upon its implementation (Deshler, 1978).

The alternative curriculum is designed to offer LD adolescents a choice other than the traditional secondary school program. If one curriculum is viewed as too difficult, irrelevant, or inappropriate, another one emphasizing functional life adjustment skills should be offered (Deshler, 1978). Students are taught grooming, survival skills for holding jobs, and enough verbal, written, and mathematical abilities to read signs, fill out applications, and carry out other consumer-related functions.

In the remedial and compensatory models, special teachers will have to work with regular educators in the planning and implementation of the IEP. A premium is placed on the ability of the special educators' human relations skills in working with parents. The helping teachers must be advocates, ombudsmen, and case managers. As case managers, the special educators are responsible for writing the IEP, scheduling classes, and working with parents in implementation. Advocate special educators work to overcome parents' reservations about having their adolescents mainstreamed, addressing such factors as the teenager's achievement in class, attitude toward school, activities, relationships with peers, and behavior in all aspects of the curriculum. As ombudsmen, the teachers must orient and educate the parents to what goes on in the classroom. It is helpful if the educators can induce the parents to describe the adolescent's behavior at home and in the neighborhood. There will be a positive effect if parents and special education teachers clarify the expectations they have of each other and the way they operate in their environments. By sharing this information, teachers and parents can clarify the reasons why the adolescent experiences difficulty in particular school situations. For example, the LD adolescent's anxiety about daily activities may be related to a fear of reading failure at school. Helping special educators may have an understanding of the reading problem and coping mechanisms that may have carryover value for use in the home.

The Vocational Planning Crisis

Invariably in working with parents, whether in a remedial, compensatory, or alternative program, another crisis will arise: vocational planning for the future for the LD adolescent. Many parents have operated on the assumption that after ten or twelve years of educational services, their LD youths will have moved into employment, although not necessarily equipped with the same skills or credentials as the normal population. Other parents watch the LD adolescent move along educationally with only one expectation: college. As they note the student's above average achievement in some areas, they are convinced that college is the right choice. Successful vocational planning and progression has not happened to LD populations (Clements & Alexander, 1975). Indeed, not until the passage of P.L. 94-142 did the emphasis on career/vocational education preparation appear in secondary preparation programs. Thus, the task of helping teachers was made more difficult by the exclusion of this group of adolescents from college preparatory and vocational education programs.

As special educators work with parents in planning the IEP, they should be prepared to advocate for entry of the LD teenager into college-bound and vocational education programs. They should not be surprised at the reluctance of parents to subscribe to this philosophy. For years, exceptional children were excluded from these programs (Abeson, 1973). Parents have not forgotten that vocational education has not served their children well (Advisory Council, 1968; Comptroller's Report to Congress, 1974). Only recently have the needs of the academically inclined adolescent been considered (Deshler, 1978). Therefore, special education helping teachers must mediate between two old adversaries—vocational and college preparatory educators and parents. Although this time parents have P.L. 94-142 on their side, special educators must realize that old feelings are not solved by law. Vocational and college preparatory educators might feel put upon at being told that they must take qualified handicapped populations into their classes (Davies, 1974; Laine, 1979).

Parents are left with an ambivalent feeling. Some react by wanting to enroll their adolescents in vocational and college-bound education programs. Others express doubt whether enrollment in programs where youths are not welcome will pay dividends. Whatever the decision, the helping teachers will have an important function to perform. As ombudsmen, they must act as buffers in the dispute between the two parties. If it is apparent that the interests of the LD adolescent will be served by a special class, the helping persons must recommend placement in vocational programs for the handicapped. However, should the LD adolescent benefit from mainstreaming, the special educator is obligated to recommend placement in regular vocational, college preparatory, or remedial education classes.

Helping special educators have not ended their work with parents when the LD adolescent is headed in the right career/vocational direction. Helping persons still operate as case managers to follow the student to high school completion. Therefore, they continue to monitor the IEP annually and to confer with parents in the interim. Interim conferences can be used to review the student's performance, to answer specific questions and concerns of the parent, to exchange information, and to keep lines of communication open between home and school.

The goal of the secondary LD helping teacher is to "reinform the parents of the reality of the situation, current and probable future, perhaps over and over again" (Clements & Alexander, 1975). Helping teachers and parents must come away from their meetings with the feeling that each has described a real person, with assets and liabilities, rather than passing out clichéd pieces of information about adolescent behavior.

Chapter 6

Involving Parents of Multihandicapped Children

The category of multihandicapped (MH) children not only has been characterized by the inconsistency of definition but also has been beset by the complex issues generated by the many exceptional classifications that are found in the subset. The MH category has paralleled learning disabilities in its growth from a single subset to include a multivariate spectrum of conditions. Again, following LD precedent, the term MH sparked the same frantic search for an all-inclusive definition to cover its wide array of exceptionalities. Finally, more than any other classification in special education, its existence has been influenced by fluctuations in public opinion caused by events of national interest. It has not been by accident that the growth and recognition of the multihandicapped category reached a climax with the passage of P.L. 94-142.

A number of events chronicle the development of the MH category. Perhaps the first instance of treatment of the multiply handicapped was recorded by a French physician, Jean Gaspard Itard, in 1798. His treatment and training of Victor, the "wild boy" who had been abandoned and seemingly was retarded, was of historical significance. Itard's teacher, Phillipe Pinel, diagnosed Victor as profoundly retarded, completely helpless, and with a poor prognosis (Balthazar & Stevens, 1975). Disagreeing with his mentor, Itard decided to institute an intensive training program. Itard's treatment of Victor, a savage-like youngster from the woods of Aveyron, emphasized a multisensory approach. Faced by a primitive, mute, and unfeeling youth, Itard used training in speech development, sensory development, stimulation, and social or physical cues to help and to teach Victor.

As a result of his work with the boy, Itard outlined his objectives for therapeutic teaching:

1. To interest the individual in his social life by providing him with greater pleasure than his former mode of living;
2. To increase his awareness of things by intense stimulations and at times by intense emotion;

123

3. To increase his experiences by giving him new ideas and needs and by increasing the frequency of his social interactions;
4. To provide him with speech by means of interpersonal contacts and by necessity; and
5. To utilize new learning experiences and apply them to new forms of instructions (Balthazar & Stevens, p. 18).

Although Itard taught Victor to recognize objects, to make sensory discriminations, to identify letters of the alphabet, to read sparingly, to copy words and apply names to objects, to speak a few syllables, and to make some generalizations, he felt that he had failed. However, to his credit, Itard made the first attempt to teach a multiply handicapped individual.

Physicians continued to dominate this period of treatment of the multihandicapped. In Europe, the work of Itard was carried on by Edward Seguin, another physician. It was Seguin, a pupil of Jean Esquirol, who modified and elaborated upon Itard's work until it became germane to mental retardation and the multihandicapped. He devised a system to lead the child "from the education of the muscular system to that of the nervous system and the senses" and "from the education of the senses to general notions, from general notions to abstract thought, from abstract thought to morality" (Salvin & Light, 1963, p. xiii).

Meanwhile, a surgeon in the United States, Dr. A.G. Goodlet, described a disease called palsy in his book *The Family Physician* in 1838. He defined palsy as:

> A disease consisting in the loss of power in voluntary motion. In severe degrees of palsy, the patient loses both the power of motion and the sense of feeling. This can be one-half of the body or the lower half of the body (p. 85).

The cause of palsy, according to Goodlet, was "a compression of the brain causing apoplexy." Five years later W. J. Little (1843), another physician, was credited with the clinical diagnosis of spastic palsy. Little described spastic paralysis persons as drooling, crosslegged, and uneducable. He felt their condition was caused by difficult labor, asphyxia, and abnormal pregnancy. Little's analysis of spastic palsy individuals assured them of a low priority position in society.

Moving into the twentieth century, there was overlap between mental retardation, emotional disturbance, and physical handicaps in the classification of multihandicapped. As Balthazar and Stevens (1975) noted:

> It is conceded that while mental retardation, emotional disturbance and physical disability are separate constructs, they quite clearly reveal a considerable degree of overlap. In fact, mental retardation together with emotional disturbance and some aspects of physical disability

along with some characteristics of neuropathic deficits present serious difficulty in classification and diagnosis (p. 5).

However, other events occurred that either enlarged or continued to have an impact on the MH population. First, in the early 1900s, Bronson Crothers (1959) found fault with Little's analysis of the intellect of cerebral palsy (CP) individuals. He discovered that some of his patients though crippled in body had average or above average intelligence. Crothers and his colleagues at Boston's Children's Hospital found that their CP patients could be assisted so as to improve their overall functioning level (Griffin, 1979).

In 1921, Edgar F. Allen founded the National Society for Crippled Children. This organization was responsible for starting the International Society for the Welfare of Cripples and the National Society for Crippled Children and Adults. Twenty-three states had societies for crippled children by 1929. The National Society for Crippled Children initiated the Easter Seal campaign as a fundraising vehicle on behalf of crippled children in the United States. This population was comprised then of postpolio residuals, osteomyelitis, and bone tuberculosis children (Wyatt, 1970).

Progress on behalf of multiply handicapped children continued at a slow pace during the middle years of the century. One of the most notable accomplishments was the development of the polio vaccine by Dr. Jonas Salk in 1953. This discovery helped reduce considerably the number of polio residuals in special education classes. A number of conferences in subsequent years focused the public's attention upon the multihandicapped category and contributed to a better understanding of the subject:

1. 1960 White House Conference on Childhood and Youth in Washington.
2. National Seminar on Research in Mental Retardation set up by the United States Office of Health, Education and Welfare (Cooperative Research Division), Madison, Wisconsin.
3. President's Panel on Mental Retardation.
4. President's Committee on Employment of the Handicapped.
5. International Congress of Cripples.
6. International Congress on Mental Deficiency.
7. National Conferences such as the following: American Association on Mental Deficiency, Council of Exceptional Children, United Cerebral Palsy Association, National Society of Crippled Children, American Speech and Hearing Association, National Society for the Prevention of Blindness, American Orthopsychiatric Association and the National Association for Retarded Children have contributed a great deal by their findings and recommendations to the prevention, research, and treatment programs for multiply-handicapped children internationally (Salvin & Light, 1963, p. xix).

The 1960 White House Conference on Childhood and Youth was called to focus attention on the sorry plight of children and to reshape public opinion into a blueprint for positive action. Although the conference did not enjoy much success in its attempt to shake the nation from its lethargy toward children, one positive note emerged: participants succeeded in coining a new term that would replace the word *handicapped* in special education literature. Instead of using that term to describe disabled children, the word *exceptional* would now be used. Exceptional children now also included multihandicapped children.

The list of other conferences held in the 1960s attests to the fact that the affected population was multivariate. Therefore, a number of handicapping conditions could be included. The characteristics of mental retardation (MR) that seemed to warrant its inclusion were:

1. MR associated with infections
2. MR associated with intoxications
3. MR associated with metabolic, growth, or nutritional disorders
4. MR associated with trauma
5. MR associated with pre-natal influence
6. MR associated with diseases and conditions due to new growths
7. MR associated with diseases and conditions due to unknown or uncertain cause with the structural reactions manifest
8. MR associated with uncertain or presumed psychologic cause with the functional reaction alone manifest
9. MR associated with impairment of special senses
10. MR associated with convulsive disorders
11. MR associated with motor dysfunction (Salvin & Light, pp. 24–26).

It thus can be seen that although mental retardation might be the major classifying agent, multiple handicapping conditions also were present. In this context, the President's Commission on Mental Retardation and the American Association on Mental Deficiency made important recommendations that not only helped define mental retardation but also caused other categories to reexamine their populations, i.e., crippled and other health impaired, and visually handicapped and deaf. Other major organizations that concerned themselves with crippled and visually and hearing impaired children met to re-examine their role in the field of multihandicapped.

The National Society for Crippled Children reaffirmed its commitment to obtain equal opportunities for its constituency. Its work was summarized in its 1959 annual report as the:

Change from the popular image of the crippled child as one who is to be pitied . . . who must live his whole life in bondage, as it were, to his physical condition . . . to the image of such a child as one who can look forward hopefully to a good and active life in which the most will be made of his abilities . . . who can achieve the maximum in physical rehabilitation, receive an education suited to his intelligence, interest and aptitudes, be offered vocational opportunities and enjoy participation in his community . . . this is a tremendous change and one that we need to be reminded of continuously.

These words in behalf of crippled children could be echoed by other organizations and associations (National Federation for the Blind, National Society for the Prevention of Blindness, Cerebral Palsy Association) in 1960s conferences.

Another organization that has illuminated the plight of the multihandicapped is the Cerebral Palsy Association. It began its efforts at the local level but later expanded nationwide. The national group, the United Cerebral Palsy Association, pushed for research and treatment centers and provided a forum for parents and professionals to work for legislation for research, professional training, and remedial programs (Haring, 1974). When it is realized that half of the CPs are mentally retarded, about 70 percent have speech problems, many have associated visual and/or auditory handicaps, and all have brain damage and motoric problems, it is not surprising that the Cerebral Palsy Association felt that the needs of its MH children warranted repeated and additional attention.

Other organizations that represented children with sensory defects also voiced their support of programs that would benefit the blind/partially sighted or deaf/ hard of hearing. Thus, meetings of the Speech and Hearing Association and National Society for the Prevention of Blindness might well have borrowed comments from the Oregon Study that dealt with the problems of the sensory impaired child.

All learning depends upon sensory stimulation of one form or another. Although each sensory mechanism plays an important role, vision and hearing are relied upon most heavily in the major learning tasks faced by humans. Impairment of one of these senses presents serious barriers to the learning process. . . . The educational system must, for these children, deal with a broader range of learning needs. . . . Rather the task education faces with deaf or blind is that of preparing them for entrance into society's main stream. For the normal child education is a means to economic sufficiency, social mobility, political capability, etc. For the deaf and blind child it is the door to society itself (p. 5).

The effort on behalf of the multihandicapped was spurred in the middle and late 1960s by events that had an impact on the exceptional child movement nationwide. First, a rubella epidemic (mothers who contacted German measles during the first trimester of pregnancy) swept through the United States from 1963 to 1965. As a result, there was a notable increase in the number of babies born with multiple handicaps or deaf and blind. Hardy (1965) gave an account of the severity of the rubella epidemic when she reported on disabling conditions in Maryland. She reported:

35 percent have cardiac disease
50 percent have hearing problems of which half are profound
20 percent have visual problems of which two-thirds are severe
54 percent have retardation of development (one-half of these are severely retarded)
60 percent have small head size—third percentile or below—and many with poor growth
less than 5 percent are normal after one year of growth.

In 1964, the New York metropolitan area reported more than 1,000 defective births due to rubella. The Rubella Birth Defect Evaluation Project at New York State University reported the following case statistics:

Deafness	252
Heart disease	182
Bilateral cataracts	58
Unilateral cataracts	50
Glaucoma	12
Psychomotor retardation	170
Neonatal thrombocytopenic purpura	85

Heart disease was the sole manifestation in 7 children and deafness was the only defect in 68 children (p. 2).

Thus, another major classification, the deaf-blind, was added to the multi-handicapped category as a result of the rubella epidemic.

Another major evolution has seen the increased involvement of the federal government in affairs of the handicapped. Strong impetus was given to special education when P.L. 85-929 was amended by P.L. 88-164. These amendments provided for training teachers under the broad concept of crippled and other health impaired. The area since has been further broken down into the specialties of the learning disabled, multihandicapped, and the crippled. Under these designations, 1970 expenditures of the U.S. Bureau for Education of the Handicapped (now the Office of Special Education in the Department of Education) for direct services to crippled children totaled about $6.2 million. Assistance also was made available to state institutions and state-supported schools. Attempts were being made to have an impact on the area of early childhood education.

Increased governmental assistance and a thrust toward prevention prompted the emphasis upon early childhood education. This awareness of prevention led to a funding of 41 projects on early childhood by the BEH prior to 1970. Seventeen of these projects involved crippled children to some extent and three were designated especially for them. These last were granted to the United Cerebral Palsy Association of New York, the New York Medical Centers, and the Curative Workshop of Milwaukee (pp. 41–42).

In 1980, $55,375,000 was allocated solely for training special education and allied service personnel. The projected funding distribution for FY 1981–82 is projected at $58 million. Of this amount, $6 million will be allocated to early childhood pre- and inservice preparation programs. Another $8 million is programmed for the severely and multiply handicapped category of personnel preparation.

Still another meaningful change that affected the composition of the MH category was the increase in children who had disabilities resulting from drugs, toxic reactions, and accidents. The National Safety Council estimated that 50,000 children (more than half of them under the age of 5) would be permanently crippled or disabled by accident in 1969. Paraplegics were being treated and kept alive while terminally ill children were being maintained medically longer than in past decades (p. 51).

Perhaps the most visible impact of the "drug culture" on the multiply handicapped population was the "monster" babies that appeared in the late 1960s. From 1966 to 1968, a number of babies were born without arms or legs and/or were disfigured because of the mother's ingestion of thalidomide and other drugs during pregnancy. Among the birth defects linked to alcohol abuse was fetal alcohol syndrome, with the associated conditions of mental deficiency, heart trouble, and facial anomalies.

THE PROBLEM OF DEFINITION

The question of definition became a difficult problem at the numerous conferences held in the 1960s and 1970s as national events spawned increasing numbers of multiply handicapped children.

The rubella epidemic of the mid-1960s focused attention upon the deaf-blind population at a number of conferences. Following the passage of P.L. 94-142 other organizations formed around a major etiology acknowledged the presence of an accompanying handicap. This acknowledgment maintained the integrity of groups (i.e., MR, ED, and Sensory Impaired) to be able to carry out the mandates of P.L. 94-142. Many different populations have a case for inclusion in the definition. Salvin and Light (1963) stressed the mental retardation linkage to the MH population and made a strong case for its membership based upon accompanying and/or aligned secondary handicaps (deafness, blindness, emotional disturbance, and physical handicaps). The population of identified young deaf-blind individuals was projected to swell from 4,414 in 1973 to perhaps 5,400 in 1980. The various degrees of handicap in the overall deaf-blind population have to be considered. Some are totally blind and profoundly deaf, many have some degree of hearing or vision, others have sensory impairments only, and many others have other exceptional conditions such as mental retardation (p. 23).

As the 1980s are ushered in, the conclusions of Moores (1978) are words of caution about the category. He said: "Although numerous studies have reported incidence figures on various types of disabilities related to deafness, present data must be treated as imprecise estimates. For the most part, the figures represent children enrolled in programs and identified by one means or another as multihandicapped . . . . Unfortunately, there has been no response to the request for the establishment of precise definitions for identification of multi-handicapped deaf children. Lacking such definition all reported incidence figures must be taken with a grain of salt" (pp. 278–281).

Visually handicapped populations can be included since they may have impairments in other body systems. These children are not new problem cases but have been given more attention in recent years. Studies reported by Lowenfeld (1968) and Graham (1970) showed a disproportionate increase of multiple impairments among blind children. Although receiving educational services for the blind, these children could be labeled properly as multihandicapped (Barraga, 1975).

The severely and profoundly handicapped child has a place in the MH category. The BEH defined the severely/profoundly handicapped as:

> A severely handicapped child is one who, because of the intensity of his physical, mental, or emotional problems, or a combination of such problems, needs educational, social, psychological and medical services beyond those which have been offered by traditional regular and special educational programs, in order to maximize his full potential for useful and meaningful participation in society and for self-fulfillment. Such children include those emotionally disturbed (schizophrenic and autistic), profoundly and severely mentally retarded and those with two or more serious handicapping conditions such as the mentally-retarded blind and the cerebral palsied-deaf (p. 1).

Vernon (1966) said that the literature on multiply handicapping conditions among deaf children was vast. He stated that prenatal rubella, premature birth,

Rh factor complications, meningitis, and genetics in addition to being the leading causes of profound hearing loss were major etiologies of mental retardation, cerebral palsy, visual defects, learning disabilities, orthopedic problems, and many other physical and behavioral anomalies. Moores (1978) acknowledged that of the five major etiologies of early childhood deafness—hereditary, rubella, Rh factor complications, meningitis, and prematurity—hereditary deafness is the only etiology not associated with a high prevalence of other handicapping conditions.

Finally, the crippled and other health impaired (COHI) area contributed heavily to the understanding of the MH population. The 1973 Leadership Training Institute (LTI) identified the COHI-MH population as "individuals with physical and/or motor handicaps who may or may not have one or more secondary conditions that require specialized educational intervention." This population is diagrammed in Figure 6-1.

The COHI-MH category has moved from its previous position of concentration upon the classic crippling diseases (polio, TB) and is becoming increasingly involved with children who manifest multisensory deficiencies, perceptual inadequacies, communication barriers, social and emotional complexities, and retarded intellectual ability. It has become a multiply disabled population (p. 95).

When viewed from these diverse perspectives, it has not been easy to find a single definition to cover all the exceptionalities represented in the MH subset. Myers (1978) defined the category:

> A multi-handicapped child is one who has physical impairments (sensory and/or motor) of such a degree that they result in delays/deficits in affective, cognitive and psycho-motor development (p. 1).

While this definition has its limitations, it is broad enough to include all of the impairments represented in the multihandicapped classification. Thus, it is accepted for this chapter.

THE ROLE OF PARENTS OF MH CHILDREN

Although the events and actions of the 1960s were noteworthy, they were only the forerunners of what was to occur in the 1970s. That decade ushered in renewed efforts on behalf of the handicapped from which the multihandicapped benefitted. In 1972, a memorable court decision, *Pennsylvania* v. *Pennsylvania Association for Retarded Children*, 334 F. Supp. 1257 (E.D. Pa. 1971) extended the right of a free and appropriate public education to all handicapped children. The passage of the Education for All Handicapped Children Act of 1975 (P.L.

Figure 6-1 Interrelationship of Handicapping Conditions

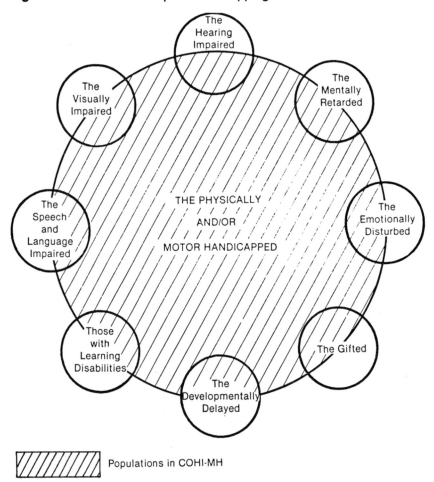

Populations in COHI-MH

Source: Reprinted from *Leadership Preparation,* F. P. Conner and M. J. Cohen (Eds.) 1973, p. 30.

94-142) gave priority to serving (a) those who previously had not been served, and (b) the severely and profoundly handicapped.

Parents of multihandicapped children welcomed the court ruling and the legislation. These included parents:

- who had been informed that their children never would advance beyond the "vegetable" stage

- whose lives might have been altered dramatically through accident, drug abuse, or other sensorimotor debilitating circumstances that affected the child

- who have lived a lonely life of isolation from the mainstream of America

- who have watched their children excluded from school

Parents of multihandicapped children have watched the pendulum of awareness and assistance swing from one extreme to another. Although parents of cerebral palsied were among the first to form parent groups, from the 1940s to the late 1960s the emphasis in special education had moved toward serving the mild to moderately exceptional child. Thus, parents of multihandicapped children had not seen a vigorous response to their pleas on behalf of their progeny. However, with the advent of P.L. 94-142 these parents have renewed the movements to gain equal opportunities for their children.

One of the positive outcomes as P.L. 94-142 moved through Congress was the addition of more parent-professional organizations to campaign for the rights of multihandicapped children. Whereas in the earlier years established organizations such as the United Cerebral Palsy Association and the National Society for Crippled Children carried the brunt of the fight, new entities such as the National Association for the Deaf-Blind (NADB) and the American Association for the Education of the Severely/Profoundly Handicapped (AAESPH) were formed to join the battle. The NADB was chartered in June 1975 and its membership was opened to any persons who subscribed to the purposes of the association, including the following:

1. To promote the welfare of the deaf-blind, multiply-handicapped person;
2. To counsel parents and State regional staff personnel on medical, educational, and recreational facilities and programs available to deaf-blind, multiply-handicapped persons;
3. To collect information from members as to the special needs of the deaf-blind, multiply-handicapped, and to make this information available to all professional workers involved;
4. To disseminate information and literature of national interest to deaf-blind, multiply-handicapped persons and their families;
5. To provide support to the various regional and state programs of benefit to this population; and
6. To raise funds for any project connected with the aid of the deaf-blind (p. 1).

The AAESPH held its first seminar in Kansas City in November 1974. While sharing ideas, the participants agreed that there was a need for a separate entity, organized and composed of those sharing an interest in the severely/profoundly handicapped. Membership was opened to professionals, paraprofessionals, and parents. The goals of the AAESPH were:

1. To function as an advocate organization for the development and implementation of comprehensive, high quality educational services for the severely/profoundly handicapped at birth throughout adulthood in the public school sector.
2. To serve as a separate entity in advocating:
   a. the development of relevant and efficient pre-service and in-service teacher training programs;
   b. the development of highly specialized doctoral level, teacher training, research, and instructional design personnel.
3. To develop, refine, and disseminate training packages, instructional programs, and materials.
4. To facilitate parent involvement in all program services for the severely and profoundly handicapped (p. 4).

Thus, two new organizations moved into the field not to challenge the efforts of established groups but to advocate for their children in the diverse field of the multihandicapped. Two distinct features marked the emergence of these parent-professional groups. The first distinction was the fact that although the MH group paralleled the LD category in multivariate populations, the choice has been not to allow a single organization to represent their interests. Therefore, each multihandicap peer organization has chosen to form its own association (AAESPH, NADB) rather than merge under one banner as did the Association for Children with Learning Disabilities (ACLD). The second distinction was the fact that this category (MH) did parallel the LD subset in moving from a medically based program to an educational setting. Thus, in the purposes of each organization strong language is found calling for the *education* of multihandicapped children.

Prior to the passage of P.L. 94-142, many of these goals probably would not have been verbalized. If they had, they probably would have fallen on deaf ears (Abeson, 1973). However, the priorities and guarantees accorded to parents of MH children gave rise to educational concerns by professionals and caused parents to voice questions that troubled them as special education moved into the P.L. 94-142 era.

PROFESSIONAL CONCERNS FOR TEACHERS

One issue that has troubled professional educators has been the medical vs. educational role for teachers of multihandicapped children. Many teachers of the multihandicapped have a feeling that their role has been essentially medically defined. Recognizing that the MH population is medically dependent in many instances, they are not resisting familiarity with classroom medical management. However, most educators have felt that too much attention has been given to these skills. Helping special educators have maintained that professionals should have the skills to analyze the behavior of the child with unique and multiple problems, to understand parental needs, and to work with community resources (p. 23). Professional educators have acknowledged that medical and other para-educational personnel have assumed their responsibilities in the past even if by default. However, they are convinced of the importance of educators' providing educational evaluation and services for MH children (Mullins, 1973). These earlier convictions have been transformed into requirements through the passage of P.L. 94-142.

Another concern has been the disagreement over the issue of mainstreaming the MH population. Some special educators have felt that mainstreaming might be pertinent for many MH pupils since the major disabling conditions (sensory or physical) may have little effect on fundamental learning processes. Others have tended to disagree. They have argued that this perception has ignored the long-term effects upon learning and behavior of traumatic experiences, atypical living environments, and prolonged experience deprivation (Rusalem, 1973).

Another conflict over mainstreaming involves regular and MH educators. Mainstream professionals have shown a reluctance to work with MH children in certain cases, but they have based this stance on the refusal of special educators to share their knowledge with them. Special education professionals have disagreed and have maintained that mainstream professionals have not taken the time to establish communication, cooperation, and understanding on behalf of MH children.

MH educators are concerned over the question of teacher training. With the many populations that have been embraced under the MH designation, teacher competencies have come into question. COHI-MH educators held three Leadership Training Institutes (at West Point, N.Y., 1970; Tucson, Arizona, 1971; and Nyack, N.Y., 1973) and each emphasized teacher competency as a central discussion area (Conner & Cohen, 1973). Although the issue of improved teacher performance is a vast one, teacher accountability will follow student accountability in the minds of parents. The most recent Gallup poll of the Public's Attitudes toward the Public Schools showed that 85 percent of respondents said yes, teachers should be required to pass a state exam in their subject areas and they should be continually tested. Seeley (1979) sees this link as the element that makes many professional educators so fearful about the competency movement. However he sees four areas that have the potential for creating an alliance between parents and professionals. They are:

1. better recruitment of persons going into teaching
2. better school principals

3. more help for classroom teachers
4. shared responsibility for education.

Professional educators of the multiply handicapped also are troubled over the issue of death and dying. With the passage of P.L. 94-142, and the *Mills* (1972) and *Pennsylvania* (1972) decisions, the United States has taken upon itself the education of everyone. No longer can the terminally or chronically ill child be sent home. This child must be helped by the MH teacher. The educator working with the chronically or terminally ill MH child has a responsibility different from that of other educators. The child that was in the classroom last fall might not be there the following year. For the teacher of the terminally or chronically ill, the responsibility does not lessen and the challenges are greater (Robbins & Kacen, 1971).

Finally, curriculum has been a major issue. Providing programs for the multihandicapped has become one of the great challenges in American education today. Individualized educational programming for the severely multihandicapped cannot be entitled "different strokes for different folks," but it must recognize that what works for a child today may not work for the same child tomorrow. A commercially packaged curriculum that meets the individual needs of each and every severely multihandicapped child has yet to be found (Writer, 1979). Thus, the constant search for *the* way, the *only* way, the *best* way of educating the multihandicapped population has placed a heavy responsibility upon special educators.

CONCERNS OF PARENTS OF MH CHILDREN

Just as professional educators have concerns about the state of the art in MH education, parents also have issues that have burdened them throughout the expansion of the population. One of the primary concerns of parents has been public education for their children. Spurred on initially by CP parents, aided later by parents of crippled children, associations of these two handicapping conditions have borne the brunt of society's inflexible attitude toward MH children. With the passage of P.L. 94-142 and changing national priorities, these organizations have been joined by others and are insisting upon a free and appropriate public education (FAPE) for their children. Previously, perhaps these were parents of "closet" children, or of those who were excluded from school (Abeson, 1973). Unable to enroll their children in public schools, these parents carried the cost of educating them. They were forced by circumstances to do it at home or to place their children in institutions or residential schools (Writer, 1977). The passage of P.L. 94-142 has allowed parents to hope that they no longer will have to bear these costs alone.

However, parents are insisting not only on a free and appropriate public education but also on one that could extend past the previously accepted regular academic school year. Parents have felt that the school year of approximately 180 days has not been sufficient for their multihandicapped children to obtain the education needed to integrate them successfully into today's society. Thus, in 1978 parents of MH children in Pennsylvania asked the courts to extend the school year. The case, *Armstrong* v. *Kline,* 1978, saw the court rule that the policy of ending the school year after 180 days violates the federal law (P.L. 94-142). The concern that has rankled parents has been the tenacity of professional educators in maintaining the 180 to 200-day school year. Parents previously were content just to get their MH children into school. Now that the children are in, the parents are concerned about the kind and extent of the education they are receiving. Having seen the gains of some of these "uneducables" during the school year, some parents are demanding that span be prolonged. Others who have witnessed positive changes in their "uneducables" in the regular school year are pressing for additional time in the classroom atmosphere to enable their children to sustain these gains (Turner, 1979).

Parents are concerned over teacher training. Some teachers of multihandicapped children have called for multidisciplinary training (Task Force II, LTI, 1973, p. 2). Others have worried about the variance among training programs, complaining about differences in preparation rather than the effectiveness of the preparation (Hammer, 1974). For some categories of MH educators, parents are dismayed to find that there is a lack of teacher competencies (Gilliam & Dollar, 1977). With so many different teacher training approaches in use, parents are confused about which is the "right" way. Since many parents have received on-the-job training with their MH children, they have grave concerns about many of the teacher training institutions that geared up programs quickly and in four years are turning out "experts" ready to work with MH populations.

Still another problem is mainstreaming. While parents of other exceptionalities have been concerned about the lack of association with their peers, parents of MH children have been worried about even getting in the door of public schools. Thus, they see two sides to the issue: (1) They question whether regular educators will be able to integrate MH children successfully into the regular classroom (LTI, 1973; Woodward, 1980). (2) They want more, not fewer, self-contained classrooms to assure that MH children will receive the best possible education (LTI, 1973). Such a dichotomy of attitudes has caused parents to have conflicting feelings about mainstreaming and least restrictive environment.

Parents also criticize the lack of foresight concerning programs for adolescents. Since these programs have been woefully lacking, the parents wonder where the programs of tomorrow are. Looking at the increasing number of students in public schools and the greater percentage of elementary programs, parents express more than passing concern about educational opportunities at the secondary level. Included in these concerns are opportunities for MH young-sters to attend college as well as services for those not planning to go to college. In the latter group, parents wonder about the welfare of those teenagers who will enter the competitive marketplace and those who will seek their livelihood in a more sheltered atmosphere. Parents ask this question about older teenagers (18–21): "Are pupils facing the same kind of educational program they received at age 16 or has a program been developed to meet the needs of the older teenagers?" (p. 48). Rusalem (1973) reinforced the need for both secondary programming and schooling of a different nature. He found that COHI-MH populations saw secondary schools for the handicapped as carbon copies of the regular secondary school and deemed this to be inadequate.

INVOLVING PARENTS OF YOUNG MH CHILDREN

> With his first breath at the moment of birth, an infant has the capacity to become a receiving, participating, interacting human being who enjoys a reciprocally satisfying and eventually a fulfilling involvement with an ever-expanding world (p. 117).

This statement by Barraga (1973) pushed special education teachers into the forefront as helping agents to parents of MH children. These educators have become the front-line troops to assure parents that their children will achieve self-actualization. Just as the population has changed, so has the relationship between teachers and parents of MH children changed with the passage of P.L. 94-142. With that law, parents of MH children have formed a deeper and closer relationship with professional educators. To assure the continuation of this re-lationship, the helping MH teachers must expand their knowledge base. They need to know:

1. Some generalizations about the experiences that these parents have encountered;
2. Some of the feelings that the parents may have undergone;
3. Some of the ways to offer encouragement and help to parents to offset their worries; and
4. Some of the community resources to be able to act as a referral agent for parents (Mouchka, 1976, pp. 79–83).

In relating to the past experiences of parents, helping teachers must have some understanding of the crisis periods and other stressful situations the parents have undergone. Since many states have instituted infant stimulation or infant-parent programs (from 0–3 years), it can be argued realistically that intervention by special educators begins early with the MH population. The helping teachers should be willing and ready to have the parents share some of the feelings that engulfed the family at the birth of the exceptional child.

For MH special educators, the key to helping parents is the ability to understand their feelings and the emotional stresses produced by their situation. The birth of an MH child may throw a family into a situation unlike that faced by any other family with a handicapped child. Many MH children have been born with handicapping conditions that threaten their lives during the first or second year of their existence. During this period of life or death, many families undergo emotional turmoil particular to their own individual and family situations. It is known that parents of MH children have different constitutional makeups and have reacted in their own individual ways to the handicap. However, there have been enough similarities in the reactions of parents to enable special education teachers to be aware of certain emotional stresses.

The first question most mothers ask following delivery of their child is: "Is the baby all right?" When told that the child is defective, parents fall into a period of grief and mourning. They grieve for the child and his suffering, frustrations, and handicaps, and—with every justification—for themselves and the burden that the care of the child brings to the household. They mourn the loss of the child-that-might-have-been. For most parents the birth of the MH child has dashed their hopes, fantasies, and dreams.

Teachers of special education must understand that assisting parents through the grief and mourning process is a time-consuming task. All parents pass through this stage, but not necessarily in the same sequence. However, certain stages should be recognized so that parents can be given support in their time of need: (a) protest, (b) despair, and (c) detachment (Hudson, 1976). An important contribution by the educator is to help the parents form a reattachment to people, activities, and things as they try to resolve their crisis.

Stage One: Protest

The initial stage of protest may be seen in parents' angry denials of the handicap such as a statement to the contrary ("It can't be true.") or in the search for a cure or answer. The defense mechanism of denial can send parents from specialist to specialist, from medical center to medical center as they look for someone who could give them a satisfactory answer. Meanwhile, protest anger can be directed at many individuals for different reasons. The physician, the nurse, and the teacher all have been objects of parents' hostility.

Helping teachers of young MH children should be prepared for these emotions and should be supporting of the parents. For many parents the search may have produced a better answer. Even if it did not, the educators must realize that the quest may have served as a useful therapeutic process for the family because, having gone through it, the parents may be ready to deal with the next phase of their problem.

This also may be said for angry parents. While anger often is thought of as an unpleasant emotion, it can be used constructively. Angry parents have the ability to mobilize for action. This is shown in their attempts to try something— or anything. Anger gets their adrenalin flowing and gives some parents the courage to do things that they otherwise would not have tried. Thus, educators of young MH children should be accepting of this phase if it does not last unnecessarily long. They should remind themselves that this is the point where parents are in their acceptance of the handicap and in the meaning that it has for them.

Stage Two: Despair

The next emotional stage is the period of despair. Parents' usual feelings are of helplessness and of resignation to their fate. Fatigue and apathy are the most visible signs. Previously well-disciplined parents come "unglued." In other words, these adults become disorganized and exhibit poor coping ability. The helplessness produces guilt feelings that are spawned by the culture that dictates that Americans don't give up but keep fighting no matter what the odds. Therefore, parents are self-incriminating and generally see problems in a perspective that makes them larger than life. This obviously is a very painful stage. However, special educators should remember that it, too, serves a useful purpose: it can be considered a moratorium for parents, a stage where they can let go as they gather the strength and the courage to attempt to manage the rest of their lives.

Stage Three: Detachment

The final stage is called detachment. Parents refuse to allow themselves to be preoccupied with the MH child 24 hours a day. This produces a guilt reaction. The parents withdraw some of their emotional investment in the child and may give the impression that they are concerned only with their own needs. This self-absorption and self-centeredness can bring parents criticism from well-meaning friends and relatives. However, helping special educators should be understanding of the fact that this, too, is a temporary phase. Parents of young MH children use it as a buffer to endure pain. Therefore, the special educators must be able to provide support in this critical phase also.

As special educators consider their roles with parents in these stages, they can expect to fulfill the functions of advocates, ombudsmen, and case managers. If the educators accept these roles under the umbrella of parent counselor and friend, they must be prepared to give time to the process. A survey indicated that parents felt more comfortable talking to their child's teacher about problems than any other staff member (Torrie, 1973). This only reinforces the contention that the parents' deepest relationship is with the MH teacher. In the parents' eyes, teachers have the primary coresponsibility for the welfare of their child because they have an expertise that can be trusted and depended upon. Thus, special teachers can help parents reorganize their lives from emotional stresses while fulfilling a coequal educational role.

The Impact of Stresses

Depending upon the stage in which teachers find parents (protest, despair, or detachment), their roles also are determined by all of the stresses operating in the lives of families of MH children. Since many MH children are born with life-threatening conditions, parents may encounter other stresses such as medical, economic, or professional during these emotional periods. Medical factors can play a major part in the stresses because many MH infants require extensive hospitalization in their first three years. Since most developmental research (McCandless, 1967; Erickson, 1968) has shown that these years are the most important for the child's growth and development, many young MH children suffer from environmental deprivation (family) because of the many hospitalizations so early in their lives. During this period, teachers must be advocates for services for the family. If parents have encountered professionals who have not listened to their concerns or simply have told them their child is hopeless and should be put away, the teachers' task is increased two-fold. Helping teachers not only must advocate for the parents and child but also must mediate any professional-vs.-parent concerns about the possibility of educating the child. If parents constantly receive negative responses and face enormous financial drains due to hospitalization, the helping professionals may face hostile, angry, or apathetic and helpless couples. Teachers have to realize that these emotions cover a number of feelings (anxiety, fear, desperation) induced by medical stresses.

In this situation the teachers may have to help parents overcome a fear of making demands upon the MH child. If parents are afraid that the child may not be enjoying good health in his early life, their anxiety about health factors may prevent them from bringing the child to class or working with him at home. All of these uncertainties about the child's future can be reflected in the parents' actions as they continue to search for a cure or an answer.

Another stress that may occur involves economic pressures on families with MH children. Hospitalization can cause unexpected and heavy expenses. The financial strains imposed by visits to specialists, obtaining glasses, braces, or other necessary aids can add to the stresses. Moreover, the loss of income from the ever-increasing number of working women who felt compelled to give up employment upon the birth of the MH child has increased the pressure on already overstrained budgets.

Still another complication is the professional factor. This can be illustrated by a case study (Yu, 1972) in which a severely multihandicapped child (deaf-blind) had a profound sensory neurological loss of hearing bilaterally. Six years old, she had "b," "p," and "n" sounds and some gutteral sounds. She had attended an oral school for the deaf for two and a half years, but her parents were frustrated by her lack of language and communication skills and her slow development and slow growth in all areas except social adaptive behavior. The parents went to a child center for an evaluation. The center offered a supplementary program so that the child could continue at the oral school while receiving individual tutorial assistance at the center. Sign language was excluded because it was not accepted by the other school or by the parents.

The center staff recommended a full-day communication skills program. Counseling and data on the total communications approach was given to the parents to facilitate their understanding of the method. The parents were given a four-month period in which to consider their options. However, they chose to send their child to a private oral camp for the summer and their application for fall entry into the school was turned down. Failing to find an oral school for their child in August, the parents agreed to send their child to the center. The moral of the story involves the different philosophical approaches that educators took. In this case, professionals had dissimilar philosophies about the total communications approach and left the parents in a bind because of the experts' biases and feelings.

In this case, helping teachers had to become advocates for the child. They had to convince the parents that the total communications program was the best possible option. Moreover, the special educators had to function as ombudsmen to mediate the conflict between professional philosophical differences that confused the parents. Finally, throughout the process, the educators had to be case managers to assure parents that the child would receive the necessary services.

Helpful Services for Parents

Parents of MH children may need transportation, babysitting services, or public health services. The helping teachers should become advocates for these services. The educators must identify available community resources that might help. Thus, when parents flounder because they do not know where to turn for help, the teachers can provide the necessary information about agencies able to offer assistance. Parents who have been drained of energy by their search for services have a high regard for teachers who have helped them acquire needed information.

In conjunction with the searches for help, long hours of care and denial of privacy may have contributed to a need for respite care for parents. Respite care should be considered a vital component of the educational program for parents with young MH children. This temporary "time out" from the constant presence of the exceptional child is an important element in the mental health outlook of parents. Respite care often causes a conflict of feelings among parents. For some, the need to get away produces guilt feelings that they are sloughing off their duties. Others would like respite care but cannot obtain it. Educators must be prepared to deal with these positive and negative feelings. Subsequently, helping special educators may have to shift roles from advocates to ombudsmen and case managers. As ombudsmen, teachers may have to help parents to ameliorate the negative and positive feelings about needing, accepting, and using respite care. If the parents waver or need additional assistance in their decision making, the teachers may have to introduce them to a parents' group or may have to form a peer group. In the former case, the helping teachers still would fulfill the ombudsman role. In the latter case, forming a parents' group, the educators' role would shift into that of case manager. With time limitations, helping teachers not only must budget their time but also must build these meeting times into the framework of their daily case load.

Teachers should not be offended if the couple shows vacillation or timidity about joining parents' groups. Parents may be reluctant to share what has been a private burden. To some parents, admission of need connotes failure. Problems and worries about other children may have to be discussed. It should not be surprising if the weariness, fatigue, and anger over the constancy of training and care dominate the conversation. Helping educators should not be patronizing but should ask questions or make appropriate responses that allow parents to express their concerns honestly and openly. In this atmosphere, trust and respect are fostered. After these concerns have been aired, attention can turn again to parent group membership.

Once the parents' group has been formed, it can be used to provide psychological support in a variety of ways. It can be a release valve. Parents will be relieved to learn that others spend sleepless nights. They can exchange complaints about the management of their child and trade ideas about methods of handling undesirable behavior. Special educators may have to introduce specific concerns when groups are in the early stages. As members of the group become more comfortable with one another, the teacher-case managers move from initiating issues to helping the parents cope with their concerns.

Children and Self-Actualization

One of the most pressing parental concerns centers on the children's self-actualization. Since this concern was fostered by the earlier inability or unwillingness of school personnel to educate the multihandicapped, parents still have reservations about whether the schools can serve their children. Having been told very early that their child was "uneducable" or needed to be put away, many parents have done the job at home. While not professionals, their efforts taught them a great deal about their children's abilities. Parents of MH children had been eager to hold the meager gains made at home and were inclined to work closely with teachers to accomplish this goal (Carter, 1974). Since the passage of P.L. 94-142, parents are assured that they can carry out these activities in a coequal atmosphere between home and school.

Helping teachers working as case managers with parents to develop skills with multihandicapped students should answer these important questions (Williams, Brown, & Certo):

1. What skill do you want the student to perform?
2. Why do you want a student to perform a specific skill?
3. How do you intend to teach the student to perform the skill?
4. How can you verify that the skill is being used or has been taught?
5. What instructional materials need to be used for the skill to be acquired and performed?
6. Can the student perform the skill across persons, places, instructional materials, and language cues?
7. Can the student perform the skill without directions from persons in authority? (1975, pp. 165–166).

The Individualized Education Program for the MH child should be a result of the teachers' being able to answer these questions and reach an accord on team planning among all who will be significant others in the child's life. Decisions about the specific skills to be taught should be made by the helping special educators, parents, therapists, attendants, and teacher aides. Answers to these seven questions will provide information to help make IEP decisions. They also will base their decisions upon:

1. The child's current level of functioning.
2. Predictions about the child's future level of functioning and/or program placement.
3. The skills that must be taught so that the child can progress from where she is now to where she needs to be (Writer, 1979).

Helping special educators, parents, and other professionals will recognize that MH populations need to be programmed individually because of the various levels of ability. For example, COHI-MH populations function at four levels. At the mainstream level, with the help of trained COHI specialists, nurses, and other personnel, they can be expected to achieve with either usual or modified methods and materials. At the second level, they can function in educational or vocationally oriented settings if provisions have been made for alternate strategies and periodic reevaluations. For third level functioning COHI-MH students, it is necessary to vary teaching strategies and the content and focus of the educational program. The fourth level must have opportunities for the development of alternate strategies and a curriculum directed toward knowledge acquisition and self-help, survival, and self-enhancement skills (Task Force II, 1973).

Another group of the MH population, the deaf-blind, also has a variety of functional levels. Smith (1974) divided the deaf-blind population into these three levels:·

1. Middle trainable and below—60 to 75 percent fall into this lowest functioning class. The best prognosis is that they will achieve levels of personal care and physical control, with a minimum capacity for social interaction.
2. Upper trainable through lower educable—15 to 25 percent fall into this category. This group can achieve independence, and, with training, acquire useful vocational skills, or some academic education, to lead semi-independent lives.
3. Middle educable and above—5 to 10 percent who can be trained and educated to very high levels of proficiency, sufficient to lead independent lives in unsheltered employment and living conditions (pp. 65–70).

Griffin (1979) advocates several levels of educational programming for CP students, another category of multihandicapped children:

1. Children with severe physical and/or mental disabilities often are placed in self-contained classrooms.
2. For moderately disabled children, the resource room concept can be used, along with the regular classroom for part of the day with special help in some academic areas.
3. Cerebral palsy children with average intelligence, adequate communication skills, and mild to moderate physical impairments can be placed in regular classrooms with structural adaptations and a buddy system.

With so many pupil characteristics and program variations in the multihandicapped population, helping special educators should work with parents to develop a readiness in the child for alternative educational programs.

At the preschool level, special educators must be available to assist parents in developing skills to care for the MH child at home. The educational program will involve them and will be designed to stress success in activities. For example, with CP children the early childhood school program should be managed by the helping educators. Teachers should make sure that mats, toys, and tumbling equipment are present to encourage floor and play movement. Physical therapists and parents can help one another place children in correct seating positions and provide them with stimulating activities. Helping teachers and occupational therapists should work jointly to assist preschool children in sampling new foods and in learning to handle eating utensils. Parents are shown how to prepare food for the child who has a tendency to choke and how to conduct toilet training.

Acting as advocates and ombudsmen, helping special educators encourage parents to observe the program, to assist in the classroom, and to participate in the parent groups (Miller, 1971). As advocates, the teachers are forceful allies to parents in their right to observe and to participate in the educational program for their child. As ombudsmen, teachers mediate differences between different team members about the amount and kind of parent participation and assistance in the program.

Dealing with the Preschool and Elementary Child

Teachers should encourage parents of preschoolers to roll, crawl, climb, scoot, and jump with the child. During this coactive movement, parent contact with the child is encouraged and parent-child communication begins. As the child grows accustomed to movement, he learns to initiate movement. Later, parents can be shown how to refer the child to his body parts—arms, legs. In this "nonrepresentational reference" phase (Van Dyck, 1973), parents give the child a point of reference about his body.

Working together, parents and teachers move the child toward the imitation stage. At this level, DB children should develop a reflective attitude. Parents and teachers stress symmetrical to assymetrical movements to facilitate learning. They sit opposite the child and raise both arms, then move one arm up and one arm down. The child reflects on these movements, then tries to imitate them. Following this achievement, the MH child is ready to imitate a drawing, i.e., a picture of a child with one arm up and one arm down.

After imitation, the child is led through the natural gesture stage when he learns what he can do with a ball (Van Dyck, 1973). Parents and teachers show the child the gesture, then put him through the gesture just before giving him the ball. Eventually, the child anticipates the gesture and finally gestures upon anticipation of the ball. Teachers and parents should be pleased when two factors in the development of natural gestures appear—decontextualization and denaturalization. When decontextualization occurs, parents tell teachers, for example, that they saw the child give the sign for drink at home rather than at school. Denaturalization occurs when the child makes a slight gesture instead of a full motion, e.g., movement of the hand instead of the motion of throwing the ball.

Case manager teachers must work intensely with parents to effect these changes in the child. Only through their combined efforts can such growth occur.

At the elementary level, helping special educators work with parents of MH children from several disability groups. When faced with moderately handicapped CP children, they should be prepared to work with the negative and positive aspects of mainstreaming. Parents may favor placement in the regular classroom and may feel good about the prospect. However, special educators should be alerted that mainstream pupils choose CP children as friends less often than other physically handicapped children (Anderson, 1975; Griffin, 1979). Thus, teachers must cope with the parents' feelings while working with the child and his classmates. Parents will have to be understanding as special educators go about changing the attitudes of some of their students. Teachers must recognize the source of the parents' complaints that the child "doesn't have any friends in class." Thus, helping special educators function as advocates for the CP child with the parent and class to advocate for the child's placement.

Helping special education teachers should be prepared to work with problems that concern other professionals and that may originate from mainstream placement. When planning the IEP for the mainstreamed CP child, certain adaptations should be considered (Anderson, 1975) involving:

1. transportation
2. modification of school buildings and furniture
3. provision of special equipment
4. personal assistance for physically handicapped children
5. therapy needs
6. information and advice to school staff
7. the need for assistance to school staff (p. 20).

As case managers, helping teachers must work with other professionals and staff to achieve success in educational programming. With so many persons involved, differences can be expected to arise. The regular class teacher is concerned about personal assistance: Who will help with the toileting and other needed academic services? Parents have reservations about the amount of time devoted to physical, occupational, or speech therapy. Ombudsman teachers must orchestrate these issues while also working as case managers to assure that all the necessary program components are included in the IEP.

The support of parents is crucial to the success of any educational program. Their help must be enlisted not only in the planning but also in the implementation of the IEP. Parents can be used to:

1. help keep the teacher oriented in the direction of long-term goal achievement
2. inform a teacher when and if a goal is achieved
3. provide valuable information on the learning patterns used by the child in achieving the goals
4. save the teacher some time in the achievement of the goals
5. provide a valuable communication link between home and classroom programming (Writer, 1979, p. 22).

Following these concepts, teachers can use parents as a valuable resource in the education of severely and multi-handicapped children.

The Place of the Team Approach

Special educators in the self-contained classroom must engage in a team approach. They must develop long-range and short-range goals with parents, occupational, physical, and speech therapists, and administrators. Once again, the responsibility for obtaining the proper services for the MH child is vested in the helping special educators. Teachers are cast in the familiar role of advocates for the child. For example, parents may be unaware of occupational therapy services offered by the school. Teachers must assure not only that parents are aware of these opportunities but also that children obtain them.

Chances for disagreements over the amount and kind of services among professionals are great. Many school districts seek to comply with the spirit of P.L. 94-142 and to supply needed services. Often, however, their finances are strained and the skills of specialists such as occupational therapists (OTs) and physical therapists (PTs) are stretched throughout the district. In this case, helping teachers will have to operate as ombudsmen and obtain the services for the child. Educators in such dilemmas face the dual task of obtaining the services while mediating the expressed needs of parents and professionals.

Because of the efforts of the helping special educators, all of the professionals (OT, PT), and parents will have joined together to implement the agreed-upon goals in the therapy and classroom settings. For the CP child such things as academic learning, motor activity, self-help skills, and free play are included in the program. Special areas for special activities are designated clearly so that children know what is expected of them in each area. In the special area for motor activity, special educators and physical therapists should develop activities that will stimulate reaching, proper positioning, crawling, and rolling (Griffin, 1979). Other items in this area might include bright toys that attract attention and encourage looking, bean bags, and objects of various textures (Robinault, 1973). Educators should encourage parents to participate in these activities with their children at home.

The area of skill-help is natural for parent-teacher collaboration. Parents may need to know the "how-to" of some abstract concept the teachers are attempting to develop. Perhaps the parent-teacher participation is desired in developing expressive and receptive communication skills in the child. Parents might need assistance in the proper use of the language board for a nonverbal child. Initially parents and teachers would work together so that the child could express himself. Then the parent would be encouraged to move gradually from nouns to verbs to adjectives. The process should be thoroughly explained to parents and their inquiries answered to their satisfaction. Parents can participate fully in self-help skills when MH children are learning to tie shoes, put on clothes, fasten buttons, brush teeth, and comb hair. When given the opportunity to reinforce these skills at home, parents work in tandem with the teachers to develop skills that the couple considers important for successful everyday living.

These joint endeavors give special educators ample opportunities to teach and counsel with parents. Many parents, when teaching these skills, may come to the conclusion that the child will never learn despite evidence to the contrary. The child's repeated failure to perform a task at home may convince parents that additional attempts to teach the skill are futile. Helping teachers must adopt understanding attitudes and may have to advocate or mediate the child's position. At times, educators should have the parents observe teaching procedures in the classroom. On other occasions, parents must spend considerable time counseling with teachers to air their concerns and to obtain a more realistic and objective view of the child.

It is not uncommon for parents to become teachers in certain situations. One of the benefits of P.L. 94-142 has been the increased interaction of parents and teachers on behalf of the child. Heretofore, the parents' knowledge of the child's adaptive behavior at home might not have been considered significant in the school's educational programming. Since passage of the act, parents not only are seen in the schools but also find their advice solicited by teachers on such subjects as feeding and nonverbal communication methods.

This kind of cooperation occurs more than just occasionally. The ability of helping teachers acting as case managers fosters such parent-professional co-operation. Educators through their advocacy and ombudsman efforts fight for or arbitrate for needed services for the MH child. Case managers involve the parents in the planning and implementation of the IEP. Through humanistic counseling and attention to the feelings of parents, teachers help the family accommodate the MH child. Special educators also work with parents to provide the child with a viable elementary education in anticipation of moving into secondary programming.

INVOLVING PARENTS OF MH ADOLESCENTS

> The rubella epidemic of 1964–65 increased the number of deaf-blind children in the United States to more than 5,000. By 1980 these children will be adolescents. Their individual and social needs will be different and their service needs will be changing. . . . And the child is not alone in his needs. He has parents whose anxiety is growing. They worry about where he can go, what he can do, and who will care for him. They wonder what possibilities the future holds for their child as a person and for themselves (Lowell, 1974, p. v).

These words on behalf of deaf-blind children can be expanded to include all MH adolescents and their parents. The key to success with parents in educational programming for the multihandicapped adolescent is best expressed by the philosophy "try another way" (Gold, 1977). This philosophy has become important in secondary programming for MH adolescents because the parents can be described as desperate and confused. Some had attempted to enroll their children in public schools prior to the passage of P.L. 94-142. To their dismay, the MH teenagers were turned away or rejected because of their inability to keep physical pace in the daily activities of the school and/or because of certain "embarrassing" physical conditions such as drooling or disfigurement or special prophylactic equipment such as catheters (Task Force II, 1973, p. 8). Other parents saw their youngsters experience so much rejection in preteen activities that they didn't even bother to attempt to enroll them. Public Law 94-142 changed the status of their teenagers and gave them hope but parents still are concerned about enrollment of their children in public schools.

Concerns over Mainstreaming

The uneasiness of parents with moderately multiply handicapped adolescents has centered on the issue of mainstreaming. Parents tend to favor the concept, especially those with teenagers with physical handicaps. Parents believe that their children can obtain a better education and benefit more socially in a regular classroom (Anderson, 1975). Many believe the regular classroom will do a better job than the segregated setting in assisting the handicapped children to adjust to the world when they become adults (Brenton, 1975).

Despite these positive feelings about mainstreaming, parents of MH children have to balance their wishes against the needs of the adolescent. Billings (1963) discovered several important factors about the physically handicapped. He found that a negative relationship existed among nonhandicapped pupils between personality adjustment and attitudes toward the physically disabled. This could be interpreted to mean that the most stable youth held the most negative attitudes toward youngsters with physical disabilities. Billings also concluded that attitudes among older children toward the physically disabled were the most unfavorable. Thus, helping teachers could face parents who insist upon mainstreaming as a viable option under P.L. 94-142. Helping educators also work with regular teachers whose classes may hold negative attitudes toward the physically handicapped. Helping teachers must become advocates for the MH adolescent in the classroom. They should have the human relations skills to produce an appreciation of individual differences in youths.

Initially, parents may feel satisfied about the mainstream placement in the regular classroom. However, after the teenager has revealed to parents his uneasiness and unhappiness in class, helping teachers must work with parents in the role of ombudsmen to mediate the ambivalent feelings. Educators also should work with the MH adolescent to increase his self-esteem and to provide coping skills. Finally, as case managers, helping teachers should support regular classroom teachers in their attempts to create a climate of acceptance for the handicapped in their classes. Functioning as advocates and as ombudsmen to the regular classroom teacher, helping teachers can originate activities designed to increase the understanding of the handicapped by nonhandicapped adolescents. Thus, special educators initiate such student development activities as the blind walk, magic circle, and self-portrait. All of these exercises are intended to create an awareness of and appreciation of individual differences and to give students a better understanding of themselves.

As a major objective, helping educators must work to provide activities to create a better understanding among adolescents and teachers. The urgency of this task is underscored by the following two findings. (1) Teachers have tended to include emotional, social, and cultural factors as well as atypical physical factors in their description of the term disabled (Sonits & Edwards, 1971). (2) Siller, Ferguson, Vann, and Holland (1967) found a cluster of attitudes in their study that they labeled "the rejection of intimacy." These factors should be noted by teachers of MH adolescents since they denote the rejection of close familial relationships with the disabled, an unwillingness to marry or fall in love with people who are physically disabled, and the rejection of bearing disabled children.

Helping educators must give high priority to regular teacher needs and teenager attitudes. At this stage adolescents form peer associations instead of close family relationships. Physical, emotional, and social changes occur that cause conflicting emotions. Parents are anxious that their teenagers are accepted by others. Secondary classroom teachers have reservations about including the handicapped in their classes, with MH adolescents low on the list of desirables (Rumble, 1978). With this evidence, it can be seen that helping special educators cannot afford to take lightly their efforts in working with parents of MH adolescents who are being mainstreamed.

The Self-Contained Classroom

Another educational alternative is the self-contained classroom. Helping teachers who work with MH adolescents in this school arrangement focus upon preparing the students for adult life. Since many of the MH students in these programs are severely handicapped, many teachers will emphasize the development of vocational skills. Most academic subject areas are linked to daily living skills. Writer (1979) suggested that the following components be included in a program for the severely multihandicapped student:

1. vocational training
2. academics
3. semi-independent living
4. independent functioning in the environment where the child resides (p. 18).

In sitting with parents to plan and implement the IEP for the severely multihandicapped youth, helping teachers must remember that all goals written should be relevant to that specific teenager—relevant to the youngster's life, relevant to the environment, and relevant to the adolescent's future. Parents may not have an accurate picture of the MH adolescent's functioning level, and confusion over the student's potential may obscure reality. Special educators must help parents assess the teenager's fuctional capacity. Both parties should carry out the assessment within the following parameters. Information should be gathered to (Writer, 1975):

1. Find out where the child is functioning:
   a. physically
   b. socially
   c. emotionally
   d. mentally
2. Observe how the child spontaneously interacts with the environment. Record behaviors
   a. in the home
   b. in the classroom
   c. on the playground, and
   d. in the community
   Determine the child's preferred avenue(s) for taking in information (mode—vision, hearing, touch, etc.; method—turning head to the side to look; smelling before touching).
3. Identify the child's best functioning space.
4. Ascertain the child's attention span.

5. Determine the child's reward system (p. 20).

Following these rules, parents and special educators strive to arrive at a program that will:

1. emphasize functional skill development
2. provide multisensory cues
3. offer results that are permanent
4. match the individual's functioning levels
5. manifest cause-and-effect relationships
6. encourage *active* participation on the part of the child

Thus, a program for the multihandicapped will have a prevocational orientation, and prevocational activities will assume a more important role. Parents and educators should work with MH adolescents to develop these prevocational attitudes about work (Bigge, 1976):

1. Work has dignity.
2. Work means different things to different people.
3. Work has different rewards.
4. Work and education are interrelated.

At this point teachers should recognize the disappointment some parents of MH adolescents feel about secondary special education and vocational education. Having noted the lack of opportunity provided to their teenagers by both areas, parents feel that their children have been shortchanged. Therefore, helping teachers not only must advocate for the vocational emphasis but also must mediate any negative feelings that parents may harbor. Special educators must advocate for prevocational training programs that parents may feel are useless. Parents may think, "why bother changing the attitudes of my youngster toward work when the adolescent isn't going to get hired anyway." These parents must be informed about Section 504 of the Rehabilitation Act of 1973, which forbids discrimination in hiring because of handicapping conditions.

Some parents may have been overprotective of their MH teenagers and may have difficulty picturing an independently functioning adolescent. Still others may want to see the youth become independent but may have conflicting attitudes about placing the teenager in a sheltered workshop situation that they consider to be demeaning to the concept of independence. Such strong feelings must be aired and information provided that will enable parents to make wise decisions. Giving parents an opportunity to be heard can provide ombudsman special educators with a wedge to explore positive options for the teenagers.

Vocational Evaluation and Vocational Education

Educators should advocate the necessary steps to be taken for vocational evaluation of the MH adolescent. They should explain the procedure thoroughly. Parents' attitudes may be influenced positively by the U.S. Department of Health, Education and Welfare's (1971) definition of vocational evaluation: "The appraisal of the individual's capacity, including patterns of work behavior, ability to acquire occupational skills, and the selection of appropriate vocational goals" (p. 1). Parents' attitudes may change further as they become better acquainted with the kinds of vocational evaluation.

For example, parents may need exposure to standardized tests, work samples, and situational assessment. This can remedy their feelings about the procedure. When this occurs, helping special educators, as ombudsmen, still should be alert to mediate any conflicting feelings that might arise as a result of the vocational evaluation. Parents of MH adolescents may have second thoughts about the evaluation and may ask for a postponement. Others may have difficulty accepting the results of the evaluation. These strong feelings may be linked to other emotions concerning a previous lack of opportunities in other subject areas. At this point, helping teachers are crucial factors because preparation for vocational training is a very crucial period in the lives of parents with MH adolescents (Barraga, 1966).

Parents face a crisis period when their MH teenager enters the stage of vocational preparation. If parents have agreed to vocational evaluation, they now must accept the fact that their adolescent will be able to work independently and hold a job, or will be considered for work in sheltered situations. In either case, the acquisition of vocational training skills cannot be looked upon as the only ones needed for the MH teenager to hold a job. Teachers should demonstrate to parents that communication and social interaction skills also are vital to an employment program. Educators acting as case managers should have reached agreement with the parents in the IEP planning that these factors would be considered in the total training program. If they were not included originally, parents should be consulted and their agreement obtained through mutual negotiations, (including the adolescent, if possible).

Under this agreement the communication skills of speech, handwriting, and spelling should be stressed (Griffin, 1979). Communication is an important capability in the employment process. Interviewing for jobs, filling out job applications, and expressing a sincere interest in employment are key elements in any job search (pp. 2–3). Therefore, parents and helping teachers should work with MH adolescents to overcome the limitations of the communications process. Teachers can use mock interviews and other simulated activities in the classroom to foster effective communication skills. To show parents that the training is not an exercise in futility, teachers should encourage community involvement by inviting resource persons from business and industry to help in the classroom simulations.

The potential for employment success for MH adolescents should be viewed also from the perspective of social relationships. Developing these skills can be linked directly to job success since the ability of a person to get along with coworkers is valued highly by employers (p. 4). One of the most desired social relationships in employment is the development of a give-and-take attitude. This often has proved difficult in MH populations. For instance, CP adolescents have been the center of attention in therapeutic and educational settings (Cruickshank, 1976). The same also can be said for DB and other multisensory handicapped teenagers who lack the benefit of hearing or vision to allow them to experience the subtleties of human interaction through direct observation or feedback.

To counteract this problem, the helping persons must advocate for activities that will provide opportunities for winning and losing situations. One way to accomplish this is to involve MH adolescents in playing competitive and realistic games in physical education. These activities can help the teenagers develop a well-adjusted personality and a strong desire to be rehabilitated.

When assisting the MH adolescent in this fashion, teachers should mediate any strong feelings of overprotection that parents might display. Educators should not be surprised if parents do not embrace these suggestions immediately. They should be mindful of the fact that parents of MH adolescents have lived a long time with the youngsters. Therefore, the suggestion of overprotection or an attitudinal change on the part of parents always should be approached cautiously. Helping persons should be alert to parents' emotions through empathetic listening. Having deciphered the parents' main concerns in this manner, special educators should have established a mutual climate of trust and respect in which counseling can take place. During these sessions, ombudsman helping teachers should stress the need for the MH adolescent to develop concern for the feelings and needs of others. Case manager teachers should provide a series of experiences that will convince parents to accept the fact that participation in "helping others" activities will decrease the self-centered attitude of the MH adolescent.

In providing these activities, helping teachers fulfill the roles of advocates, ombudsmen, and case managers. However, their job is not complete without community involvement. Special educators must advocate in the community for MH adolescents, particularly to destroy the myths that have been perpetuated about these populations. Thus, as ombudsmen, teachers should provide information about the truths and capabilities of the MH teenager with the understanding that only an informed public can be an intelligent consumer of information (p. 7).

Finally, case manager helping teachers work with the various publics to assure that all the functioning parts are fitted into the IEP. The helping teachers and parents work together from the inception of the plan to seek community involvement. Long-range and short-range involvement goals will have been agreed upon mutually. Objectives will have been changed constantly through a continuing informal evaluation process. Through this constant evaluation and reevaluation, MH adolescents can be helped to progress toward developing an independent and better quality of life.

In conclusion, the future of MH adolescents can be summed up best in the words of Benjamin Smith:

> It is the conviction of this writer that this population . . . can be self-supporting, can be . . . independent, can make a contribution to our social order, and can have in return enriched and fulfilled lives that will be well worth the efforts we make (1974, p. 70).

Chapter 7

Involving Parents of Behaviorally Disordered Children

By the most conservative estimate, at least 1.4 million children under the age of 18 have emotional problems of sufficient severity to warrant urgent attention. As many as 10 million more require psychiatric help of some kind if they are ever to achieve the potential that medical progress on other fronts has made possible (p. 52).

These words by Dr. Joseph D. Noshpitz (1974) of the American Academy of Child Psychiatry document the plight of the behaviorally disordered or emotionally disturbed (BD/ED) child. As late as the early 1970s the behaviorally disordered or emotionally disturbed child could be called an "endangered species." Regardless of their circumstances, the chances were high that they were not receiving services. Moreover, parents of BD/ED children and youths continued to be overwhelmed by never-ending daily problems and faced unending community indifference to their needs. These were the "families of crises."

BD/ED children and youth have been called the principal's and teacher's dilemma (Morse, 1971). Many kinds of behaviors or disorders are included in the category. At the core can be found the autistic or schizophrenic children. These BD children generally are helplessly withdrawn from the realities of the world and live in an inner world not entered frequently by parents and strangers. More than 1 million BD children can be labeled "hyperkinetic." These youngsters have a tendency to destroy schoolrooms and homes and to traumatize teachers and parents through their frantic and uncontrollable physical activity. Neurotic symptoms also plague some of these children. They are traumatized by nightmares, caught in the web of depression, terrified about going to school, or trapped in the grip of mysterious compulsive rituals. However, the hardest to identify but equally troubled are the children and youths who fail to function in society. They are branded as failures in schools by educators, are known as fighters and/or thieves, and eventually fill reformatories, jails, and penitentiaries.

The state of the art was captured in these words of Matt Clark (1974):

. . . until recently, childhood emotional disorders have been tragically neglected as a national health problem of dramatic proportions. Be-

cause of his bizarre and often repellent behavior, the emotionally disturbed youngster has never made an appealing poster child for
mother's marches and annual fund raising drives. While most of the
nation's 7.6 million physically handicapped receive educational and
medical services through a variety of public and private channels,
fewer than 1 million of the emotionally handicapped are receiving the
help they need. All too often the disturbed child has been expelled
from public school as unteachable, or shunted into special classes for
retarded children with brain damage (p. 52).

These comments can be understood better if the terms behaviorally or emotionally disturbed are examined in the context of schools. Both terms have
carried a connotation of the disturbed or disturbing pupil (Morse, 1971). For
these students the school was seen as the least likely place to be found. In fact,
schools were not considered to have much say in the mental health effort for
children (Allinsmith & Goethals, 1962). The sequence of events for the child
could be forecast in the following manner. In step one, the child considered
disturbed or disturbing was taken out of class and referred to a mental health
specialist (social worker, psychologist, or psychiatrist). A child exhibiting maladaptive behaviors and facing the best chance for referral was most likely to
be described in these terms by the teacher:

He is just like the others. That whole family is crazy. Either you get
him out of here or I quit.

or

I understand about the waiting list. But I've got 30 other kids in the
class that I've got to take care of. What am I going to do in the
meantime?

In step two, the emotionally disturbed or behaviorally disordered child became
a client, to be diagnosed and to become a long-term patient of a therapist. While
this process was going on, step three, a "holding action" pattern, was initiated
by teachers and educators. They were expected not to interfere in the process.
They were consoled with the fact that they would get the BD/ED child back
after therapy had been completed.
   There were those who disagreed with this medical model with its methodical
processes and its emphasis upon "sickness." These educators advanced the
theory that all behavior was learned. Basing their findings upon behavioral
operant conditioning, they (Hewett, 1968; Haring, 1969; Kauffman, 1977) attempted to dispel the favoritism extended to psychotherapy as a preferred treatment for BD and ED children (Morse, 1971).

Others, however, were of the opinion that the behavioral model was not the panacea for the mental health and education of these children. Hobbs (1964) took a broader conceptualization of the problems. He theorized that the mental health and learning ability of the child was affected by his interface with his environment. This ecological approach propelled schools into the forefront as a dominant resource in the well-being of BD and ED children. Schools were accorded a role as one of the provocateurs or exacerbaters of mental health in children. Since schools see children and youth over long periods of time in a realistic setting, they were regarded as an opportunity to become the scene for prevention. Finally, a reversal of priorities has taken place. Teachers are seen as critical persons or mental health agents in the mental health and education effort on behalf of BD and ED children (Morse, 1971).

What these changes have meant for special education and schools cannot be overestimated. First, special educators cannot be overly concerned about whether the child is called behaviorally disordered or emotionally disturbed. Rather, their concern should focus on the principle that the child needs help. Whether the child is "acting out" or has "poor concentration," under P.L. 94-142 it is the school's responsibility to be more effective in providing positive rather than negative rewards for students. The terms behaviorally disordered or emotionally disturbed will not enable teachers to avoid being accountable for the achievements of pupils regardless of the nomenclature. Hence, the terms BD and ED are used interchangeably in this chapter.

Parents have been elevated to positions of coequals with teachers through P.L. 94-142. Teachers similarly have been accorded a leadership role in the mental health and educational rehabilitation efforts on behalf of BD or ED children and adolescents. Therefore, mutual efforts for insights concerning both what to do and how to do it for the student should be undertaken by both parties. Parents and teachers should make use of a wide array of strategies to find an effective plan that will benefit the pupil. These processes may not be found in any single model. Educators should be prepared to adopt several methods to provide the needed help.

In the parent-teacher relationship under P.L. 94-142, educators of BD and ED children are assigned another critical role: they may be the only positive adult models these pupils are likely to see over a sustained period. Since children and youth learn by imitation, teachers have a responsibility to show them a responsible, mature, and productive form of adult behavior. Teachers also provide modeling behavior patterns for parents. This teacher-parent-student relationship is a critical mental health and educational factor. Often a good adult-to-adult school-home relationship becomes the only resource for correction of unfavorable child-parent interaction.

Working with parents of BD/ED children and adolescents presents a renewed challenge to special educators under P.L. 94-142. These parents live with such a diversity of handicapping conditions that the guilt/deficit model previously assigned to them cannot be accepted unquestioned. Parents ask that professionals commit themselves to help bring about positive changes in the education of their children and in finding strengths and fostering self-esteem in the family circle.

ISSUES FACING EDUCATORS OF BD CHILDREN

One of the primary issues confronting educators of BD/ED children is the problem of identification. Despite the definition in P.L. 94-142, there still is considerable disagreement among professionals as to what constitutes the nature of a BD child (Rubin & Balow, 1978; Farber, 1975; Blackham, 1967; Hewett, 1968). In fact, so much dissonance has emerged that Hobbs (1975) said that "the diagnostic classification of emotional disturbance and cognate conditions in children remains a thicket of thorny problems" (p. 57).

Another issue troubling educators is the problem of implementing the P.L. 94-142 definition of special education in public schools. Programming in BD/ED is hampered by problems of measurement of personality constructs. Projective techniques and personality inventories used in measurement attempts generally have not been too reliable or valid (Bower, 1957).

Still another problem is the inability of schools to conceptualize a workable model. Generally BD educators operate from the knowledge base of their training. Since there are five generally accepted conceptual models now operating, it has been difficult for educators to agree upon a best one or to compromise upon best ones (Grosenick, 1978). Thus educators continue to rely upon the medical model (Rimland, 1964), the behavioral model (Haring & Phillips, 1962; Kauffman, 1974), the psychodynamic model (Freud, 1949; Jung, 1958; Adler, 1956; & Morse, 1971), the ecological model (Hobbs, 1975; Lewis, 1967) and the sociological model (Kvaraceus, 1959).

A closely related problem is the concern about teacher training programs. Gilliam and Dollar (1977) found very little literature on competency-based instruction for teachers of the seriously emotionally disturbed. Yates and Shirley (1978) projected a need of 2,656 teachers in the ED category over the next decade in a single southwestern state. Berkowitz (1974) noted another feature of BD teacher training programs: a shortage of teachers to work with these children existed because of the low number of teacher preparation programs. Gilliam substantiated this lack of teacher training programs in his survey that showed only seven out of 40 institutions of higher education offered programs in autism (Marion, 1979). Thus teacher training institutions face a two-fold problem: (1) Teachers are not being trained in sufficient numbers to meet the demand for services. (2) Accumulated evidence suggests that teachers need to increase their preservice competencies to be able to work with BD/ED children.

A final issue that faces BD educators is the lack of qualified programs and services for adolescents. Adolescent programs are inadequate for other categories, and BD adolescents have not fared well either. Nelson and Kauffman (1977) listed several reasons for the scarcity of programs for BD students at the secondary level. Chief among these were departmentalization, lack of qualified teachers, long histories of academic nonachievement, and dropouts (after the 16-year-old attendance requirement is completed). Morse (1964) summarized the high school population when he said:

> By the time disturbed children reach high school age, they are much more difficult to handle, their pathology is likely to be deeply ingrained, and their anti-social behavior as often as not has taken them out of school into the hands of a secondary social agency. Their less bright prognosis, and the limited efficacy of educationally oriented remediation makes the schools less willing to undertake special programs of this sort for them (p. 21).

While all of the issues discussed in this section are worthy of the concern of educators of BD children, certain challenges are deserving of further explanation and examination. Specifically, the choice of educational and treatment models and the widespread use of drug therapy have provoked much controversy and discussion among special educators. In the case of educational and treatment models, five different approaches have tended to dominate the field of BD/ED. Each model is examined in fuller detail.

1. The Medical Model

In this approach, the definition of BD/ED is linked to an absence or presence of biological symptoms. In the biological presence of distress symptoms, the behavior of the child is considered abnormal; in the absence of complicating signs, the disturbance of the youngster is characterized as normal. The assumptions of the model are vested in the premise that the pathology of the BD/ED child is caused by biological conditions and that sociocultural factors are not relevant to diagnoses or treatment. The medical model has several distinguishable characteristics (Coulter, Gilliam, Morrow, & Coulter, 1978):

- Bipolar model: pathology—health
- Evaluative: pathology "bad"—health "good"
- Not culture bound
- Deficit model

- Pathology, attribute of person

- Biological cause produces effect

- Pathology can exist unrecognized

The chief therapists of this model have been physicians who have tended to treat emotional disturbances or behavioral disorders as they would any other illness. Physicians generally have dispensed tranquilizing medications to calm the overactive child and have administered invigorating stimulants to rejuvenate the depressed and melancholic one. They also generally have counseled the hyperactive child to get more rest and the depressed youngster to arrange a program with the potential to stimulate new interests. Under the medical treatment plan, neither parent, teacher, nor child could be expected to have much contact with the attending physician (Clarizio & McCoy, 1970).

The teachers in this model can be considered referral agents. Their role in the educational and treatment process is limited on two accounts: (1) the physician has been the dominating force in the educational and medical process, and (2) the length of time that the child is removed from classes has created continuity problems in the pupil's educational process.

2. The Sociological or Social System Model

In this model the definition of BD/ED is related to society's acceptance of the child's behavior. Thus, socially deviant behavior is considered abnormal since it violates social system norms. Conversely, actions that have met society's expectations are considered normal behavior. Furthermore, the social system is imbued with particular characteristics and infused with certain characteristics. Three assumptions of the model can be stated: (1) The model has multiple definitions of normalcy and norms are established for each role in each system. (2) Norms are determined by biology but are defined in terms of the political process. (3) Tests are used to enforce the norms of the dominant or majority society (Coulter, Gilliam, Morrow, & Coulter, 1978). Moreover characteristics of the social system model can be outlined in this manner:

- Multidimensional model has norms for each role in each system.

- Local values of powerful groups are enforced.

- Abnormality is social system and role bound.

- Deficit and asset mode is operative.

- Deviance is judgment about behavior, not viewed as an attribute of a person.

- Biological cause is not sought; the political process defines deviance.

- Deviance is an interpersonal assessment and cannot exist unrecognized.

The educators' role in the sociological model is limited to the teaching of conformist behavior and modeling. Specifically the model has been applied to youthful offenders and juvenile delinquents. Rewards and punishments are not overly used but rather the focus is placed upon having children acquire a mastery of "coping skills."

3. The Behavioral Model

This model is based on learning theory, and BD/ED behavior is characterized by the interfering behaviors exhibited by the child and considered as "learned" maladaptive behavior. Two assumptions are made with the behavioral model: (1) The child can be assisted in modifying maladaptive behavior and thereby his success in and acceptance by the environment can be increased. (2) Positive and negative consequences resulting from inappropriate behavior should be the major focus of the program (Hewett, 1968).

Behavior models attempt to modify two types of maladaptive actions. One kind is classified as involuntary and is not under the child's control. The second kind is categorized as voluntary and is under the control of the child (Hewett). In the former case, negative reinforcement can be expected when the child is thrust into threatening conditions or fearful stimuli. The latter can be expected to occur when a response to an action by an individual to a particular stimulus is punctuated by positive or negative reinforcements.

The teachers' role in the behavior model is enhanced since they serve as pivotal figures in changing and controlling the maladaptive behavior of the child. They function as learning specialists (Hewett) and assist the child by presenting him tasks the youngster needs to do, is able to do, and can find satisfaction in doing. A starting point is established and the complexity of tasks assigned is increased depending upon the child's readiness. Upon successful completion of the task, children are rewarded; conversely, they are not rewarded if what they do is not correct. The strategies used in a systematic approach to develop adaptive behavior for learning are called behavior modification. Behavior modification techniques are applied without regard to racial, cultural, or social considerations. They generally take the form of token economies, operant conditioning, points and time-outs. In summary, behavior modification strategies focus upon "what" the child presents in the classroom, and attempts to reshape deviant behavior in line with required standards of learning.

4. The Psychodynamic Model

This model is concerned with the psychic origin and meaning of maladaptive behavior and the child's interpersonal relationships with others. The definition of normal behavior is linked to the successful resolution of crises that occur during various developmental stages of the child's growth and maturation. Initially influenced by Freud (and later by Erickson and by Adler), BD/ED behavior is seen as internal to the individual and is maladaptive if the person cannot mesh the ego, id, and superego into a working system that can resolve the oral, anal, phallic, latency, and genital stages of development. Similar conflicts had to be resolved during the eight stages of Erickson. Later disciples of modified psychodynamic approaches have been Morse (1971) and Hewett (1968).

The teachers' role in the psychodynamic model is that of team members and educational therapists. Special educators are expected to work with social workers, psychometrists, guidance counselors, speech therapists, and other specialized personnel. Special educators on the team must be totally accepting of the child and must interpret his behavior within a psychodynamic framework. Thus the teachers must make use of psychoanalytic concepts. Within the instructional role, the crisis teacher model with life space interviews has been the most dominant form used in the management and education of the child in the classroom. The crisis teacher stays with the child, helps him to gain control, assists the child in understanding what caused the blow-up, and finally shows the child how he can cope with frustration and anger.

5. The Ecological Model

In this model, disturbance is viewed as a dynamic interface between the child and his environment. Chief proponents of this model have been Hobbs (1966), Rhodes (1967), and Lewis (1967). Behavior is seen as abnormal if the child is performing below the standards of his own sociocultural group. Normal behavior is defined as actions that reflect the average behavior of the child's sociocultural group. Thus, the ecological model assumes that the disturbance does not reside in the child but in "the ecological system of which the child is an integral part" (Hobbs, 1975, p. 113). Ecological system is defined narrowly as "the child and the settings and the individuals within these settings that are a part of the child's daily life" (Hobbs, 1975, p. 114) and can be considered in a broader sense as "extending to the community and its cultural context which surround the child" (Rhodes, 1970; Rhodes & Paul, 1978).

The teachers' role in the ecological model is that of systems analyst. Teachers must locate the disturbance in the interactions between the child and the environment and then focus upon eliminating the disturbance through an assessment and planned intervention program. The objective is not merely to change or improve the child but to make the total system work (Hobbs, 1975). Special educators have a concern that any intervention that attempts to remove a child from his environment to change his behavior and to return him to his previous unchanged environment is unethical (Rhodes, 1970). Thus the special educators work with three systems in the ecological network to change the child's behavior: (1) the behavior or physical setting, (2) patterns of behavior across settings, and (3) the community and culture.

CONTROVERSY OVER USE OF DRUGS

The second major controversial area in services to BD/ED children (educational and treatment models was the first) is the use of drugs. Since Charles Bradley (1937) first used Benzedrine to reduce the hyperactivity of children who exhibited disturbed behavior in schools, the use of drugs with BD/ED children has grown tremendously. The number of children using drugs to control their hyperactivity is estimated between half a million and two million (Offir, 1974). Huntsinger (1970) reported a 1970 National Institute on Mental Health survey that computed the number of children who could benefit from tranquilizers at close to four million.

These data indicate that the use of drugs with BD/ED children is widespread. Hyperactivity is the problem behavior for which most drug therapy is prescribed. For the hyperactive child, the amphetamines and their chemical cousins are the most widely dispensed medications. Principal tranquilizers such as phenothiazine and its near chemical kin, chlorpromazine, also are used as calming agents (Axelrod & Bailey, 1979). Despite this wholesale use of drugs, the controversy surrounding the approach has not abated.

According to Zukow (1975) much of the furor has arisen because the two terms "hyperactive" and "hyperkinetic" have been used interchangeably. He made the following points:

1. All hyperkinetic children are hyperactive.
2. All hyperactive children are not hyperkinetic.
3. All learning or behavior problems are not the result of hyperkinesis.
4. About 75 percent of hyperkinetic children do have a learning problem as a direct or indirect result of the condition.
5. A youngster does not suddenly, at age 6, become hyperkinetic (p. 40).

A January 1971 report of the U.S. Department of Health, Education, and Welfare also begged that the two terms not be confused. It gave the following definition of hyperkinesis:

"There is no known single cause or simple answer for such problems. The major symptoms are an increase of purposeless physical activity and a significantly impaired span of focused attention. The inability to control physical motion and attention may generate other consequences, such as disturbed moods and behavior within the home, at play with peers, and in the schoolroom. Thus, the evidence has indicated that a child can be hyperkinetic without being brain damaged. Furthermore children can be brain damaged without being hyperkinetic."

In addition to the confusion about the terms "hyperactivity" and "hyperkinesis," there has been considerable controversy about the effects of drugs on hyperactive behavior and on children taking the medication. Axelrod and Bailey (1979) examined four controversial areas where evidence has been inconclusive: (1) whether drugs paradoxically affect hyperactive children differently from nonproblem behavior children, (2) whether medication lowers the amount of improper behavior, (3) whether academic performance is increased by use of drugs, and (4) whether different kinds of adverse physiological or psychological reactions occur over the long run or short run.

In the case of paradoxical effects, it had been thought that amphetamines or Ritalin acted as stimulants for normal children while calming other children. Grinspoon and Singer (1973) found that this argument could not be maintained consistently. Experiments on the ability of drugs to reduce undesirable behavior showed conflicting results, some of them not positive. (McConnell, Cromwell, Bealer, & Son, 1964; Strong, Sulzbacher, & Kirkpatrick, 1974). Freeman (1970) and Conners and Rothchild (1968) found that drugs were instrumental in curbing behavior disorders. Academic performance can be increased by drug usage in certain instances when self-control is improved (Zukow, 1975; Eisenberg, 1972). Finally, physiological and psychological side effects of drugs often are cited as being harmful to the well-being of the child. Elevated blood pressure and prolonged quickened heart rate due to ingestion of medication over a long period of time has been a concern (Sprague & Sleator, 1973). Other noticeable effects are irritability, nausea, depression, and insomnia (Offir, 1974).

Beset by so much controversy, a nonbiased assessment of drug therapy has been difficult to obtain. Connors (1973) offered several guidelines for consideration when attempting to evaluate a proposed drug therapy program. He suggested that:

1. a simple diagnosis not be accepted; a detailed developmental history, medical and neurological examination, family and child psychiatric interviews and educational and psychological examination are all required.

2. the effect of stimulant drugs is more complex than a simple reduction of activity level. The effects of the drugs can only be ascertained by a close liaison of the treating team with the school and the family.
3. the drug treatment by itself is seldom a sufficient remedy for the child's total set of symptoms and maladaptive behavior. When any portion of the educational, psychological or medical total treatment program is missing, communication problems occur. These form the basis for mismanagement of drug therapy programs.
4. careful follow-up of the course of treatment is essential, both to regulate dosage and to evaluate the side effects and behavioral effects of drugs.
5. despite these cautions, it is important to remember that these drugs have uniformly been shown to produce substantial academic and behavioral improvement, and therefore, when indicated, they deserve to be used under proper circumstances (pp. 349–351).

These guidelines should be considered by all involved in the drug therapy program to prevent overreliance upon medication. However, teachers involved in a drug therapy program should be warned that the possibility of a liability action does exist. Attempts to ascertain teachers' liability generally have been viewed in the context of reasonable and prudent actions. Since "reasonably prudent" action has been given different interpretations by the courts, Axelrod and Bailey (1979) suggest that teachers follow these protective actions:

1. A copy of the doctor's prescription should be on file containing the date of prescription, name and dosage, specific time to be administered and expiration of the drug if applicable.
2. A statement of the purpose for administering the drug should be on file.
3. The parents' request form should ask that the drug be administered during school hours for a specified duration of time.
4. Medication should be sent to the school only via a responsible adult.
5. Medication should be fresh, clearly identified, labeled with the child's name and dosage and kept in a secure location.
6. Medicine that is not going to be immediately administered should not be kept in the classroom.
7. Whenever medication is administered, a precise record should be kept of the child's name, medication's name, dosage administered, exact time given, and the signature of the person administering the drug (pp. 548–549).

This examination of drug therapy has not been exhaustive. However, enough evidence has been presented to support the notion that its use is a popular form of treatment for BD/ED children and youth. Parents and special educators have the responsibility to see that it is not abused under the pretext of aiding educational achievement.

CONCERNS OF PARENTS WITH BD CHILDREN

The first issue about which parents are perplexed is the exclusion of their children from schools. The Children's Defense Fund found that "in sum, out of school children share a common characteristic of differentness by virtue of race, income, physical, mental or emotional *handicap* and age" (emphasis added) (p. 4). Furthermore, many BD/ED children and adolescents have not left school by choice but have been excluded. This lack of choice has been documented further by the fact that suspensions have played a major role in keeping youth out of school. Age has been an important factor in the process since "secondary students were nine times more likely to be suspended than elementary students" (1975, p. 60). Thus, parents of emotionally or behaviorally disturbed children have had to fear that their youngsters might have been excluded or suspended from school in the primary grades, a fear that increased as they grew into adolescents.

A second concern of parents is the lack of services and programs available to their BD children. Morse (1971) postulated that only 13 percent of school-aged emotionally disturbed children received any special education and that there was a shortage of 200,000 teachers of the emotionally disturbed (p. viii). Jasper Harvey, Director of the Division of Personnel Preparation, Office of Special Education, U.S. Department of Education, stressed that preservice or teacher training funds were limited to institutions of higher education and that the areas of the severely emotionally disturbed and autistic were critical need areas in the 1980s. Prior to the passage of P.L. 94-142, only 12 percent of emotionally disturbed children were being served in public schools (President's Committee on Mental Retardation, 1976, p. 18). Moreover the President's Commission on Mental Health (1978) found that:

> Because diagnostic criteria vary so widely different surveys of general population show that the overall prevalence of persistent, handicapping mental health problems among children aged three to fifteen ranges from 5 to 15 percent. These conditions include emotional disorders, the so-called conduct disorders, and impairments or delays in psychological development (p. 8).

Parents have been shocked to learn that less than 1 percent of children between the ages of 3 and 21 actually are receiving special education services.

A third troubling issue is the stigma that the label emotionally disturbed has brought to the family of a BD/ED child. This label causes parents to become misfits and isolated from other families, saddled with guilt, and made to feel that "it's your fault" (p. 6). This feeling of guilt undermines the parents' ability to enter into a healthy relationship with the child. The crippling impact of "I'm the cause" guilt weakens the foundation for effective interaction between parents and child.

The lack of educational programming for BD/ED adolescents is a fourth concern. Nelson and Kauffman (1977) found that most school programs for BD students were located at the elementary level. In their survey, Morse, Cutler, and Funk (1964) reported that 32 percent of public school districts offered classes for BD students at the junior high level and 11 percent at the senior high school level. Bullock and Brown (1972) in a survey of public and private educational programs in 16 Florida counties found 69 percent were at the elementary level and only 15 percent served adolescents. The concerns of parents about the low incidence of programs for adolescents were captured in this statement from *Closer Look* (1979):

> The passage in 1975 of The Education for All Handicapped Children Act (P.L. 94-142) breathed new life into school programs for children with handicaps.
>
> But the growth in programs for children for those who are emotionally disturbed has been extremely slow. On the high school level, programs are almost nonexistent (p. 5).

This progression shows that not many changes have occurred in ED programming for adolescents in the past 15 years.

The fifth and perhaps greatest concern of parents of BD children is the question of definition. Parents are confused enough by the behavior of their children. Their lives are further complicated when a multitude of labels is applied to their children and youths—emotionally disturbed, behaviorally disordered, or socially maladjusted. Parents wonder what utilitarian value the terms have for education and treatment. Hewett (1968) defined the term emotional disturbance as maladaptive behavior because it implied that the child was a socialization failure. Furthermore he believed that the term emotionally disturbed had very little pragmatic value in the classroom. Morrow, Coulter, Gilliam, and others (1979) in a survey of Texas practitioners of emotionally disturbed reported that most respondents viewed emotional disturbance in the form of behavioral patterns (disruptive, inappropriate, or immature) rather than the P.L. 94-142 definition. Thus the practitioners' definition of emotional disturbance is dominated by overt behaviors mainly disruptive to teachers.

All of this is of little consolation to parents. First, they hear their children described in Freudian terms. Later, they observe that a more eclectic philosophy exists. The prevailing view holds that childhood mental ills arise from three intertwining influences: predisposing physical and hereditary factors, forces within the family—including the Freudian traumas—and stresses imposed by contemporary life (Clark, 1974). Within this prevailing doctrine, in the late 1970s parents share the following feelings expressed by one mother:

> I know from experience that schools accept emotionally disturbed children—but that's all . . . . The child is allowed to sit in a classroom, oblivious to everything around him (if that is the way he responds to reality). He may get violent—then the chances are that he'll be thrown out. These children are the forgotten children (*Closer Look*, 1979, p. 5).

Thus, parents are fearful that no matter what their BD/ED children are called or labeled by the professionals, their needs will not be met.

INVOLVING PARENTS OF ELEMENTARY BD CHILDREN

> I've had it. I can't take it any more. Either he goes or I go.
>
> *Elementary teacher of BD child*

> He just needs a good sympathetic teacher. If you give him a chance, he will respond and change for the better.
>
> *Mother of elementary BD child*

These two statements characterize the relationship between teachers and parents of elementary BD children. In the eyes of many professionals it has become a relationship of despair brought about through ineffective child-rearing practices. Blackham (1967, pp. 53–54) summarized ten key ineffective child-rearing practices and the resulting effects on the child (Table 7-1). In each instance the attention of professional educators focused upon ineffective parenting practices as a direct causal agent in the behavioral disorders exhibited by the child. Using this frame of reference, many professionals caused parents of BD to harbor doubts about their ability to function as guardians of the well-being of their children. However, with the passage of P.L. 94-142, parents of BD elementary children began to shake off the stigma of the label and to enlist the assistance of educators in obtaining a free and appropriate education for their children.

Table 7–1 Child-Rearing Problems and Effects

Parenting Practices	Child's Behavior
1. Unreasonable or punitive discipline	1. Conformity or hostility
2. Emotional deprivation and rejection	2. Emotional instability and inability to love
3. Marital conflict	3. Tenseness and anxiety
4. Sex-role confusion	4. Difficulty in formation of sex roles, effeminacy, latent homosexuality
5. Authoritarian	5. Stereotyped, rigid, submissive, obedient
6. Ambivalence and inconsistent discipline	6. Extreme anxiety and insecurity, vacillation when dealing with problems
7. Perfectionism and unrealistic expectations	7. Unrealistic standards leading to frustration, guilt, and self-deprecation
8. Overprotection (indulgence)	8. Selfishness, low frustration tolerance, bossy, hyperactive
9. Overprotection (domination)	9. Lack of initiative and feeling of inadequacy, submissive, passive, conforming, dependent
10. Excessively high morals	10. Strict, rigid superego, guilt, low self-esteem and self-condemnation

Source: The Deviant Child in the Classroom by G. J. Blackham. Reprinted by permission of Wadsworth Publishing Co., Belmont, Calif., © 1967.

Indeed, educators should be prepared to face the parent:

1. who has been isolated from family and friends
2. who has lived with hostile behavior, physical violence, humiliation, and despair
3. who has sought help from schools in the past only to be turned away
4. who often has been shunted from agency to agency, mental health worker to mental health worker
5. who perhaps has a low self-esteem as a person

When viewing the assets of these parents, helping teachers could be trapped into assigning a deficit model to their working relationship. However, special educators should be cautioned against acceptance of this viewpoint. Instead, they should regard these parents as resources to be used in the rehabilitation of their BD children. If helping educators adopt this stance, it will be possible for them to work with two kinds of parents with less severely impaired children to establish an effective home-school working relationship:

1. those coming to the school without a clear conception of what the terms BD/ED mean in the educational program

2. those coming to the school with a full knowledge that their child's behavior requires special attention but uneasy about the reception they will receive

Regardless of the situation, special educators still have the three previously noted principal roles facing them when working with parents of BD/ED children: advocates, ombudsmen, and case managers.

In the case of the less severely impaired child and parent for whom the school becomes the principal labeling agent, the sequence of roles might have to be altered when working with parents, the child, or the regular teacher. For instance, parents who are informed for the first time that their child might be disturbed or have maladaptive behavior are being hit with unfamiliar terms. While they may have heard the words, many parents will be in the dark or feel that the teacher is overreacting to the child's behavior in class. Parents' reactions in such an instance could be:

> You're the principal. You either tell that teacher to quit picking on my daughter and suggesting she belongs in a class for the loony ones or I'll go to the superintendent (Morse, 1971, p. ix).

In this situation, special educators must enter the negotiations as ombudsmen, helping to mediate differences between the regular teacher, parents, and child prior to the assignment to special education classes. This is particularly important in the case of the less severely impaired BD/ED child who is programmed for regular class placement with resource room assistance. In such a situation, teachers should seek to assist the troubled child. Parents who have felt like outcasts will see a sympathetic helping human being who also is an advocate for their child. Observing special teachers functioning in this fashion, parents have less apprehensions about sharing information.

From the General to the Specific

Ombudsman special education teachers can solicit the following information from parents while mediating the conflict with the regular educator:

1. What are the child's reactions to school?
2. What activities does the child enjoy the most?
3. Who have been the child's favorite teachers in the past?
4. What are the child's favorite activities at home?
5. What kinds of activities does the child enjoy doing with parents?
6. What do parents enjoy most about the child?
7. What do parents consider desirable and undesirable behavior on the part of the child?

8. What things frustrate or upset the child the most? (Blackham, 1967, pp. 65–66).

These questions move from the more general aspects of the child's life to the more specific; they are couched first in light of a school experience, then turn to home-family activities.

Helping teachers attempt to convey a sense of warmth and belonging to these frightened, angry, or confused parents. Through a combination of calm mannerisms, empathetic and carefully posed responses, and attentive listening, teachers meet the affective needs of parents with BD/ED children. Thus, these parents now begin to have a sense of belonging.

As the relationship grows, special educators can answer other questions that relate to specific parental concerns about the education and curriculum of their children:

1. What happens when the child blows up?
2. Are there skilled teachers who work with the child?
3. Are social relationships stressed in the curriculum?
4. Does the school foster the attitude that everyone makes mistakes, that no one is perfect?
5. Are times provided during the school day for teachers and children to talk about problems?
6. Are parents accepted as allies in the program?
7. Does the IEP reflect specific and relevant goals for changes? (*Closer Look,* 1979, p. 12).

As helping teachers tune in to these questions, they still exude warmth to the parents. They communicate to parents that crises interventions are used rather than the traditional punitive style of dealing with disruptive pupils. Parents and helping educators are drawn together in a discussion that explains how crisis intervention works. Extensive time is allowed so that parents are assured that should the child get caught in an emotional storm, the crisis teacher, instead of sending the pupil to the principal's office, has the responsibility to stay with the youngster until he gains control and is able to return to class. Parental anxieties are relieved upon learning that helping teachers have the ability to assist the BD/ED child to understand what caused the blowup and to help him acquire coping skills, so he can handle similar situations better at a later date.

Parents' worries about mainstream education are evidenced by their concern about the social relationships of the BD/ED child. Helping teachers can become a major relaxing force for parents. Together they can discuss why the teaching of interpersonal relationships is considered vital to the curriculum of the BD/ED child. The special educators should emphasize that they will stress skills of daily living, self-awareness, communication, and handling difficult or embarrassing situations in teaching this child. Moreover, they must assure parents that they will be treated as coequals in the educational partnership. Helping teachers acting as case managers should accord parents the respect of adults who have had the responsibility of a 24-hour-a-day job of caring, coping, teaching, training, and managing a BD/ED child. The case managers work with parents to develop a meaningful IEP for the child, discussing with them proposed plans and agreeing upon goals for learning and development.

Orchestrating Implementation of the IEP

When implementing the IEP, case manager special educators must orchestrate the desires of the parents together with the needs of the child. If the IEP agreed upon with parents had input from the child, the working task can begin in a cooperative atmosphere. If the IEP was drawn up without the involvement of the child, then his viewpoint must be considered. Helping teachers should attempt to discover:

1. What is the child's self-concept?
2. What are the child's hopes? His fears?
3. What are the child's expectations?
4. What is the child's view of school?
5. What are the child's goals in life? (*Closer Look,* 1979, p. 13).

Working with the BD/ED child is not considered a simplistic, one-approach decision by helping educators. These children have a multiplicity of behavioral problems. Some have failed to develop an adequate set of values. This group includes several kinds of behavioral patterns: (1) the sociopathic child who seeks to satisfy his own impulses regardless of the effects on others, (2) the narcissistic student who believes that his slightest wish is someone else's command, and (3) those with a maladjusted view of group responsibility, limiting it to the gang or family rather than accepting a broader societal perspective (Morse, 1971).

Case manager teachers must monitor the progress of these children. They assist parents in helping pupils to learn the "three Ls"—love, limitations, and letting them grow up (Chapmen, 1965). Advocate helping teachers work with parents to avoid overly punitive discipline that might lead to counteraggression; instead, they show parents how to restrict the misused freedom and how to learn other behavioral management techniques. Ombudsman helping teachers exchange information with parents so that both can model appropriate behavior at home and at school. In this manner BD/ED children are afforded the opportunity to identify with strong, purposeful adults. Together, teacher/parent efforts concentrate upon:

- increasing individual attention through task structure, with definite limits set for acceptable behavior

- decreasing permissiveness and less opportunity for choicemaking

- concentrating training in desirable habit formation, checking work, organizing work, following step by step direction

- reducing environmental stimulation and

- involving the child in tasks that are concrete rather than abstract (Carberry, 1976, p. 82).

A fourth category of BD/ED children seeking help from special educators in addition to sociopathic, narcissistic, and maladjusted includes the disenchanted or passive dependent pupil. Educators must be advocates for this child. They seek the support of parents in the following behavior:

- reinforcing risk-taking behavior in other children to serve as vicarious reinforcement for the child

- using role play to build "assertive behavior" patterns

- assigning the child a responsible role in a small group activity (Carberry, 1976, p. 82).

A fifth kind of child seen by special educators is termed those with loss of hope (Glasser, 1969). For these children, effort has been replaced by fate as the determiner of their futures (Morse, 1971). Teachers and parents face major problems motivating these pupils. Helping educators should attempt the following educational interventions:

- focusing initially on guaranteed success learning situations

- using a step-by-step approach beginning with a task the child can be sure to do

- avoiding confrontations which result in a will struggle

- initially reducing the criterion for correctness

- settling for a "thimbleful" of accomplishment rather than a "bucketful" (Carberry, 1976, p. 82).

The remaining category involves children who are disintegrated and disorganized—those who cannot cope with life's experiences and are driven by the need for attention and survival. Some of these children have grown up in the city's slum areas, where life is a continuous struggle. Others have been left in a psychologically battered state from a life filled with rejection, family violence, hate, alcoholism, and other high-risk situations (Morse, 1971).

Helping teachers who work with these BD/ED youngsters have to become ombudsmen for parents and children alike. They must mix a blend of individual and group counseling, structure, and fun things to do. As teachers work with the children in this fashion to calm the stranger behaviors and to achieve more normal patterns, students conquer their fears and develop skills for a better quality of life. The combination of these efforts can be summed up in the words of one mother of such a BD/ED child:

> I can still feel the panic when I hear the phone ring. . . . I automatically think someone is calling to tell me my son has just hurt a kid or broken a window . . . even though things are better now. The teacher he has now has made a tremendous difference. . . . I can get through a day without constant fear (*Closer Look*, p. 1).

Although schools are continuing their mainstream efforts, some attention is being given to the more severely impaired BD/ED child. The most notable object of this attention is the autistic child.

The Problem of the Autistic Child

Autism is a term coined 30 years ago by Dr. Leo Kanner of Johns Hopkins. Kanner used the term to describe young children who showed the following characteristics: rigidity or limpness, deafness to some sounds, insensitivity to pain, monotonous rocking, and whirling dervishness (Clark, 1974). That definition has evolved to the point where it now is included in the criteria for the Bureau for Education of the Handicapped (now Office of Special Education) definition of severely emotionally disturbed children. Under P.L. 94-142, seriously emotionally disturbed is defined as follows:

1. The term means a condition exhibiting one or more of the following characteristics over a long period of time and to a marked degree, which adversely affects educational performance:
   a) An inability to learn which cannot be explained by intellectual, sensory or health factors;
   b) An inability to build or maintain satisfactory interpersonal relationships with peers and teachers
   c) Inappropriate types of behavior or feelings under normal circumstances
   d) A general pervasive mood of unhappiness or depression; or
   e) A tendency to develop physical symptoms or fears associated with personal or school problems.

2. The term includes children who are schizophrenic or autistic. The term does not include children who are socially maladjusted, unless it is determined that they are seriously emotionally disturbed.

Parents have raised objections about the lack of a separate definition for autism. These parents—especially mothers—have grown weary of defending themselves against the Freudian theory that "refrigerator parents" produced autistic children. Under this theory parents were supposed to play "dead" or to be without feeling for their children. However, studies have shown that parents of autistic children do not display any unusual emotional traits that differentiate them from other parents (Clark, 1974). Additional research suggests that the handicap of autism shows signs of being a neurological impairment with a distinct and separate set of physiologically related characteristics and symptoms. Accordingly, in May 1979, the National Institutes of Health published the following definition:

> Autism is the severely incapacitating, lifelong developmental disability which usually appears during the first 3 years of life. . . . In most cases, the cause or causes are unknown. There appear to be several types of autism, each with a distinct neurological basis. No known factors in the psychological environment of a child have been shown to cause autism, and most scientists believe the cause is physical. Symptoms include: slow development or lack of physical, social and learning skills. . . . Immature rhythms of speech, limited understanding of ideas and use of words without attaching the usual meaning to them. . . . Abnormal ways of relating to people, objects and events (pp. 7–8).

In addition the Bureau for Education of the Handicapped stated that: "The definitions of handicapping conditions provide convenient categories for counting children for both state and federal distribution of funds. . . . These definitions do not serve as a basis for development of individualized programs." The significance of this statement for parents of autistic children is reflected in the point that the diagnosis "autistic" can be used to count those children who fall into the category of severely emotionally disturbed, but services have to be offered to meet the distinct individual needs of the child.

Helping special educators must recognize what these calendars of events have meant to these parents, who are desperate and confused. They feel the effects of a long search that generally had started and ended under the banner of false hopes. Most parents have echoed the sentiments of this mother:

> Everytime you go to someone you're desperate. They say they'll treat him. But then they can't reach him and they give up (Clark, 1974, p. 55).

Parents of autistic children not only have spent endless hours searching for the cure but also have been alienated and burdened with guilt. They have lived alone with the stress of rearing a difficult child. Mostly they have felt that:

> When your child is seriously emotionally disturbed, you need other parents to talk to who know what it's like . . . or else you end up totally alienated from other people . . . . totally alone.

or have been told:

> For years I kept being told I was a bad mother, I was to blame. They said my child should be institutionalized for life. It almost destroyed me (*Closer Look*, 1979, p. 1).

For these parents, finding a helping person who can understand these feelings can be the turning point in their lives. Helping special educators face the challenge of assisting emotionally drained and desperate parents attempting to find alternative educational opportunities for their children.

To help parents achieve these objectives, teachers can offer services for autistic children in a variety of ways. Parents who are not knowledgeable about P.L. 94-142 might have numerous questions about their rights under the law. Other parents might seek information about educational arrangements open to their children or about institutionalization vs. home programs. When these or related questions on the treatment of autistic children arise, educators should be guided by the following principles:

1. Be prepared to talk about educational programs for autistic children—parents are desperate for information about model or training programs for their children
2. Be prepared to work with parents in a school-based program or to offer suggestions for institutional programs for serving autistic children—parents have a right to education in the least restrictive environment for their children
3. Become knowledgeable about community resources that can help parents with autistic children—parents have a need for respite care
4. Inform parents about other parents who share similar concerns and needs in the rearing of difficult children—parents want to reduce the alienation that they feel in their lives.

Helping special educators who follow these guidelines demonstrate to parents of autistic children that they care about an often-forgotten child. They also show parents that educators are seriously committed to following the intent of P.L. 94-142—providing an appropriate education in the least restrictive environment.

INVOLVING PARENTS OF BD/ED ADOLESCENTS

Perhaps the greatest crisis in special education involves the inability or failure of the schools to treat and educate BD/ED adolescents successfully. The figures are distressing:

Of 160,000 behaviorally disordered adolescents only 20,000 were receiving instruction (Metz, 1973, p. 19).

Despite expanded efforts to reduce and control juvenile delinquency in recent years, youth arrests for all crimes rose 138 percent from 1960 through 1974 (Subcommittee to Investigate Juvenile Delinquency, 1975, p. 6).

Between 1950 and 1975, the suicide rate for white adolescents rose from 2.8 to 7.6 deaths per 1,000 (Wynne, 1978, pp. 307–308).

Pupils showing severe behavioral disturbances constitute another low incidence group that has been traditionally underserved by the public schools (Sabatino, 1979, p. 336).

All of these statements have one denominator in common: parents of BD/ED adolescents have been in need of assistance for a long time. These are the parents:

1. who have been crying for help for a long time due to meager services
2. who have been "coping" throughout the BD/ED child's preadolescent years
3. who are concerned about the future of the adolescent that "nobody wants"
4. who have been isolated because few parents of other teenagers can "stand" the abuse of the disturbed adolescent

Special teachers operate within this framework to provide understanding and support to parents to improve their self-esteem and to enhance the credibility of the special education program. Regardless of the severity of the disturbing condition, teachers must take great care not to abuse these parents. Although P.L. 94-142 has given new impetus to special education programs, teachers should be warned that parents have not easily forgotten the isolation they felt as they encountered a scarcity of programs for their adolescents (Morse, 1971). Nor have parents discarded completely the fear of expecting their teenagers to be excluded from school. Parents also have remembered the numerous warnings about the proper behavior expected of their adolescents upon reentry into school if they were fortunate enough to achieve this goal.

Special educators must assume the role of advocate for these parents, who are likely to have been alienated for a long time. These parents generally have not found the school environment a friendly place for their offspring (Sabatino, 1979; Kelly, 1978; Children's Defense Fund, 1975, 1974). Thus, helping teachers often work with parents who are apprehensive about being in foreign and threatening surroundings. In such instances, teachers should take the initiative to relieve the anxiety and to show by verbal and nonverbal actions that they respect the parents' rights. Much of the advocacy approach of the helping special educators must appear in actions since parents of BD/ED adolescents are prone to take a "doubting Thomas" attitude.

Special educators should adopt the role of advocate to provide information to parents about the choice of programs open to the adolescent. Recognizing that certain options may not be available in the school system in spite of P.L. 94-142, educators have the responsibility of providing correct information about what services are available and needed to serve the BD/ED teenagers. Parents should not have their rights violated because they lack information about program and service options. Therefore, teachers should develop their reservoir of knowledge about the kinds of programming most frequently used with these students. Helping special educators should be familiar with these program alternatives:

1. Regular classroom programs—an intensive focus upon teacher consultation, inservice and problem solving sessions, efforts to remove noxious environmental influences, affective education and assistance to parents
2. Special programs—the regular classroom—various teaching assignments that team special education and regular classroom teachers to work in heterogeneous groups
3. Resource room—crisis intervention focus, in-school problem solving and facilitation, coordination of other services and primary intervention
4. Diagnostic classroom—placement of youth for short periods of time, not to exceed 4 to 6 weeks, use of educational assessment to be translated back into classroom action
5. Short term special classes—definite time limit, might or might not involve partial integration with regular school activities
6. Day school settings and associated residential/community mental health centers—carefully designed inter-disciplinary approach
7. Short term residual treatment—therapeutic school program; assessment of planning for re-entry.

8. Long term residential care—cognitive stimulation, socialization and normalization of living experiences to the extent possible (pp. 9–10).

In addition to these models, helping special educators should be knowledgeable about the alternative schools that parents and educators of BD/ED teenagers have explored. These schools can be grouped under one or more of the following types (Nelson & Kauffman, 1977):

a. Open schools—Learning activities are individualized and organized around interest centers within a building
b. Schools without walls—Interaction with the community is emphasized with learning activities occurring throughout the community
c. Continuation schools—Drop-out centers, re-entry programs, pregnancy-maternity centers, evening and adult high schools are featured that offer a broad range of services
d. Learning centers—Learning resources are concentrated in one center
e. Multi-cultural schools—Cultural pluralism, ethnic and racial awareness are emphasized and they generally serve a multicultural student body.
f. Free schools—Curriculum development from the present needs and interests of the student is stressed
g. Schools-within-schools—They are organized around teachers and students who choose to become involved in a different learning experience
h. Freedom schools—These are organized to build academic skills, ethnic pride and community power and are less inclined than other alternative schools to "do your own thing" (pp. 111–112).

Dissemination of this kind of information about programs will not negate the special educators' roles as ombudsmen and case managers. On the contrary, these two roles can assume greater importance in the education of these adolescents and in working with their parents.

Supporting Data Are Scarce

Helping educators should be warned that they have very little concrete data to support their choices of intervention programs (Nelson & Kauffman, 1977). This has been due to (1) the lack of follow-up studies because of the instability of the teenage BD/ED population and (2) the lack of agreement among special educators about the goals of special education for maladjusted and delinquent adolescents.

In addition to these problems, case manager special educators must work with parents to develop an IEP for the student. The regular school program is one possibility. When discussing this, parents and teachers should be aware of the educational mainstream's difficulty in dealing with the BD/ED adolescent (Schreiber, 1967; Children's Defense Fund, 1974, 1975; Kelly, 1978). Ombudsman educators should be prepared to cope with the feelings of anxiety-ridden parents about the ability of their teenager to be mainstreamed. Having already experienced the effects of regular school intolerance, these parents have good reason to be apprehensive about allowing their BD/ED adolescents to continue in the regular classroom with consultation. Ombudsmen should use interpersonal skills such as verbal and nonverbal communication to assist parents to overcome this reluctance. Empathetic listening plus open and honest feedback are essential.

Helping teachers must play all three roles of educators, ombudsmen, and case managers to achieve the full-service goal. First, case manager special educators should outline the services that will or might be available. If consultants are to be used, their roles should be discussed. Helping teachers should stress the problem-solving suggestions and mental health support that will be given to the mainstream educator. Second, advocate special educators should work with parents for inclusion of the BD/ED adolescent in such a full-service program and to advocate for the teenager with the regular classroom teacher. Third, ombudsman helping teachers must be available to parents and regular educators to ameliorate conflicts in programming and attitudes that may arise over the performance of the adolescent. Otherwise, the youths can experience so much dissonance with the regular educator that they will join the ranks of the dropouts, malcontents, or alienated school leavers.

Resource rooms and/or regular classrooms have been used for BD/ED adolescents with varying success. Special educators seeking to involve these youths in these kinds of educational arrangements can facilitate parent involvement by emphasizing that educational intervention resources will focus heavily upon the teenagers. Special educators must share their knowledge of behavioral management strategies and remedial education methodologies with the parents. Showing such a positive advocacy on behalf of the youth will help the parents to adopt a truly coequal partnership position with the teachers. Any IEPs developed by the parents and special educators will reflect joint teacher/parent thinking on crisis teaching and support. Ombudsman teachers should remind parents of the attention given to life-space interviewing—verbal discourse on the spot at the time of crises (Morse, Long, & Newman, 1971). They will alert parents and regular educators to their availability in possible crisis-precipitating occasions.

As case managers, special educators have shared responsibilities concerning the amount of time BD/ED students spend in regular classrooms and the resource room program alignment. They have let it be known through the specificity of the IEP and the consent of all parties that negotiated agreements are blueprints for action. Helping educators must allocate class time after advocating with parents and regular classroom teachers for needed academic and interpersonal instruction. Educators must balance their feelings of what is desired for the parents by what is needed by the adolescent, so they must work with parents to bring about a sense of reality to the educational program. Case managers must program their own time commitments so that they are prepared to mediate conflicting notions by parents and regular educators as to the "rightness" of each party's opinions and desires about the educational program for the adolescent.

Case manager teachers should be concerned that they not allow their expertise to railroad the parents into a resource room arrangement because it is the popular feature of the day. The managers should not be lulled into accepting the job of writing the IEP under false pretenses. They must determine that parents of BD/ED have not been talked into acceptance of this program because of their desire to see their teenager accepted rather than ostracized. Case managers must exercise care to make sure that the parents' rights have not been abused. Agreement should have been reached by the three (regular educators, special educators, and parents) and the fourth (the teenager) if possible. All should be assured that this focus is the most appropriate educational intervention.

Special Classes and Residential Schools

Special class placement and residential schools also are used in educating BD/ED teenagers. Self-contained classroom placement has enjoyed the most popularity of the secondary school options (Bullock & Brown, 1972; Morse, et al., 1964). Parents may be for or against this form of placement. Some may be so overjoyed at the prospect of any schooling for their previously excluded/suspended students that they readily agree to this segregated arrangement. Others may be caught up in the aura of mainstreaming and will not hesitate to discount the self-contained classroom option.

In the case of those against the self-contained classroom, special educators should discuss all options with parents to convince them that this placement is the best possible alternative—if in fact it is. Helping teachers should resist the temptation to program for mainstream education and should work to make parents aware that the self-contained classroom might be the least restrictive environment for the teenager. Educators base their decision on the fact that very few severely disturbed students failed to be integrated into regular classrooms before P.L. 94-142 (Morse, et al., 1971). This fact has not changed dramatically with the passage of P.L. 94-142. Therefore, the special educators' judgment has not been impaired by popularity but rather has been tempered by the fact that the self-contained classroom does have advantages over other types of educational intervention. Even in self-contained classrooms, parents must feel that the teacher is a caring person. Moreover, parents must be assured that socialization skills are taught to their BD/ED teenagers regardless of the label attached to environmental surroundings. Parents must be convinced that their roles as allies will not be diminished through this arrangement.

Parents in the first group (for the self-contained classroom) may have informational needs that must be satisfied for a better understanding of the meaning of the placement. Helping educators should not be annoyed if parents have a multitude of questions about the educational intervention process. Instead, they should be pleased that parents have not been brow-beaten and still have enough self-esteem to inquire into the nature of the program. Helping teachers should be reminded that despite the popularity of the self-contained classroom, the little research available (Dunn, 1968) has not supported this model as the most viable approach for educating BD/ED adolescents. Special teachers should advocate for the self-contained classroom as the least restrictive environment for both groups of parents whenever they feel that the option is a viable one for the teenager. After all, much of the criticism and ultimate recommendations related to the special class as a delivery model were made with the mildly handicapped in mind. These educators have an obligation to seek a proper blend of academic and vocational instruction for the BD/ED teenager. Realizing that parents of severely handicapped pupils have more faith in the teacher than in any other professional (Carter, 1974), special educators must face being put on display as "Exhibit 1" since they will have the major responsibility for the academic portion of the teenager's program.

Vocational Education

Special educators also must advocate for vocational education in the adolescent's program. In light of P.L. 94-142 requirements, vocational education is considered a vital part of BD/ED adolescent programming. However, this can produce another crisis period in the lives of parents. For parents of BD/ED youths, the concern about vocational training is well-placed. Evidence about the effectiveness of these programs has been mixed. Balow (1961) indicated vocational education was too difficult and technical for maladjusted pupils to master. A later study by Irvine (1970) found that work-study programs did help BD/ED students make better progress toward work role adjustments in late adolescence. Morse (1977) suggests that a major problem is the lack of vocational education because of the difficulty in maintaining BD/ED students in the vocational program.

Special educators should seek to mediate parents' ambivalent feelings toward vocational education. Since parents' attitudes are influential in shaping students' perceptions about work, helping teachers can work to change any unfavorable opinions that parents might hold about vocational education. Ombudsman special educators have a responsibility to assist parents to make a wise decision about enrolling the teenagers in regular vocational education or in vocational education programs for the handicapped. Moreover, the ombudsmen will be expected to mediate any differences that might arise once the choice of options has been made.

Case manager special educators should continue to exhibit ombudsman sensitivities when managing the IEP process. Parents and vocational educators will have to agree upon the kind and amount of vocational training that the BD/ED teenager will receive. Special educators must monitor the program to ascertain that each party—parent and vocational educator—is satisfied with the progress of the student. These teachers must mediate differences in terminology that precipitate communication differences. This has caused considerable dissonance between special and vocational programs for the exceptional student (Fair, 1976; Lain, 1978).

The World of Work: Shared Responsibility

Special educators are expected to be available to help with any curriculum modifications needed in the vocational education program. Although chiefly responsible for the working program, vocational educators have not seen prevocational training as a vital part of their program (Lain, 1978; Fair, 1976). Therefore, special educators should share with parents the responsibility of totally preparing the BD/ED adolescent for the world of work. Helping teachers and parents will have to model appropriate responsible work behavior at home and at school. Moreover, operating in a totally developmental capacity, case manager educators must attempt to arrange a sequence of home-school work-related academic experiences that will assist the adolescent to become functional in the adult world of work.

Although residential schools generally have been popular placement alternatives for BD/ED teenagers with severe disturbing conditions, many formerly existed outside the purview of public school control (U.S. Bureau of the Census, 1972). With the advent of P.L. 94-142, the majority of residential programs continued to exist as training schools for delinquents (Nelson & Kauffman, 1977). Residential institutions also serve youths from detention homes and federal and state prisons. Many of the studies to date have not supported the possibility that these youths can return to the regular school program (Sabatino & Mauser, 1978; Budnick & Andreacchi, 1967). Although many might be able to function in a regular class if they receive appropriate support services, Kelly, Bullock, and Dykes (1977) found that regular classroom teachers need considerably more inservice and preservice training in behavioral disorders to be more competent in their ability to work effectively with them.

Special educators should be alerted to the strengths and weaknesses of these alternatives for BD/ED adolescents. They then will be better equipped to exchange information with parents concerning out-of-school placement and will have a better information base from which to act as a referral agent for parents desirous of seeking this form of educational alternative.

Alternative programs have attracted teenagers who have encountered trouble in conventional school environments. Most of the adolescents filling the rosters of alternative programs can be identified as drop-outs, truants, underachievers, nonreaders, and discipline problems (Nelson & Kauffman 1977; Mayo, 1974). Offerings available to BD/ED students were listed earlier in this chapter. Helping educators should be reminded that alternative schools are not for everyone and especially not for all BD/ED adolescents. Miller and Keene (1973) listed 10 reasons why alternative schools are not for everyone:

1. Alternative schools aren't appropriate for certain types of students.
2. Alternative education requires especially careful counseling, more attention to motivation.
3. Alternative education requires that teachers pay more attention to individual progress of students.
4. Alternative learning methods make special demands on students.
5. Alternative learning tends to proceed at a slower pace.
6. Alternative programs that share a campus with a regular school have more drawbacks than those that don't.
7. Alternative schools usually have to cope with an army of detractors.
8. Alternative teaching definitely is not for every teacher.
9. Like it or not, alternative programs do compete with the regular schools.
10. Alternative schools may not be the solution to many long-standing educational problems (pp. 39–41).

Even with these limitations in mind, special educators must be alert to the possibility that they will be called upon either to provide instruction in an alternative setting (Mesinger, 1965) or to act as referral agents for parents of BD/ED adolescents with disturbing conditions. In either instance, helping teachers should have a working knowledge of community resources to assist them with their advocacy, ombudsman, and case manager roles. Advocate special educators are concerned that the community have a clear understanding of the handicapping condition and be responsive to BD/ED teenagers. Ombudsman special education teachers should arbitrate disagreements among employers, parents, and vocational educators concerning the educational approaches used in the IEP of these adolescents. Case manager special educators must involve the community, business, and industry, and concerned parents in the educational program. Helping educators working with parents and youths in an alternative environment should be guided by the following compelling principle:

While the alternative movement may provide incentives for improvement . . . it has not yet invented the effective formula for effective learning and teaching. That answer . . . lies in the quality of the individual teacher and especially in his ability to inspire individual students, his respect for unique personalities, and his competence in individualizing instruction (p. 443).

In summary, working with parents of BD/ED children and adolescents is an exacting and challenging assignment for special education teachers. Problems of definition have plagued the field, particularly causing problems in providing different kinds of services for BD/ED children and youths. Parents have been caught in a torment of feeling about their exceptional children while searching for educational and supportive services. They have been aided in their quest by P.L. 94-142, which decrees a free and appropriate education for all exceptional children and youths, including BD/ED students.

Helping special educators are being challenged to provide these educational services in the spirit of the act. Moreover, they are being asked to work with parents of BD/ED children and youth as coequals and to plan and implement an IEP in which a good program can be built by tailoring approaches to in-depth knowledge of the child. Helping teachers must agree with parents so that both have a complete picture of what needs to be done, so they do not go off in irrelevant directions or repeat interventions that already have failed.

Chapter 8

Involving Parents of Abused Exceptional Children

Most people take for granted the fact that the United States is a highly civilized society. They also presume that the well-being of children is one of the foremost concerns of the civilized community. However, recent developments in the area of human rights in this country have focused upon one area of child welfare that challenges this assumption and calls into question the sincerity of the claim to be civilized people: the area of child abuse. Yet only recently has child abuse become a major concern. Although abuse-prone parents have neglected and abused large numbers of children, society has been slow to respond.

Traditionally, the responsibility for the physical and emotional well-being of children has been relegated to parents and families. Since the home was sacred, child abuse went largely unattended and abusive parents went largely unreported although society recognized their existence. This was so despite the fact that Congress in 1912 established the Children's Bureau as a part of the then U.S. Department of Commerce and Labor (since 1913 in the Department of Labor) to be responsible for investigating and reporting on all matters relating to the welfare of children (GAO, 1976). Today, however, in this era of human rights, new efforts are being made in the health, social service, and educational areas coupled with legislation to call attention to the needs of young children who require the assistance of adults to survive in society.

THE HISTORY OF CHILD ABUSE

Child abuse is not new in the world. Various forms have been in existence for centuries, with various societies tolerating differing levels of acceptance. In primitive societies, deviant children often were left to die or were killed if found to be defective. Some analysts have used theological doctrines to explain abuse, relating the saying "Bring up the child in the way he should go" to excessive physical punishment. Early tales by Dickens pictured the plight of the exploited and abused child.

Moving through time, abuse of children was linked more closely to their economic oppression than to their physical and mental well-being. In 1860, only four states had a minimum age law for full-time employment of children. Not until 1874 did the first legal interference on behalf of an abused child appear. In that case, the decision was prompted by action by the American Society for the Prevention of Cruelty to Animals. It gained legal protection of a malnourished and physically abused child on the claim that she was a member of the animal kingdom. In fact, not until the late 1960s and early 1970s did most states begin to enact laws that required child abuse to be reported and/or to provide immunity to those who called attention to the plight of the abused child.

Even health caregivers were reluctant to report incidents of abuse. Although Caffey (1972) recognized the connection between abuse and childhood bone injuries or abuse and hematoma in the early 1920s, he was skeptical about reporting it in the late 1940s. Slowly awareness of child abuse grew, and in 1962, C. Henry Kempe and associates coined the phrase, "the battered child syndrome." Their survey focused public and professional attention on the problems of the identification and the incidence of child abuse. This in turn sparked a flurry of writings and activities that has resulted in increased public awareness of the problem. Research has produced reliable criteria that can be used to identify and diagnose child abuse. While early detection of child abuse is important for preventive and intervention purposes, health care workers have a legal responsibility to report suspected cases of child abuse. Reports made in good faith afford legal protection to vigilant observers (McCaffrey, 1978).

There probably is no disagreement about the extreme cases of abuse. It is the borderline and mild cases that are the most difficult to diagnose and substantiate. These present the greatest challenge to classroom teachers and other educational personnel since failure to recognize and report these incidents may result in dire consequences for the child. According to the General Accounting Office, 64 per cent of abused children were in serious or critical situations that threatened their well-being prior to their acceptance into protective services (1976, p. 17).

In the case of teachers and educational personnel, there are additional incentives to work with abusive parents and abused children. For one reason, 43 states as of 1978 require teachers to report suspected cases of child abuse. A second and more important reason affects teachers and personnel in special education. Soeffing (1975) says that the abused child also is an exceptional child. She cites studies that show a relationship between handicapping conditions and child abuse and neglect. Additional studies show that different (exceptional) children are seen as difficult to raise by parents. Therefore, persons working in special education should be acutely sensitive to the needs of abused children.

FORMS OF CHILD ABUSE

Congress defines child abuse and neglect as: the "physical or mental injury, sexual abuse, negligent treatment or maltreatment of a child under the age of 18 by a person who is responsible for the child's welfare under circumstances which indicate that the child's health or welfare is harmed or threatened thereby" (p. 3).

From this definition, it can be discerned that there are several forms of abuse and neglect: physical abuse and neglect, emotional abuse and neglect, and sexual abuse. Moreover, several kinds may be found in combination. Therefore, teachers and educational personnel should be alert to the various forms and combinations that may be recognizable in the classroom and/or school. The following forms of abuse are most likely to be seen by educators:

Physical Abuse

Physical abuse is nonaccidental injury to a child. This injury may be caused by a single incidence of abuse or may happen repeatedly. It may occur in mild or severe forms and can be fatal.

Physical Neglect

Physical neglect is the failure by parents and caretakers to provide the basic necessities of life for a child. Lack of supervision, absence of medical care, insufficient nourishment, and inadequate clothing and shelter all are causative factors in neglect.

Emotional Abuse and Neglect

Emotional abuse and neglect is a relatively new concept. The Model Child Protective Service Act defines it as "injury to the intellectual or psychological capacity of the child as evidenced by an observable and substantial impairment in his ability to function within a normal range of performance and behavior with due regard to his culture."

Sexual Abuse

Sexual abuse can be either interfamily or intrafamily sexual activity between adult and child. Sometimes it can be direct and result in injury and trauma for the child. At other times it can be nonassaultive and may constitute minimal trauma and injury.

As the forms of child abuse and neglect are understood, it is obvious that the teacher and other individuals are in a unique position to address the question of such abuse in families (McCaffrey, 1977). First, in the early grades, teachers—despite reports to the contrary—still are operating "in loco parentis." This affords them the opportunity to observe the child over an extended period and to give validity to questions by talking with parents and other children, including siblings. Second, teachers, still being accorded a position of respect by the public, are in an enviable situation to help parents and children seek remediation of the stressful condition through counseling and referral.

CHARACTERISTICS OF ABUSE AND NEGLECT

Research shows that abused and neglected children range in age from infants to adolescents. Some 50 per cent of this group is 6 years of age or younger and the most seriously injured are infants. Hartly (1969) and Sussman (1968) agreed in separate studies that abused children generally were below the age of 3 years. The number of reported cases of battered children—15,000 to 25,000—represents only a fraction of the total and the incidence of abuse is higher among the handicapped, premature, multiple-birth, adopted, foster, and stepchildren. McNeese and Hebeler (1977) state that the estimated rate of incidence of child abuse is 10 per 1,000 live births. Thus, the number of cases ranges from 70,000 to 4 to 5 million; a more realistic calculation is that 1.6 million children are abused each year and that 2,000 are killed. (p. 4). These data give additional weight to Soeffing's (1975) contention of the relationship between handicapped and/or different children and child abuse. The role of the special education professional is crucial in working with abusive parents and their families. Moreover, P.L. 94–142 has intertwined their interests in the child so closely that it is impossible for the issue of child abuse and neglect to be overlooked.

OVERVIEW OF CHILD ABUSE AND NEGLECT

When examining child abuse and neglect, there appear to be three major contributing variables that should be of interest to special educators. Helfer (1972) identifed these variables thusly:

$$Parent + Child + Situation = Abuse$$

Furthermore, he found that the same factors operate in cases of neglect. Special educators should recognize that child abuse is a family affair. Although all three elements are present, child abuse and neglect may take the form of an isolated incident or may be repeated over time. Therefore, special educators should be alert for these three prerequisites: (1) There is a child who is either difficult to manage or considered different (Sandgrund, Gaines, & Green, 1974;

Morse, Sahler, & Freidman, 1970). (2) There should be parents and family who exhibit abuse-prone behavior (Silverman, 1972; Kempe, 1962). (3) There is a stressful situation that contributes to incidences of child abuse and neglect (Giovannoni & Billingsley, 1970; Helfer, 1972).

Characteristics of Abuse-Prone Parents

The first variable in the abuse equation is the abuse-prone parent. Abusive parents are a heterogeneous group and are found in all levels of socioeconomic, racial, and ethnic groups. Special educators should keep the following reminder very much in mind when assessing the abuse-prone parent: a parent is, first, a parent. Only in the family dynamics of child-rearing practices do parents assume the role of child abusers. This usually is an outgrowth of parenting practices that they learned from their parents. Some characteristics of abusive parents are:

- Immaturity and dependency
- Low self-esteem and sense of incompetence
- Difficulty in seeking pleasure and finding satisfaction in the adult world
- Social isolation and reluctance to seek help
- Role reversal
- Fear of spoiling the child and strong belief in value of punishment
- Lack of ability to be empathetic and respond to the child (Steele, 1975, p. 4).

Abusive parents cling tenaciously to the adage "My home is my castle." Therefore, the term child abuse can be viewed rightfully as family abuse since it exists "in house." Because they are "family matters," abusive parenting practices tend to be passed on from generation to generation and to occur most frequently in the home.

In light of these views, Helfer (1975) has reconstructed a schema that pictures the child-rearing history of the abusive parent. It is called "The World of Abnormal Rearing" (WAR) (Figure 8-1). Within this schema, Helfer identified five questions that could combine to be contributing factors and could result in an adult's becoming an abusive parent:

1. Are the parents a product of inadequate rearing?
2. Have the parents become isolated individuals who cannot trust or use others?

Figure 8-1 Schema for 'The War of Abnormal Rearing'

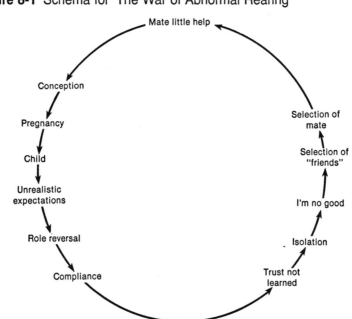

Source: "Child Abuse and Neglect: Diagnostic Process and Treatment Programs," Office of Child Development, Publication #OHD 75-69.

3. Do these adults have a spouse whose personal realities are such that he/she cannot give or provide support?
4. Did the parents' development structure a poor self-image?
5. Do these parents have very unrealistic expectations for their children? (p. xiv).

Although Helfer approached the study of abusive parents from a psychiatric point of view, Gil (1970) postulated a sociological perspective. He identified five elements in the parental sociological lifestyle that contribute to child abuse:

1. cultural attitude toward violence and physical punishment
2. social stress and frustration
3. family/community relationships
4. interaction of sociological forces
5. a combination of all of the above. (pp. 135–136).

In either perspective, the characteristics listed at the start of this section accurately picture abusive parents.

In spite of the fact that abusive parents are not a homogeneous population, several parent groups deserve special mention. Several studies point out child abuse is on the increase among military personnel (Satlin & Miller, 1971), certain religious sects, and families with severe financial problems (Giovannoni & Billingsly, 1970). The latter families with limited incomes specifically are the victims of misplaced cultural myths.

From previous data and from an historical point of view, it could be contended that lower income families are overrepresented among abusive parents. This statement gives rise to the supposition that child abuse and neglect is a phenomenon of racial minorities and poor parents and families. While early statistics reflected this fact, they were not true indicators of the nature of child abuse and neglect. There were several reasons for this misrepresentation of data. (1) Minorities and poor families had to use public facilities, welfare agencies, and public hospitals, and therefore were more vulnerable to reporting. (2) Private physicians of more financially able parents were reluctant to report child abuse cases for fear of endangering their relationship with the families. (3) Some family practitioners failed to recognize cases of child abuse when they saw them.

These factors contributed greatly to the misconceptions surrounding child abuse, minorities, and the poor. In reality, child abuse cuts across all economic levels and racial groups. Steele (1975) emphasized this fact when he said:

> Unfortunately, because so many of the early reports and descriptions of child abuse came through welfare agencies and municipal hospitals, it became a common belief that abuse and neglect of infants were associated with racial minorities and poverty-stricken groups of people. Such ideas still persist in many quarters, despite the increasing knowledge that child abuse and neglect occur among families from all socioeconomic levels, religious groups, races and nationalities (p. 3).

However, evidence of social and economic deprivation, substandard housing, unemployment, and racial prejudice should not be discounted as stressful factors in the life styles of parents who abuse and neglect their offspring. It is well documented that these stress factors affect the quality of life and often precipitate abuse and neglect. They always should be considered in any program that seeks to assist and remediate abuse-prone families.

Characteristics of the Situation

The second variable in the abusive parent syndrome is the crisis situation. Helfer (1972) attached a great deal of importance to the crisis situation in the abused child. He was convinced that even if one period of stress was resolved, given the two other variables of abuse-prone parent and special kind of child, the risk of abuse was not alleviated since the next stressful incident would precipitate a crisis and would result in an abusive incident.

Although the ability of a family to withstand stress will vary, the following factors can precipitate a crisis:

1. Emotional factors—Stresses that may cause abuse are: serious illness of a family member, death in the family, and separation and/or divorce of the parents.
2. Medical factors—Stresses that may contribute to abuse are: long periods of required hospitalization for the infant, child, or youth; elaborate and expensive medical hardware, and costly prescriptions and medications.
3. Economic factors—Stresses that may precipitate abuse are: loss of a job, impoverished circumstances, or a drastic change in economic lifestyle.

Although these stressful events may cause incidents of child abuse, it always should be remembered that the situation is combined with the other predisposing characteristics of the parent and child. That is to say, all three elements must be present for abuse to occur.

Characteristics of Children

This is a third element that is significant in the abused child syndrome. Gil (1970) reported in a nationwide study that 25 percent of the children studied for abuse had exhibited "persistent behavior atypicality." Finally Steele (1975) stated that "the already difficult problem of misperceptions can be complicated by the presence of real abnormalities in the infant. Some babies are inevitably more demanding and less rewardingly responsive to their parents because of prematurity, congenital defects, illness, genetically determined hyperactivity, and many other things" (p. 14). Helfer (1972) specifically mentioned the special or exceptional child as a precipitating element in the abused child interaction. Other studies have shown that there is a definite relationship between child abuse and a child that is seen as difficult or different to raise by parents. Stern (1973) designated the premature infant as "high risk" and a prime candidate for abuse. The weak "mother-infant bond" associated with prematurity is reported to make the premature infant more susceptible to injury (Klaus, 1972; Klein & Stern, 1971). Sandgrund, Gaines, and Green (1974) found that the neurologically or cognitively impaired child with provocative or unmanageable behavior had a high probability of abuse when the crisis situation was linked to an abuse-prone parent. Thus, all of these studies reinforce the contention that children who are different or difficult to raise are prime contributors to their own abuse. Consequently, special educators should be especially alert to behaviors and physical/emotional indicators in children that are peculiar to their abuse.

Behavioral Indicators of Abused Children

Abused or neglected children may exhibit behavior that is extreme or inappropriate for their age. Since these behaviors form the abused and neglected child's mode of operation, they can be categorized into these general classifications:

1. Passive, undemanding, and overly compliant behavior
2. Aggressive and demanding behavior
3. Overly adaptable behavior
4. Developmental delay-related behavior (McCaffrey, 1977).

There are differences in the behaviors of mildly and severely abused children. Mildly abused children are likely to exhibit hyperactivity, temper tantrums, short attention spans, and aggressive behavior. Severely abused children also show recognizable behaviors: dependence, wariness of physical contact, excessive crying or shyness, or lack of curiosity.

These behavioral indicators of physical abuse may be translated into the classroom by:

- Poor classroom attendance

- Underachievement

- Aggressive behavior

- Quiet, withdrawn behavior

- Frequent, chronic absences

- Early arrival at school, late departure

- Complaints of pain without cause

- Hypervigilancy

- Anxiety (McCaffrey, 1977).

Physical Indicators of Abused Children

Abused children show the following distinguishable physical symptoms:

1. Bruise and welt injuries related to abuse
2. Burn injuries related to abuse

3. Laceration and abrasion injuries related to abuse
4. Skeletal injuries related to abuse
5. Head injuries related to abuse
6. Internal injuries related to abuse (McCaffrey, 1977).

SPECIAL EDUCATOR RESPONSIBILITY

Gil (1969), reporting on the educators' important role in child abuse, observed that the classroom teacher's "daily contacts put him in a strategic position to observe early indications of abuse." Therefore, special educators should first observe the child to see if signs of physical abuse are present. The professional then can raise questions concerning the physical appearance of the child, such as:

- Are the bruises extensive?

- Could the bruises have been caused by a particular instrument?

- Are the injuries inconsistent with the explanation offered by the child? by the parent?

- Are burns caused by particular instruments or by immersion in hot water?

- Does hair appear to have been pulled out forcefully?

After these and other questions have been answered to the professionals' satisfaction, special educators should document the occasions. The professionals should keep close check on the data to ascertain if a pattern is occurring. By proceeding in this fashion, special educators can gear up to report in a professional, validated method. Evidence gathered methodically over time forms the basis for the objective reporting of abuse by special educators.

Neglect

Indicators of neglect. Children who are neglected show the following physical symptoms:

1. Abandonment
2. Inadequate supervision
3. Inadequate clothing and poor hygiene
4. Lack of medical or dental care
5. Inadequate education
6. Inadequate nutrition
7. Unsafe and/or lack of shelter (McCaffrey, 1977).

Emotional neglect. This form of neglect is extremely difficult to define. The problem of definition is complicated by the fact that it is hard to distinguish what constitutes ineffective parenting and what implies emotional neglect. Since a fine line separates the two forms, special educators can look for the following indicators:

1. Overly compliant, passive behavior
2. Overly aggressive behavior
3. Lags in physical, emotional, and intellectual development (Mc-Caffrey, 1977).

Responsibility of special educators. In cases of suspected neglect, special educators should continue to document specific behaviors of parents, children, and the parent-child interactions. The educators should continue to make notes for possible reporting later. They also should work with the parents and encourage them to seek help voluntarily. Finally, the teachers should familiarize themselves with the supportive and social services and community resources available to the professional for referral and assistance.

Sexual Abuse

Underlying family conditions. Sexual abuse in families usually occurs under stressful situations. The following conditions are present usually:

- loss of spouse through death or divorce

- severe crowding in sleeping arrangements

- alcoholism

- multigenerational pattern of incest

- parental lack of "coping" skills

- denying husband or wife

- culturally determined standards of body contact (McCaffrey, 1977).

Physical indicators of sexual abuse. Physical indicators of sexual abuse are best detected by a physician. However, special educators may observe the following signs in young children:

- bruises in external vagina, genitalia, or anal areas

- bleeding from external genitalia, vagina, or anal areas

- venereal disease in young children
- semen on clothing or around the genitals (McCaffrey, 1977).

For older children, these conditions may exist:

- venereal disease
- pregnancy
- broken hymen (McCaffrey, 1977).

Although special educators can learn much from observing physical evidence, certain behavioral clues may add additional evidence to substantiate the case for sexual abuse, including:

1. Regression into fantasy worlds or into infantile behaviors
2. Delinquency or aggression
3. Poor peer relationships
4. Drug usage or abuse
5. Runaway behavior
6. Unwillingness to participate in physical activities
7. Fear of going home (McCaffrey, 1977).

Responsibility of special educators. Special education professionals must continue to document the case. Collection of hard evidence is to be desired if the case is to go to court. Therefore, a complete interview should be conducted and a physical examination should be requested for the child. Moreover, special educators should gather information in a nonthreatening interview atmosphere that is removed from the physical examination. If conducted in this fashion, needed information can be gathered and will negate the need for further questioning. Above all, special educators should keep in mind that without medical evidence to substantiate their suspicions, there is not much hope of proving sexual abuse.

EFFECT OF UNRESOLVED ABUSE AND NEGLECT

To observant special educators, the immediate effects of child abuse are obvious. Fractured arms, burned palms or hands, and badly bruised eyes are readily visible. However, although the short-term effects are illustrated dramatically, the long-term effects may be more devastating to the child. Physical abuse may result in brain damage culminating in mental retardation. Sandgrund, Gaines, and Green (1974) reported a significant difference between abused, neglected, and nonabused children on verbal and performance IQ measures of 60 abused, 30 neglected, and 30 nonabused controlled subjects. Caffey (1974) found that shaking could lead to brain damage and become a major cause of retardation. He reported that "casual, habitual, manual whiplash shaking of infants is a substantial primary frequent cause of later mental retardation and permanent brain damage."

Other injuries or developmental delays are likely to occur from abuse and neglect. Glaser et al., (1968) in a follow-up study of 50 abused children found that 17 were below height/weight (third percentile or bottom 3 per cent of a normal group, 6 were mentally retarded, 4 were psychotic or emotionally disturbed, and 7 had minor behavioral disorders.

Psychological consequences of abuse and neglect, although difficult to define and diagnose, are beginning to be recognized. Since child abuse and neglect are linked to ineffective parenting, an abused child is most likely to become a socially deviant and abusive parent.

The short-term and long-term effects of child abuse and neglect now are documented. However, additional research and documentation suggest that this abuse and neglect tends to perpetuate itself within a family cycle. Therefore, with the exceptional children so vulnerable in the home, special educators have a unique opportunity to work with parents and child to assist in resolving an abused or neglectful situation.

CONCEPTS FOR WORK WITH ABUSIVE PARENTS

In working with abuse-prone parents and their children, special educators have two main areas of responsibility: (1) to identify and report the abused child and (2) to work with parents of abused children.

Identification and Reporting

To identify properly and report reliably on cases of child abuse and neglect, educators must develop the same attitude toward sharp observation about abuse as characterizes their teaching and learning activities. Hence, one of the most useful tools that special educators can use is the power of observation. The child should be observed for signs of any of the symptoms and behaviors of abuse and neglect mentioned earlier in this chapter.

Special education teachers should be alert to the attitudes and behaviors of the parents when conferring with those who have abused and neglected children. While caution should be exercised to differentiate between cultural differences of families and differing philosophies of parenting practices, special educators should distinguish between inappropriate parenting skills vs. their total absence.

Any lack of concern about the child's well-being or overconcern about minor injuries may be justification for continued scrutiny.

The most valuable tool for special educators in situations of suspected child abuse is a case study for documentation purposes. Using documentation over time, observant special education teachers can build a case history that will be invaluable for reporting. The case history also is a viable instrument for educational personnel. Such an in-depth study records the feelings of parents and children, their treatment (abused or neglected), and family relationships (Helfer, 1975).

Special educators should familiarize themselves about state legislative requirements and provisions, about their school policies, and about local reporting procedures (Soeffing, 1977). Only by educating themselves in this manner can special teachers report reliably and be assured of a reasonable chance of success. As stated earlier, and as we move into the 80s, 43 states require teachers to report child abuse. Educators must realize that without medical documentation the success rate in prosecuting sexual abuse cases will be low. Finally, special educators must recognize that while reporting is sometimes difficult, their responsibilities are clear: they are charged to report suspected cases of child abuse and neglect.

The Need for Trained Educational Professionals

In the area of child welfare, educational professionals, paraprofessionals, and other individuals are becoming increasingly aware of the need to develop their intervention skills for working successfully with parents and families of "high risk" children. This is especially true for those who work with parents in areas where the physical and mental well-being of children is at stake. However, only in the area of child abuse and neglect are the feelings and emotions of special helping teachers so strongly intertwined with those they seek to assist: parents and other caretakers. Some of the strongest human emotions—anger, love, denial, guilt, sorrow, shame—are invoked from within parents. These feelings often precipitate acts of violence that sometimes result in the death of the child. On the other hand, involved workers react with feelings along a continuum that ranges from disgust and anger to identification. Many special educators register feelings that translate out as "I could never hurt a helpless child," or "Thank God it was him and not me because I've had the same feelings so often." Regardless of the origin of the perception, the problem of child abuse and neglect means getting involved in parents' rights, children's rights, human rights, parenting practices, and civil rights. These complex issues, viewed from either end of the spectrum, constitute a serious strain on the ability of either of the affected parties to communicate with one another.

This is so mainly because it is hard to maintain an accepting point of view when consumed by such strong feelings. However, working with abusive parents requires a nonpunitive point of view. Special educators must keep in mind that working with parents is one way of ensuring that the problem of child abuse is recognized by the family and, most importantly, that the child is protected. In this parent-centered treatment process, the family is perceived as a unit by special teachers, who recognize that family members do not operate in isolation from one another or from society.

It should be emphasized that working with parents adds another preventive dimension to the child abuse rehabilitation process. If parents are seen as allies and not adversaries, the child is the ultimate benefactor. Recognition of the fact that the pendulum is swinging away from permanent removal of the child from the family home advances the concept of parent involvement as a preferred mode of treatment. Therefore, greater effort on the part of special helping teachers to ensure good relationships between themselves and the parents can bring increased dividends. This will come about as more successful shared intervention opportunities increase the chances for improvement in parenting practices.

Another factor that enters into a cooperative parent-educator relationship is the theory of punishment vs. help. Abusive parents whose children are removed temporarily and then returned to them are more inclined to accept the special education helping teacher who has been a friend and not an antagonist if temporary foster placement outside the home had to be effected. It is not hard to relate in a positive fashion to a person who has refrained from a ''punish the guilty offender'' attitude. This parent-educator relationship has significance as a way of protecting children as well as fostering positive mutual attitudes.

However, by its very nature, working with parents produces an interesting paradox. Many of the special education teachers on the front line of child abuse treatment still are not being trained to view parents positively. Similarly, in many instances parents have been influenced to regard special education professionals negatively and with distrust. This culturally oriented bias is at the root of many of the dilemmas experienced by special educators in child abuse and involvement situations. Resolution of this paradox is fundamental in working with the abusive parents.

Skills for the Family Encounter

Having discussed the variables that are present in any abusive or neglectful family situation, and having recognized the need for trained people, educators now can focus on specific skills they need to be effective in a parent involvement program.

No matter where the initial meeting with parents takes place, intervention will have a more useful beginning if special educators have the skills to work with adults who don't want their help or don't think they need it. Therefore, the most valuable skill is participatory listening as noted throughout this book in many other types of situations. Abuse-prone parents need a sympathetic, responsive, and nonjudgmental ear. People who have never been listened to without fear of reprisal or threat will have a difficult time feeling at ease. Thus, if the ombudsman special educators can wait and can provide an opportunity for parents to talk by open, attentive listening, they will increase the opportunity for the parents to relate to them. In this manner, parents will feel less threatened and distrustful; teachers can show by their ability to listen that they have honest respect for the parents' feelings.

Participatory listening can fulfill another important function. Abusive parents were characterized earlier as immature and dependent, lacking in self-esteem, and typed by role reversal. Awareness of these factors allows the ombudsman special education teacher to listen for role discrepancies. Ross (1972), describes three kinds of role discrepancies—cognitive, allocative, and goals—that are pertinent to the educator working with abusive parents. Cognitive discrepancy exists when one or more of those involved in the family role system do not know, or are not sufficiently familiar with, the roles required of them by other family members. Allocative discrepancy results when individuals refuse the role allocated to them or when other family members fail to complement the role. Goal discrepancy occurs when the goal of one family member is to obtain some form of gratification from another, but the latter fails to meet the demand because the individual's goal is related to withholding or the person is unable to satisfy the demand.

Cognitive discrepancy can occur when the universal role ascribed to the child by the parents is not fulfilled. This could happen in situations when the parents expect the child to be still or to be quiet when teething or when ill at an early age. Sometimes the child is not capable of satisfying this demand. The child has not yet learned his prescribed role in the family system. When this happens, the parents' demands are not met and abuse may follow. These parents' unreasonable demands were fostered by their previous recollection of parenting practices. The cognitive discrepancy was accelerated by unrealistic parental expectations that brought about a disequilibrium in the family system. Abusive parents often assign roles to their children and then are angered, sometimes to the point of violent aggression, when the children cannot fill the role.

In allocative discrepancy, role reversal occurs when abusive parents adopt the role of the child; that is, they have needs that were not met when they were children and they now desire the child to fulfill these needs for them. The result is that the requirement that roles be complementary is not met and abuse of the child follows.

An understanding of goal discrepancy is an extremely important ingredient of participatory listening. These discrepancies can be either motivational or biological in origin. Illness, immaturity, or intellectual deficiency generally are paralleled by a restricted capacity for goal attainment. These biological (and any motivational) limitations may cause disequilibrium. This is especially true when parents are unable or unwilling to change their level of expectancy concerning the child's goal attainment. Thus, one role partner—the parents—may be disappointed and cannot accommodate the limited biological or intellectual functioning of the child. The child has disappointed the parents by not fulfilling their expectations. These situations occur frequently in the families of abused children and are commonplace where children are thought to be different, deviant, or handicapped.

Thus, expressions of tension, anxiety, and hostility may be verbalized in the encounter between parent and special educator. Open listening can do much to (1) create a friendly atmosphere, (2) defuse tension and hostility, and (3) identify what discrepancies exist within family systems.

As parents begin to talk, special teachers initially take the role of the ombudsmen. Later, as the parents become more comfortable, the special educators as advocates can respond to the central concerns of the parents. Allowing the parents to talk can lead to an opportunity to exercise the second skill—feeling focused feedback (the first is participatory listening). This is the skill of responding verbally to parents, usually by paraphrasing, without passing judgment.

Advocates can begin to assume a more active role in the involvement process. However, the nature of the teachers' responses can do much to dictate the course of the encounter. It is critical in this phase of parent relationships that special teachers not be influenced by the nature of the abusive act. Advocates must continue to be accepting of the abusive parent. Special educators should listen and be alert to recognize that the feelings being expressed may not be the true attitude of the parents. It may be that the parents need to air feelings that otherwise might consume them. Advocate special educators should remember that they are working with parents who have the following needs:

Someone to help them to feel good about themselves, to make up for the belittling they've experienced in their own lives.

Someone to comfort them when they are hurt, to support them when they feel weak and to like them for their likeable qualities, even when these are hard to find.

Someone they can trust and lean on, someone who will put up with their ill temper and someone who will not be tricked into accepting their low sense of self-worth.

Someone who will not be exhausted with them when they find no pleasure in life and defeat all attempts to help them seek it.

Someone who will be there in times of crisis (Danvoren, 1975, p. 39).

Feeling Focused Feedback

If special teachers respond to the attitudes of abusive parents through the medium of feeling focused feedback, they can avoid registering whether they are approving or disapproving. This also allows ombudsmen to be able to respond to the nature of the feeling (negative, positive, or ambivalent) and the direction of the feeling (toward police, counselor, or self) without being misunderstood. Therefore, teachers can nod their heads, ask relevant questions, or replay the feeling back to the parent.

Feeling focused feedback can help parents work through goal discrepancies. Through feedback and paraphrasing (replaying what the parents have said in their own words) advocates can be effective in holding up reality without arguing the point. If parents deny the severity of the abusive behavior, advocates can reflect or clarify the discrepancies by replaying the information back to them. In this manner, parents can begin to discover potential alternatives for dealing with their concerns and needs. Advocates should remember that many couples are not aware of the discrepancies in their parenting practices and the concomitant inconsistencies in their communication to the educators. It is in the encounter meeting that advocates have the opportunity to help the following parents:

> Those who need someone that understands how hard it is for them to have dependents when they have never been allowed to be dependent themselves.
>
> Those who need someone that will not criticize them . . . that will not tell them what to do or how to manage their lives.
>
> Those who need someone that will help them understand their children without making them feel imposed upon . . . or stupid.
>
> Those who need someone that will give to them without making them feel of lesser value because of their needs (Danvoren, 1975, p. 39).

These parental needs vividly make the point for feeling focused feedback. In this mode, teachers promote discussion by responding only to what the parents really are saying and by encouraging them to express their feelings. This means that the advocates' goal in responding is to understand what the parents are expressing and to communicate ''I am with you.'' It would be inappropriate for teachers to pass on interpretations to the parents. It already has been noted that parents need someone who will help them without making them feel of lesser value, who will not criticize, or tell them what to do or how to manage their lives. With feeling focused feedback, advocates can assist parents to identify and choose alternative socially acceptable behavior rather than abusive parenting practices.

Finally, the skill of directive summation makes it possible for helping special education teachers to assume their role as advocates or ombudsmen. Directive summation is the ability of teachers to "put it all together" for the parents. Without this skill, teachers will find themselves at a loss in dealing with abusive parents. Therefore, while maintaining an open and accepting attitude, teachers also must look for ways to summarize the feelings heard in the encounter and be able to go beyond feeling focused feedback to help the parents. The abusive parents should hear the substance of their feelings as a "complete" replay rather than as an "instant" replay. This is the major difference between directive summation and feeling focused feedback. Directive summation might occur at the beginning of the counseling encounter, several times during the meeting, or at its conclusion.

The strength of directive summation lies in the fact that it allows teachers in the counseling encounter to choose a path of action with the parents. If parents are moving toward resolution of the dilemma (e.g., goal discrepancy), teachers can function as ombudsmen and can continue to mediate the problem. If it appears that the parents are having difficulty in resolving the goal discrepancy, then teachers may become advocates for alternatives. These may take the form of (1) referrals for psychotherapeutic intervention if the denial is too rigid, (2) continuing to work conjointly with the parents in a support role, or (3) regarding the situation as hopeless and unchangeable.

Most case manager special educators who seek to help abused and neglected children probably never give way to the third alternative. Rather than viewing the child as an unfortunate victim of negative parental influences about which nothing can be done, most special educators continue to exhaust their energies in attempting to.work with abusive parents. They develop skills and help parents grow into tolerant human beings.

Chapter 9

Involving Parents of Exceptional Children in Transcultural Settings

Historically, a primary function of the family has been the education of its children. Legally, the educational function has been vested in state educational agencies and then largely delegated to local school districts. However, the precedent remains that the family still is the primary educator of children. Although most parents have accepted this fact, some parents and families still doubt the sincerity of this philosophy in schools. For these families, the education of their children has been considered the province of educators and other related professionals with the parents playing a secondary role. In short, these parents, of racial minority origin—particularly black and Mexican-American—generally have been expected to fulfill two roles in the educational planning process: a good scout and loyal supporter of the educational system and an accepting recipient of child reports. Although these convictions have been directed primarily toward the regular educational program, racial minority parents are equally vociferous concerning their lack of participation in special education programs for exceptional children.

The passage of P.L. 94-142 has given these parents equal status with teachers in the education of their children. This legislation makes it mandatory that minority parents be consulted in any educational plans developed for their exceptional children. This legislation obviously demands a more sophisticated special educator approach to working with these minority parents. This usually has been a weak link in special education professional preparation. Providing experiences for educators who are expected to work with minority parents has not been a priority item in either inservice or preservice training. However, the passage of P.L. 94-142 emphasized that special educators must expand their efforts to involve minority parents in the planning processes. In essence, the act assumes that schools will increase their efforts to communicate with, and involve, minority parents successfully in the educational planning of their exceptional children.

SETTING THE STAGE

When considering the act's mandate, it is necessary to trace the historical and social evolution of minority parent participation in the schools. It then will be possible to highlight critical variables and relevant events that have shaped the perceptions of minority parents toward schools and special education. The two traditional institutions that have influenced the life style of the minority exceptional child—the school and the family—will be traced.

The Schools

The schools have not served minorities, notably blacks and Mexican-Americans, well. This also is true in special education. While Anglo parents of exceptional children sought relief in the schools as early as the 1930 White House Conference on Children, minority parents were struggling for recognition of equal educational opportunity under a dual schooling system. As the 30s and 40s came to a close, most minority children—in both North and South—still were in segregated school settings. Parent participation was of a mixed nature. In the North, where the Parent-Teacher Associations (PTAs) were the dominant force for participation, minority parents' involvement was minimal and the future of their children usually rested in the hands of white middle-class parents. The South in the 40s presented a different picture. With the dual system of education in effect, minority parents had their own schools and for the most part were active participants. These separate activities were decreed by law (*Plessy* v. *Ferguson,* 1896) to be carried out in isolation from whites. Even under such circumstances, these parents felt a sense of community and loyalty to their schools.

With the advent of desegregation (*Brown* v. *Board of Education,* 1954), the situation changed. Two conditions emerged that made minority parents suspicious of the mission of schools and special education. In the South, formerly active minority parents felt disenfranchised as their schools were closed or converted into lower level educational centers. Because of the sometimes violent nature of desegregation (U.S. Commission on Civil Rights, 1964), these parents did not attempt to participate in PTAs and other school-related activities. At the same time many minority children who were enrolling in previously all-white schools were labeled "mentally retarded" and were placed in disproportionate numbers in special education classes.

Although most black parents harbored strong feelings concerning the appropriateness of these placements, they usually were given two choices: they could accept these placements or they could watch their children being forced out. Racial minority children in northern schools received much the same treatment.

These parents saw their children concentrated in neighborhood schools by de jure segregation patterns. Since many had migrated from rural areas where schooling was nonexistent or insufficient, these urban migrant children brought with them educational deficiencies perpetuated by past discrimination. Their school situations often were complicated by their school systems' failure or lack of flexibility in meeting their needs. At that point in history, two theories emerged that stamped special education programs as the curriculum for students who were different by reason of pigmentation, behavior, social class, or learning style: the scapegoat theory and the mental illness theory. This emotional tide was linked with middle-class teaching values that then were pervasive in the public school system. The impact of these theories upon minority children in school teacher-learner situations lasted until the 1960s.

The Scapegoat Theory

The foundation for this theory and its application to minority children had its roots in desegregation in the South and integration in the North. According to its opponents, the scapegoat theory became operational following the *Brown* decision that outlawed the dual system of education. These educators reported that minority students were the recipients of misplaced hostility resulting from bitter school systems and administrators following the desegregation decree. They cite the following descriptors of such a theory. Ashmore (1954) noted the plight of black students when the color of their skin was considered. He said that because of their pigmentation, Negroes remained a "visible minority." Jones (1974) reported that minority children suffered a "double jeopardy" syndrome: those in special education were discriminated against by the system, then "labeled" mentally retarded. Hickerson (1966) spoke of the alienation that these students felt by virtue of the fact that they were perceived to be different by dress, life style, or color.

The crucial denominator of this theory rested in the importance attached to IQ testing as a primary indicator of intelligence. At the heart of the conflict was the belief that intelligence was innate, hereditary, and largely a function of race. Citing the works of Galton (1976) and Cattell (1947), the advocates of the scapegoat theory made extensive use of the IQ tests in schools to separate students on the basis of ability determined by such assessments. Opponents of the theory assailed testing from many perspectives.

First, they attacked the premise that IQ testing should be the sole criterion for determining intelligence. These educational professionals contended that tests as they were being used and constructed never would allow minority students to gain access to the mainstream of school life. Second, many fought the concept of group intelligence tests (Johnson, 1969; Dunn, 1968). Despite these protests, minority children continued to increase in educable mentally retarded classrooms. They seemed destined to bear the brunt of harsh feelings in the aftermath of the *Brown* ruling. The outcome of the testing issue is still unsettled as we move into the 1980s. A California judge (Packham) made permanent his ban on the use of IQ tests for placement in special education classes in California. However, a Chicago judge (Grady) ruled that Chicago public schools could continue to use IQ tests to place students in classes for the educable mentally retarded.

The Mental Illness Theory

The scapegoat theory with its bases in desegregation did much to influence the notion that minority children were different on the basis of innate intelligence, but it could not account for all of the labeling practices applied to them. During this same period, the scapegoat theory was coupled with another concept to provide additional "evidence" for placement of minority children in special education.

The mental illness theory was based upon the behavior of minority children that was judged atypical in relation to that of middle class white children. Opponents of this theory describe how it was used to place children in special education classes. McCandless (1967) reported that the values of many teachers (mostly middle class) in the public schools differed distinctly from the pupils (mostly lower class) they taught. Specifically, he listed several essential differences that mirrored these dissimilarities of pupil/teacher interaction. McCandless concluded that teachers most likely faced pupils who shared few of their values, who on the whole were more aggressive, and who perhaps were less well dressed than their middle-class counterparts. When this happens, teachers, who need satisfaction and rewards yet receive few from such pupils, reject the children. Dent (1976) described the process strictly in behavioral terms. He reported that teachers were unprepared to accept the active, aggressive behavior of black boys and interpreted the pupils' behavior as hostile. Since the students did not subscribe to the teachers' expectations of compliant, docile, and conforming children, they were determined to be unmanageable. The final step in the process is recommendation to special education and, more specifically, to emotionally disturbed classes. Gaston (1970) described this behavior problem wherein aggressive black children were placed summarily in special education classes.

This set of circumstances led to a disproportionate number of minority students, mostly black, in special programs for the mentally retarded and emotionally disturbed. Desegregation decreed in *Brown* (1954) was unpopular and unacceptable to a large proportion of southern school personnel. The companion scapegoat and mental illness theories combined to cause large numbers of minority children to be assigned to special education classes.

Another Contributing Variable

The combination of theories and desegregation in the 50s might have been sufficient for minority parents to harbor deep feelings concerning special education. However, regular educational programs contributed to those negative feelings. It was during this period that minority parents experienced the push-out syndrome. The Southern Regional Council (1973) documented that there was a push-out problem that was related directly to desegregation. This organization found a substantial cause-and-effect relationship between students who were suspended or expelled, on the one hand, and those who were labeled as dropouts on the other. Edelman (1975) also concluded that there was a high correlation between students who were minority and poor and those who were out of school.

1960s, SPECIAL EDUCATION, AND MINORITIES

As special education moved into the 1960s, it was affected dramatically by movements in regular education. Often called the decade of the disadvantaged, this period was punctuated by another prevailing theory and resultant actions that once again changed the course of special education for minority children. The theory was cultural deprivation, the action was the work of minority and other concerned educators in the field, and the result was a change to an educational philosophy called cultural pluralism.

The Cultural Deprivation Theory

Proponents of this theory (Passow, 1963; Ravitz, 1963; Goldberg, 1963) argued that minority children were deficient in the cultural background they brought to school with them. In 1970, even such an impressive group as the Task Force on Urban Education directly chaired by Wilson Riles, the Director, Division of Compensatory Education, now State Superintendent of Public Education in California, equated the inappropriate behavior of poor minority students in urban schools with the behavior seen in the mentally retarded, the emotionally disturbed, and the physically handicapped. Others such as Reisman (1962) and Harrington (1962) fueled the implication that the failure of minority and poor children in school was due to factors similar to those of exceptional children in the three aforementioned categories.

However, opponents of the culturally deprived theory assailed this hypothesis as being deficient in describing the schools' failure to educate the poor and minorities. Hurley (1969) stated that the culturally different might be environmentally deprived rather than mentally retarded. He concluded that although education was not solely responsible for the failure of the poor to learn and their overrepresentation in mentally retarded classes, it was more responsible than any other single factor. Similarly, Edelman (1974) reported that in many states— but particularly in five largely rural southern states—the percentage of black children in mentally retarded classes was three to five times as high as that for white children. In many cases the proportion was ten times as high. Prillmen (1975) reached the same conclusion from his study that was limited to Virginia school populations.

. During this same period Mexican-American children, because of language differences, suffered the same fate. The U.S. Commission on Civil Rights (1974) reported on the overrepresentation of Mexican-American children in mentally retarded classes. In its report *On Quality Education for Mexican-Americans,* it said these children were assigned to educable mentally retarded (EMR) classes mostly on the basis of IQ tests but that these tests seldom were in the child's primary language.

The cultural deprivation theory was functioning although its utilitarian value was being challenged seriously by minority professionals aided by sympathetic majority educators.

The Challenge to the Theory

The most serious challenge to the cultural deprivation theory came in the area of testing. Education as a profession already was under fire for its seeming inability to educate children who were different from those usually prescribed for middle-class schools. Having seen what the overemphasis on testing had done in the ability grouping sets in schools, analysts put special education under close scrutiny for its use of IQ tests for entry into its programs. Dunn (1968) in his classic position paper was one of the first to cast doubts on the use of tests, self-contained classrooms, and special education as *the* only curriculum for minority culturally different students. Johnson (1969), Dent (1976), Jones (1972), and Green (1972) spoke out about the cultural biases inherent in test construction and administration for blacks. DeAvila (1974) and the U.S. Commission on Civil Rights (1974) made the same comments regarding test use with Mexican-American children. Hillard (1975) and Gay (1973) discussed the problem of assessor bias in evaluation. Both believed that the orientation of the testers and their views of the use of tests with minority students were linked. For the first time the theory had been joined to the challenge of the appropriateness of IQ tests. This period also marked the first time minority professionals had joined in the argument over the appropriate placement of minority exceptional children in special education programs. Equally important was the fact that they had been joined by other equally concerned majority educators.

CHANGE IN PHILOSOPHY

Prior to the mid-1960s, educational philosophy in the U.S. had been geared to the melting pot doctrine, which was based on the historical process of assimilation. Its basic ingredient was the desired concept of "sameness." Stated plainly, it meant that all children could be acculturated into American society through the same principles and practices of education that had served immigrants and their generations through the evolution of that society. However, too many Americans came to disagree with this philosophy in the mid-1960s and the doctrine of cultural diversity emerged. This philosophy is based on the inherent positive values assigned to the culture of each racial ethnic group. Middle-class values are not considered to be the yardstick against which other children are measured. Education, in particular, was the institution questioned concerning its adaptability to this change.

For special education, the change signaled the end of the acceptance of disadvantaged or deprived youngsters as prime candidates for programs for exceptional children. This challenge prompted the 1969 Advisory Committee on Handicapped Children to recommend that priority be given to preschool disadvantaged children. However, the committee begged the question of the practice of identifying a disproportionate number of disadvantaged children as "retarded" or as "emotionally disturbed." As a final note, the Bureau for Education of the Handicapped and the Council for Exceptional Children showed their concern about the placement of vulnerable poor children of any race or color by hosting a conference focused on this issue. Out of this conference came seven major recommendations related to the identification, labeling, and placement of minority children in special education:

1. provide early childhood stimulation, education, and evaluation as part of the continuum of public education.
2. conduct a study of histories of successful inner-city families who have learned to cope effectively with their environment.
3. restructure education of teachers, administrators, counselors; retrain those now in the field.
4. reexamine present system of intelligence testing and classification.
5. commit substantial additional funding for research and development in educational improvement for disadvantaged children and youth.
6. thoroughly delineate what constitutes accountability, allocate sufficient funds to carry out the responsibility entailed and hold the school accountable for providing quality education for all children.
7. involve parents, citizens and citizen groups, students, and general and special educators in a total educational effort.

MINORITY PARENT PARTICIPATION

The 1960s also marked the initial attempt by schools to allow minority parents to participate in their decision-making apparatus. This participatory action came in the form of advisory councils, chiefly through government-funded programs. Programs such as Title I and Head Start stipulated that parents sit on advisory councils to ensure their continued involvement in the education of their children. As these programs developed, educators became increasingly aware that parents indeed were vital in assuring their success. Early childhood educators were the first to recognize that parents were the primary foci in their children's lives. After observing the success of these programs, preschool educators conceded that parents did indeed play vital roles in determining the gains made and maintained by their children. Separate studies (Smith, 1963; Jones, 1971; Gordon, 1972; and Sullivan, 1970) reported that parents' behavior and modeling in their various roles in the child's early years did influence intellectual performance.

These programs also realized that it sometimes was difficult to involve parents meaningfully in the education of their children. Educators were frustrated because many parents were apathetic to, or refused to be guided by, the school establishment interpretations of the program. Despite this frustration, other studies (Grotberg, 1970; Jones, 1971) found that continued early parent involvement outweighed any disadvantages. The Grotberg study showed that the performance of children whose parents were assisting them at home, with or without the teacher materials being used by the classroom teachers, definitely was superior to that of a control group of children who were not receiving help of any kind from home. Both groups of children, experimental and control, were exposed to the same instruction and materials in the classroom. Jones' study (1971), dealing with low-income families, reported that low verbal ability too often was equated wrongfully with a lack of intellectual potential. Another study (Rodin, 1971) outlined the effect of varying degrees of participation by low-income parents in preschool programs. She found that active parent involvement significantly increased children's reading readiness scores.

Most studies related to Title I parent participation have concluded that more rather than less involvement was to be desired. Chilman (1968) recommended that advisory committees be strengthened and provided with a functioning structure. Reyes and Gezi (1973) studied Title I programs in California and made 12 recommendations, the last of which contained several key points:

> . . . If advisory committees are to contribute meaningfully to the compensatory education program, school districts must show that they are committed to the right of the community to share in the educational decision making process by earnestly seeking and implementing the advice of the school district advisory committee. Workshops and in-

service training sessions for committee members should be provided to help them become more knowledgeable in the development and implementation of compensatory education programs and to aid them in developing the skills needed to evaluate such programs (pp. 16–17).

In the 1980s school districts are still seeking means to successfully implement the conditions of the recommendation. Based on these Title I and Early Childhood studies, it can be seen that regular education programs provided a challenge for educators to involve minority parents in special education.

MINORITIES AND SPECIAL EDUCATION

While minority parents' involvement with schools in general has not always been pleasant for them, their experiences with special education have been even less satisfying. At first glance it might appear that this statement is questionable in light of recent developments. However, in past litigation, minority parents demonstrated that they were disappointed with the accountability provided to them and the placement and services given their children.

As early as 1963, minority parents served notice that they were discontented with the placement of their children. In *Mills* (1963) they obtained a judgment against the District of Columbia schools to stop the "tracking" of a disproportionate number of minority children into the general curriculum in their schools. In the 1970s a series of cases underscored the disenchantment parents felt toward the schools and special education programs. *Larry P. v. Riles* (1972) contended that black children had been placed in mentally retarded classes as a result of inappropriate testing procedures. The landmark suit was the *Pennsylvania* (1972) case that accorded a free public education to all handicapped children. Although relief was sought on behalf of another minority—handicapped children—the *Pennsylvania* decision was applied liberally to include all children. This decision helped the cause of minority children considerably since it halted the exodus of those excluded from schools. Finally in *Diana* (1973), Mexican-American parents challenged the placement of their children in mentally retarded classes because of language differences and solely on the strength of IQ tests. Again, minority parents received a favorable judgment.

Thus, the perception of minority parents toward special education has been prejudiced by the fact that they believed the curriculum was for (1) those who were dumb (mentally retarded) and (2) those who were troublemakers (emotionally disturbed). However, a changing social order and a shift in educational philosophy caused minority parents to raise their aspirations concerning schools and special education. The shifting social order and a changing educational outlook led black and Mexican-American parents to take a different look at their family structures. Based on these perceptions, they concluded that their families had strengths that should be regarded more highly by educators rather than the pathological concept formerly accorded them. Moynihan (1965) and Munuchin (1967) were two of many experts who assigned attributes to low-income minority families (Exhibit 9-1).

Minority researchers rejected these views and argued against these as negative stereotypes. Billingsley (1968) and Hill (1972) presented strong arguments for a positive perspective of black families. Hill's study listed five strengths that are persuasive arguments for a different approach to black families: (1) strong kinship bonds, (2) strong work orientation, (3) adaptability of family roles, (4) high achievement orientation, and (5) strong religious orientation. Hill emphasized that a reevaluation of black families would show strengths that could help in understanding the qualities that previously had been ascribed to weaknesses. He contended that these newfound strengths could lead to a more constructive program for meeting the needs of minority families.

In considering Mexican-Americans, Castenada (1974) and Flores (1972) found family solidarity to be a strength. Rubel (1971) and Murillo (1971) stressed expressiveness as a family asset. Flores (1972) and Evans and Anderson (1973) also found high achievement to be a source of family solidarity. Another source of strength, religious orientation, was cited by Madsen (1964). Murillo (1971) and Ramirez, Harold, and Castenada (1974) concluded that cooperation also was a major strength.

From these investigations, a new structure of minority families emerged that emphasized the following basic strengths: (1) kinship, (2) adaptability of roles, (3) strong religious orientation, (4) high achievement orientation, and (5) strong work orientation. If these strengths are accepted, minority parents and families of the 1980s face challenges similar to those that confronted parents of educa-

---

Exhibit 9-1 Family Stereotypes

Black	Mexican-American
1. Matriarchal	1. Patriarchal
2. Unstable	2. Cohesive
3. Productivity lack	3. Subservient/low esteem
4. Multiagency families	4. Multiagency families
5. Low value of education	5. Low value of education
6. Pathological	6. "Unplanned" parenthood

Source: Robert Marion, Minority Parent Involvement in the Lazy/Dishonest IEP Process: A Systematic Model Approach. *Focus on Exceptional Children,* Love Publishing Co., © 1979. Reprinted with permission.

tionally handicapped children in the 1960s. When complaints by parents covering the two decades are compared, they are fundamentally similar in nature (Exhibit 9-2).

When viewing such comparisons and reflecting upon history, it is not hard to understand the unwillingness of minority parents to accept decisions that place their children in special education or to become involved in IEP development. Whereas other parents viewed special education as an alternative, minority parents were categorized by the stigma of two labels: emotionally disturbed for those "hard-to-handle kids" and mentally retarded for "not-too-bright" children. These labels inferred to minority parents that their children were mentally ill, socially maladjusted, or not too smart. Many were not knowledgeable concerning the fact that special education also served the visually handicapped, learning disabled, deaf, and physically handicapped.

The task for teachers who seek to involve minority parents in special education programming is two-fold: (1) When the child needs special education and the parents in all probability still are relating to the old stereotypes. The special educators must work with minority parents to change the stereotype and help them develop the best educational plan for the child. (2) When the minority child already is enrolled in special education. The presence of the reluctant parents is needed to draw up the IEP and their participation in and their understanding of the process is essential. The challenge to the special educators is to be able to work with minority parents to gain the desired outcomes.

Educators often must deal with these circumstances when working with minority parents in special education. Therefore, knowledge of the history of schools and minority families can be helpful in implementing intervention and involvement strategies for including them in the planning and design of the educational program.

Exhibit 9-2 Comparison of Parents' Complaints

1960s	*1980s*
1. Overemphasis on testing and IQ scores (culture-free and group)	1. Discriminatory testing
2. Middle class values	2. Second-class citizenship
3. General curriculum tracking	3. Least restrictive environment
4. Language differences, dialects, and second language	4. Primary language of the child and mode of communication
5. Individualized instruction	5. Individualized Education Programs

Source: Robert Marion, Minority Parent Involvement in the Lazy/Dishonest IEP Process: A Systematic Model Approach. *Focus on Exceptional Children,* Love Publishing Co., © 1979. Reprinted with permission.

INVOLVING MINORITY PARENTS

Working with minority parents has added a new dimension to the life of special educators. Involvement has grown from being purely parent conferences with a ritualized meeting between two adults to an open informative exchange between minority parents and teachers. P.L. 94–142 assumes that schools will treat minority parents as coequals and not as adversaries. It also requires schools to comply in good faith with minority parents in fulfilling the act's guarantees. Special education teachers who can use intervention strategies with the attendant skills of interviewing, communicating, assessment, and educational planning can work better with minority parents of exceptional children.

The Past

In the past, working with minority parents was one of the helping teachers' least enjoyable tasks because special educators felt:

- that the parents blamed the teachers for the child's problem
- that the minority parental criticism of the teachers' techniques and methods was harsh
- that the minority parents wasted valuable teacher time in useless conversation
- that the minority parents appeared to be apathetic and unconcerned about the child's school activities

or the minority parents perceived:

- that the teachers blamed the parents for the child's problem
- that the teachers were critical of parents who interfered with the management of their classrooms
- that the teachers were annoyed by parents' involvement in advisory committees or school activities
- that the teachers had difficulty understanding parents' lack of participation because of economic or other financial worries

When these teacher-minority parent responses are viewed in the light of past parent-teacher relationships, it is not hard to understand why contacts have been infrequent. One of the principal reasons for limiting contact with minority parents to so few meetings was that these conferences seldom seem to produce any positive dividends for teachers or parents. Therefore, to maximize dividends under P.L. 94-142, the following steps are proposed:

1. All involved (teachers, parents, and, if possible, the child) should agree upon the purpose of the learning activity as stated in the IEP. This plan should contain explicit terminal goals.
2. Any learning activities directed toward achieving the terminal goals should be arrived at through joint decision-making.
3. When the IEP has been implemented, there should be open and frank feedback between parents and teachers to foster a climate of trust where information can be exchanged freely.
4. The child's IEP should be evaluated jointly on the actual data related to the terminal goal criteria. In this fashion, all persons feel they have an equal share in the success or failure of the plan.

With these four steps in mind, the question of minority parent-helping special educator cooperation can be addressed from this premise: parents "tune out" teachers when teachers fail to "tune them in." Thus, working with parents has a three-dimensional phase that can be likened to the diagrams here. If minority parents are being listened to, the diagram looks like Figure 9-1.

Communication is open and honest and both parties are listening to one another. However, the diagram will resemble a diamond when minority parents feel they are not being heard. Thus, the picture changes to look like Figure 9-2.

Figure 9-1 When Teachers Heed Minority Parents

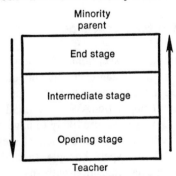

Minority
parent

End stage

Intermediate stage

Opening stage

Teacher

Source: Robert Marion, Parent Involvement in Educational Planning Education Service Center Region XI, Fort Worth, Tex., 1977.

Figure 9-2 When Teachers Ignore Minority Parents

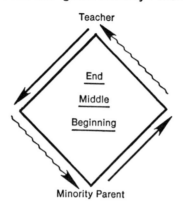

Source: Robert Marion, Parent Involvement in Educational Planning Education Service Center Region XI, Fort Worth, Tex., 1977.

This diagram illustrates the contention that today's minority parents generally are a more heterogeneous group, are demanding more accountability, and are rejecting the "teacher knows best" concept traditionally espoused by some educators. Barsch (1969) said this type of approach made adversaries of parents instead of allies. As he stated, parents were concerned about being treated with some dignity as individuals and not simply as objective, impersonal entities called "the parents of a handicapped child." Barsch added that as teachers were able to convey a feeling of acceptance of the individuals, the parents reciprocally were more accepting of whatever assistance the teacher might offer.

Minority Parents and Special Teachers

Traditionally many parents of exceptional children have regarded teachers with a positive attitude. Barsch substantiated this with citations from more than 12,000 sets of parents and related experiences with numerous teachers. Minority parents constitute a different population. While a small number may support Barsch's viewpoint, the majority are more likely to have moved away from the good feeling that special education offered small classes, good teacher/child ratios, and professionals who were special people. Instead, minority parents are more predisposed to view special education with suspicion. They are inclined to believe that teachers hold the view that the minority child is inferior and needs less of a challenge, including much less of the monies set aside for special programs (Silberberg & Silberberg, 1974).

The passage of P.L. 94-142 tends to dim that view somewhat but it also provides additional impetus to the conviction that teachers should feel compelled to recapture their positive image in the eyes of minority parents. At the same time, they should seek to diminish the negative image currently ascribed to them by these same parents. This outlook will have the dual effect of meeting the guidelines set forth in P.L. 94-142 and of elevating minority parents to the status of coequals in the educative process.

Fearful Parents and Anxious Teachers

In approaching the teacher-parent encounter, many minority parents inevitably ask: What's the problem? What has the child done now? In spite of the compulsory legislation and supporting court decisions, most minority parents still are apprehensive about meeting their child's teacher. These fears may have originated from:

1. their own school experiences
2. the apprehension of learning that their child is not performing satisfactorily in school
3. the fear of being blamed by the teacher for much of their child's problems
4. previous contacts with schools that proved to be embarrassing for parents.

These fears in addition to teachers' anxiety about the meeting often combine to signal a less than satisfactory session. The problem then becomes two-fold: (1) special educators must alleviate feelings of insecurity within themselves, and (2) they must counter the feeling that minority parents are at fault for the child's problems.

The first positive step that case manager special educators can take is to build and maintain the trust factor underlying the basic assumption that parents are sincerely concerned about their child. However, case managers must keep in mind the variables mentioned earlier that undoubtedly will influence the parents' response to the call for a conference. It is important for case managers to understand that it is not unusual for minority parents to react angrily, to be unresponsive, or to give a defensive response to a contact whether by telephone, in person, or by note. The parents' initial response may originate from a single factor or a multiple of the factors cited. While these sources of conflict are important, several specific predetermining factors also may be operating to the detriment of the special educators. Therefore, unaware of these conditions, the teachers may be the recipients of angry or defensive reactions that arise from the following conditions:

- Immediate family crises such as inadequate housing, insufficient nutrition, illness or death of a family member, loss of a job, drug problems, or other problems, one or all of which may be a causative factor; the net effect may be one more burden that weighs down already overextended parents.

- Parents' lack of previous information that their child is having a problem in school; this lack of notification is particularly upsetting if prior contact has been impersonal.

- Prior ambiguous or misleading information concerning the child that causes parents to place the blame for the pupil's problems on someone else (teachers, the school, other children).

- Specific negative responses to the parents by the school or teachers; for example, the teacher in the previous grade might have been unwilling to work with minority parents.

- Negative attitudes toward the school system; many minority parents may believe that low-income children are not tested properly before being placed in special education programs.

When special educators grasp an awareness of these predetermining conditions, the case manager teachers and parents can begin to work together in a position of mutual trust and respect. In the face of these perplexing problems, there are some methods that can be used by case manager educators to build that respect and trust.

Building Trust and Respect

The first bridge is the realization by both sides that they must learn to enter into their interactions believing that each is committed to the education and well-being of the child. Teachers and parents by role definition are the primary educators of the child. Barsch (1969) speaks of the reality of the situation for special education teachers. He says that rather than regarding parents as adversaries, teachers must regard them as associates and allies. Barsch adds that there is no value in an attitude of mutual helplessness because the middle ground is occupied by the child struggling to find the highest possible level of personal integration. This means that the learning efficiency of the child is the primary issue and should be of paramount consideration to teachers and parents. Therefore, the best method for the minority parents and the special educators to gain mutual respect is to work toward a common goal and to achieve success. This common goal must be the education and well-being of the children.

To obtain this respect, teachers—whether fledgling or experienced—must display basic communication skills. These are necessary not only if the teachers are to gain respect and trust but also to enable the partners in the communication process to exchange information concerning the child. Therefore, educational professionals must learn to listen, to respond, and to give feedback to the parents.

Participatory Listening

Earlier in this chapter, the helping special educator was reminded that parents stop listening when they are not being heard. In the parent-teacher interaction context, the first skill—participatory listening—becomes extremely important. Case manager special educators must remember the sources of anxiety that cause minority parents to react in certain ways. This parent-teacher encounter may come at several points of intervention: when there is the suggestion of a placement in the special education program, when there is a local support team meeting, or when there is a discussion of the Individualized Education Program.

Although there may be other instances where minority parents and teachers interact, these illustrate the importance of the skill of participatory listening. If the initial contact is by phone and is the first with the parents, the listening skill becomes even more paramount. When teachers initiate the interaction and the minority parents assume something is wrong, the reaction may be anger, hostility, or resentment. The question then becomes: are the teachers able to listen intently to the parents' reply without building up value judgments in their own minds?

What may appear to be a routine phone call home by a teacher may very well be threatening to the minority parents and a signal that something has gone wrong at school. They may feel that their parental judgment is being questioned and that their guidance is faulty. Even under the most favorable circumstances, the first call home tends to elicit a scary feeling.

Special educators should keep in mind that they are interacting at two levels—in both the cognitive and affective domains (Kendall, 1978). The minority parents may be operating at the fourth level of Maslow's (1954) hierarchy in their cognitive response to the special educators. Therefore, their response may be inarticulate, hesitant, and vague. On the other hand, the parents may be found at the bottom level in their affective needs. With the basic needs of shelter, food, and sleep unmet, the parents may not want to become involved in school problems in any way. After all, the parents' concern at home may be focused on having sufficient shelter and food for the child. Thus, teachers who can listen attentively for any discrepancies that might come from the parents' discussion of their feelings will begin to gain their respect and trust.

Parent-teacher meetings may take place in the home, at the school, or in other physical settings where the participants are in a face-to-face situation. When this occurs, King (1973) says there are three key ideas that the ombudsman teachers should keep in mind to convey the posture of an attentive listener. The first rule is to relax physically and to center attention on the parents. Ombudsman teachers will find that they will be more effective listeners when they forget about themselves and concentrate their attention upon the parents. Participatory listening also means acceptance of the parents' values. It is important for the teachers to have a positive self-concept if they are to withstand some of the emotions or feelings of parents who might be overwrought over the disclosure that something might be wrong. Empathetic listening ombudsman special educators can permit the parents to have a catharsis and can go to where the parents are without them feeling threatened personally by a disdainful sounding voice. It means much to parents to have listeners who will not pass judgment upon them or consider them less than equals.

The second rule is that teachers should use eye contact to help them focus upon the parents and to communicate to them that they are being heard. They need not gaze at the parents with a highly intense stare or attempt to fixate them; rather, their eyes should convey to the parents, "I'm with you." The eyes form a formidable channel for nonverbal communication. Teacher ombudsmen should resist the temptation to be judgmental through the power of the eyes.

The third rule is that teachers should follow what the parents are saying. This is important in working with minority parents who often are not afforded the courtesy of being heard. Frequently, their views are not considered because of language differences or lack of facility with the "King's English." Even if experiencing difficulty, special educators may be able to capture the essence of the situation. By concentrating upon this skill, educator ombudsmen can keep the meeting from dissolving into meaningless dialogue simply because the teachers assumed that the problem was similar to a thousand others that they had heard before. By listening and following, teachers can avoid this trap and can respect the uniqueness of each situation brought before them by minority parents.

Feeling Focused Feedback

The second set of skills for empathetic teachers is the ability to be able to respond accurately to the parents and to provide feeling focused feedback. Responding can be channeled through two methods of communication, verbal and nonverbal. In nonverbal reflection of feeling, the special educators simply mirror the emotions or feelings being expressed by nodding the head or through facial expressions that correlate to parental concerns. The teachers, without commenting, become the mirror that reflects exactly what the parents are saying. Minority parents have sensitive antennae and will tune in to persons who can reflect the depth of their feeling without speaking. The verbal reflection of feeling not only involves a worded response but also contains feedback for the parents. Teachers should be aware of the following conditions involving their responses:

1. Teacher responses should *be* as nonauthoritative as possible.
2. Teachers should *be* truly accepting, empathetic, and responsive without giving the impression they are making value judgments.
3. Teachers should *ask* open-ended questions, i.e., those that encourage further discussion rather than close off additional inquiries.
4. Teachers should *be* considerate of parents' vulnerability to the child's problem.
5. Teachers should *accord* parents of all economic, racial, and ethnic groups the same respect and rights as they work together for the welfare of the child.

Exchange of Information

It now is obvious that as teachers make accurate responses and begin to use feeling focused feedback, they can move from a passive to a more active relationship with parents. This stage ushers in the third set of skills—the ability to exchange information. It is during this stage that teachers begin to help parents become intelligent consumers of information. For example, after the initial trauma has receded and the parents have been given feedback, both sides should be in a position of trust and respect whereby information can be exchanged and tasks mutually agreed upon. This can be done by the teachers' summarizing the information that is being shared, which also allows the parents to repeat the information.

The exchange of information can be facilitated if both teachers and parents are speaking the same language. For instance, P.L. 94-142 requires that parents be involved in any decisions regarding the assessment, placement, and programming of their child. Clearly understood language, communicated between equals and in lay terms, will do much to alleviate minority parents' insecurity and anxiety. It will enhance the teachers' stature in the eyes of the parents. Better yet, it will ensure the parents' continued cooperation and consumerism in educational planning.

Finally, the skill of information exchange makes it possible for teacher human services helpers to assume the responsibility for case management. From this role, they can become advocates or ombudsmen. Summarization is the ability of teachers to capsule the problem for the parents. Therefore, while exuding warmth, the teachers also must look for ways to summarize minority parents' feelings so that together they can plan to advocate or mediate for resolution of the problem.

The Emotional Issue: Testing

One of the most common complaints of minority parents is the cry that they are accorded treatment different from other parents (Edelman, 1975). Frequently they charge that they are left out or are not given sufficient information to make proper decisions for their children. Testing is an area that encompasses all the fears and apprehensions that minority parents share.

Earlier it was mentioned that working with minority parents means becoming involved at the affective and cognitive levels. On testing, both levels are involved. Testing is an emotional issue (affective) with minority parents. They construe it as another way to single out their child for "dummy" classes (PCMR, 1971; U.S. Commission on Civil Rights, 1974). Emotions run high and feelings often take precedence over other elements.

On the other hand, testing is a cognitive issue for minority parents. Although most know about the tests, they know very little about test item selection, construction, and administration (Dent, 1973). Therefore, one of the tasks facing advocate special educators is to help the minority parents become informed consumers. Information must be disseminated in lay language. Special educators must summarize the information and become much more directive in their approach. This means that they must ask for instant playback of their comments. Working back and forth in this fashion, the teachers call upon minority parents to repeat the shared comments and information. An approach of this type enables the advocate special educators to verify that the minority parents have reached an acceptable level of understanding.

Special education advocates must consider at this stage the cultural diversity among minority parents. While Mexican-American and black parents may be at the same place affectively, there may be vast cognitive differences between the two culturally different groups. Therefore, special educators should understand the "locus of control" concepts espoused by Rouche and Mink (1976) in their work with culturally different youths. A wise special educator will check the perceptions of the adolescent's parents to ascertain how much control they feel that they have over their lives. Realizing that their approach must be therapeutic, ombudsman special educators will work with minority parents to assist them to develop coping skills to deal with their anxieties and frustrations. This approach implies that special educators will be knowledgeable about "life space" principles. Having this knowledge, they can function effectively. They continue to convey data in language that the minority parents can understand. If the parents have limited knowledge of English or it is not the dominant language in the home, the special education advocate assists them by enlisting the aid of a translator.

If assessment data must be reported, the special educators show themselves to be sensitive to minority parent concerns about testing and the labeling of children. They are prepared to interpret and to discuss the assessment implications (Oakland, 1973; Gay & Abrahams, 1973). In their efforts to assure continuation of mutual trust and respect, the special educators take pains to allay any fear or anxiety that minority parents may feel about misuse of the test results. The teachers explain the practical applications of the findings in simple terms by telling the minority parents and child the implications for placement or for return to regular programming.

As summarization and information exchange continues, special educators encourage the minority parents to have input into the dialogue, making special efforts to solicit their opinions and to ensure that the main concerns of both parties are voiced and not lost in translation. To accomplish this, ombudsman educators make extensive use of the skills of participatory listening and feeling focused feedback cited previously.

As these examples indicate, working with minority parents is not easy. The task requires patience, understanding, and the ability to work with a hybrid of parents and situations. Public Law 94-142 is an affirmation of the belief that schools working with families can serve the different. It also implies that the different are not inferior but possess special needs. Special educators have a commitment to serve children who are exceptional and not just racially or culturally different. Many educational professionals are developing the skills necessary to serve minority exceptional children. They cannot handle the task working in isolation. Therefore, skilled case management special educators will seek the assistance of their best allies—minority parents.

Bibliography

Abeson, A. *Legal change for the handicapped through litigation*. Arlington, Va.: Council for Exceptional Children, 1973, p. 1.

_____. Movement and momentum: Government and the education of handicapped children - II. *Exceptional Children*, 1974, *41*, pp. 109–115.

Ackerman, N. W. *Treating the troubled family*. New York: Basic Books, Inc., 1966.

Adler, A. *Individual psychology of Alfred Adler: A systematic presentation in selections from his writing*. New York: Basic Books, 1956.

Alexander, R. N., & Clements, E. J. Parent training: Bringing it all back home. *Focus on Exceptional Children*, 1975, *10*, 1–11.

Allinsmith, W., & Goethals, G. W. *The role of schools in mental health*. New York: Basic Books, Inc., 1962.

American Association on Mental Deficiency. A survey of AAMD education division. *Proceedings of Education Division*, Portland, Ore., May 1975, pp. 1–19.

A message for Michael: You're equal under the law. *Austin American-Statesman*, October 23, 1967.

Anderson, E. A research study on the integration of physically handicapped children in ordinary primary schools. In J. Loring & G. Burn (Eds.), *Integration of handicapped children in society*. London: The Spastics Society, 1975.

Anderson, S. V. Introduction. In American Assembly, *Ombudsman for American government*. Englewoods Cliffs, N.J.: Prentice-Hall, Inc., 1968.

Ashmore, H. S. *The Negro and the schools*. Chapel Hill: The University of North Carolina Press, 1954.

Axelrod, S., & Bailey, S. L. Drug treatment for hyperactivity: Controversies, alternatives and guidelines. *Exceptional Children*, April 1979, *45* (7), 544–549.

Bailey, J. S., Wolf, M. M., & Phillips, E. L. Home-based reinforcement and the modification of pre-delinquents' classroom behavior. *Journal of Applied Behavior Analysis*, 1970, *3*, 233.

Balow, B. Delinquency and school failure. *Federal Probation*, 1961, *35*, 15–17.

Balthazar, E. E., & Stevens, H. A. *The emotionally disturbed mentally retarded: A historical and contemporary perspective*. Englewood Cliffs, N.J.: Prentice-Hall, Inc., 1975, p. 18.

Bane, M. J. Is the American family dying out or just technology stunned? San Angelo, Texas: *San Angelo Standard-Times*, August 21, 1977.

Barraga, N. *Parental needs versus affiliate services.* Paper presented at the Texas State United Cerebral Palsy Conference, Fort Worth, 1966.

——————. Utilization of sensory-perceptual abilities. In B. Lowenfeld (Ed.), *The visually handicapped child in school.* New York: The John Day Co., 1973, pp. 117–154.

——————. Parental needs versus affiliate services. In E. Hammer (Ed.), *Families of deaf-blind children: Case studies of stress.* Paper presented at the American Orthopsychiatric Association first regional conference, Dallas, November 17, 1972.

Barsch, R. *The parent-teacher partnership.* The Council for Exceptional Children, Inc., Arlington, Va., 1969.

——————. A critical review, another plea for perspective and a fond hope. D.C.L.D. Newsletter, 1976, p. 13.

Beaird, J., McDonnell, J. J., & Carl, L. M. *Education of Oregon's sensory-impaired youth.* Monmouth, Ore.: Oregon Board of Education, Teaching Research, 1972, p. 5.

Beers, C. *A mind that found itself.* New York: Longmans, Green & Co., 1921.

Bell, N. W., & Vogel, E. F. (Eds.). A modern introduction to the family. Glencoe, Ill.: The Free Press, a division of Macmillan Publishing Co., Inc., 1960.

Berkowitz, P. H. In J. M. Kaufmann & C. D. Lewis (Eds.), *Teaching children with behavioral disorders: Personal perspectives.* Columbus, Ohio: The Charles E. Merrill Publishing Co., 1974, pp. 24–29.

Bigge, J., & O'Donnell, P. A. *Teaching individuals with physical and multiple disabilities.* Columbus, Ohio: The Charles E. Merrill Publishing Co., 1976, p. 251.

Bijou, & Sloan, H. N. Therapeutic techniques with children. In I. A. Berg & L. A. Pennington (Eds.), *An introduction to clinical psychology* (3rd ed.). New York: Ronald Press, 1966.

Billings, H. K. An exploratory study of the attitudes of noncrippled children toward crippled children in three selected elementary schools. *The Journal of Experimental Education,* 1963, *10,* 381–387.

Billingsley, A. Black families in white America. Englewood Cliffs, N.J.: Prentice-Hall, Inc., 1968.

Blackham, G. J. *The deviant child in the classroom.* Belmont, Calif.: Wadsworth Publishing Co., Inc., 1967, pp. 53–54, 73.

Bower, E. *The education of emotionally handicapped children.* Sacramento, Calif.: California State Department of Education, 1957, pp. 143–147.

Bradinsky, B. Annual list of ten major events. In Special education: A major event in 1973 (editorial) *Phi Delta Kappan,* 1973, *8,* 513.

Bradley, C. The behavior of children receiving benzadrine. *American Journal of Psychiatry,* 1937, *94,* 577–585.

Braginsky, D. D., & Braginsky, B. M. Surplus people: Their lost faith in self and the system. *Psychology Today,* August 1975, *9*(3), 66–72.

Brenton, M. Introduction: In M. Watson (Ed.), *Mainstreaming the educable mentally retarded.* Washington, D.C.: National Education Association, 1975.

Brewer, G. D., & Kakalik, J. S. Serving the deaf-blind population: Planning for 1980. In C. E. Sherrick (Ed.), *1980 is now: A conference on the future of deaf-blind children.* Los Angeles: John Tracy Clinic, 1974, 21, 23.

Brolin, D. *Vocational preparation of retarded citizens.* Columbus, Ohio: Charles E. Merrill, 1976.

Bronfenbrenner, U. To nurture children. Conversation with Burt Kruger Smith, Hogg Foundation for Mental Health, University of Texas, 1977.

Brown, B. F., & Task Force. *The adolescent, other citizens, and their high schools: A report to the public and the profession.* New York: McGraw-Hill, 1975.

Brown v. *Board of Education,* 347 U.S. 483, 745. Ct. 686. 1954.

Brown, G. W. Suggestions for parents. *Journal of Learning Disabilities*, 1969, *2*, 94–106.

Budnick, A., & Andreacchi, J. Day schools for disturbed boys. In P. H. Berkowitz and E. P. Roth-man (Eds.), *Public education for disturbed children in New York City.* Springfield, Ill.: Thomas, 1967, 57–77.

Bullock, L. J., & Brown R. K. Research bulletin: *Educational provisions for emotionally disturbed children: A status report.* Florida Educational Research and Development Council, 1972, *8*, 1.

Caffey, J. On the theory and practice of shaking infants. *American Journal of Diseases of Children.* August 1974 *124* (2), 161–169.

Carberry, H. How can this child be helped? *Instructor*, January 1976, *85* (5), 5.

Carter, R. *The teacher's role in the family process.* Paper presented at Midwest Regional Center New Staff Orientation Workshop, Collier Center of Communication Disorders, Dallas, October 15, 1974, p. 2.

Castenada, A., et al. *The educational needs of minority groups.* Lincoln, Neb.: Professional Education Publications, 1974.

Cattell, P. *The measurement of intelligence of infants and young children.* New York: Psych. Corp., 1947.

Cawley, J. F., Fritz, M., Shaw, R. A., Kahn, H., & Bates, H. Math word problems: Suggestions for LD students. *Journal of Development for Children with Learning Disabilities*, 1979, *2*, 28.

Chapmen, A. H. *Management of emotional problems of children and adolescents.* Philadelphia: J. B. Lippincott Co., 1965, p. 3.

Charles, D. C. Longitudinal follow-up studies of community adjustment. *New vocational pathways for the mentally retarded.* Washington, D.C.: American Personnel and Guidance Association, 1966.

Children's Defense Fund. *Children out of school in America.* Cambridge, Mass.: Author, 1974. 101–110.

——————. *Suspensions: Are they helping children?* Cambridge, Mass.: Author, 1975.

Chilman, C., et al. *Parents as partners.* Washington, D.C.: U.S. Department of Health, Education and Welfare, 1968.

Chilman, C., & Kroft, I. *Helping low income families through parent education.* Washington, D.C.: Department of Health, Education and Welfare, SRS, 1967, pp. 1–10.

Clarizio, H. F., & McCoy, G. F. *Behavior disorders in children.* New York: Thomas Crowell Co. 1970, p. 156.

Clark, A. D., & Richards, C. J. Learning disabilities: A national survey of existing public school programs. *Journal of Special Education*, 1968, *2*, 223.

Clark, M. Troubled children: The quest for help. *Newsweek*, April 8, 1974, 52.

Clements, J. E., & Alexander, R. N. Parent training: Bringing it all back home. *Focus on Exceptional Children.* Denver: Love Publishing Co., 1975, p. 3.

Clements, S. D. *Minimal brain dysfunction in children.* Washington, D.C.: Cosponsored by the Easter Seal Research Foundation of the National Society for Crippled Children and Adults and the National Institute of Neurological Diseases and Blindness (NINDS Monograph No. 3, U.S. Public Health Service Publication No. 1415), Washington, D.C.: U.S. Government Printing Office, 1966, p. 3.

Cohen, D. Immigrants and the schools. In Education for socially disadvantaged children. *Review of Educational Research*, 1970, *40* 1, 14.

Cohen, P. C. The impact of the handicapped child on the family. In *Casework services for parents of handicapped children.* New York: Family Service Association of America, 1963, p. 18.

Cohen, S. *Casework services for parents of handicapped children.* New York: Family Service Association of America, 1963, p. 18.

Cole, L., & Hall, I. N. *Psychology of adolescence* (7th ed.). New York: Holt, Rinehart & Winston, Inc., 1970, 4.

Coleman, J., et al. *Equality of educational opportunity.* Washington, D.C. Department of Health, Education and Welfare, U.S. Office of Education, 1966.

Commonwealth of Pennsylvania v. *Pennsylvania Association for Retarded Citizens* 343 F. Supp. 279, E.D. Pa., 1972.

Conner, F., Wald, J. R., & Cohen, M. *Pre-institute expression of opinion: Status, problems and trends.* New York: Columbia University Teachers College, 1970, p. 23.

Conner, F. P., Wald, J. R., & Cohen, M. J. (Eds.). *Leadership preparation for educators of crippled and other health impaired, multiply handicapped populations.* Nyack, N.Y.: 1973, p. 29.

Connors, C. K., & Rothchild, G. H. Drugs and learning in children. In J. Hellmuth (Ed.), *Learning disorders,* Vol. 3. Seattle: Special Child Publications, 1968, pp. 191–223.

Connors, C. K. What parents need to know about stimulant drugs and special education. *Journal of Learning Disabilities,* June-July 1973, 6(6), 349–351.

Council on Vocational Education. Vocational education: The bridge between man and his work. Washington, D.C.: U.S. Government Printing Office, 1959.

Coulter, W. A., Gilliam, J. E., Morrow, H. W., & Coulter, J. L. *Making sense of emotional disturbance: Practical approaches for identification and intervention.* Paper presented at the Annual Meeting of the American Pychological Association, Austin, Texas, September 1979.

Crothers, B., & Paine, R. *The natural history of cerebral palsy.* Cambridge, Mass.: Harvard University Press, 1959.

Cruickshank, W. M. *Cerebral palsy: A developmental approach.* Syracuse N.Y.: Syracuse University Press, 1976.

——————. Myths and realities in learning disabilities. *Journal of Learning Disabilities,* 1977, *10,* 61.

——————. The development of education for exceptional children. In W. M. Cruickshank & G. O. Johnson (Eds.), *Education of exceptional children and youth.* (2nd ed.). Englewood Cliffs, N.J.: Prentice-Hall, 1967, p. 22.

Cubberly, E. *Changing conceptions of education.* Boston: Houghton Mifflin, 1909, pp. 18, 19.

Dalton, J., & Epstein, H. Counseling parents of mildly retarded children. *Casework services for parents of handicapped children.* New York: Family Service Association of America, 1963, pp. 22–23.

Danvoren, E. Working with abusive parents: A social worker's view. *Children Today,* 1975, *39.*

Davies, J. A. *A crisis of confidence.* Unpublished class paper University of Texas, Austin, 1974, p. 1.

DeAvilz, E. A. Some critical notes on using I.Q. tests for minority children. In *Toward quality education for Mexican-Americans.* Report VI. Washington, D.C.: U.S. Commission on Civil Rights, 1974, pp. 17–33.

DeGenero, J. J. What do you say when a parent asks, how can I help my child? *Journal of Learning Disabilities,* 1973, *6* (2), 102–105.

Dennis, W. Causes of retardation among institutional children: Iran In C. B. Stendler (Ed.), *Readings in child behavior and development.* New York: Harcourt, Brace & World, Inc., 1954, pp. 93–100.

Deno, E. Special education as developmental capital. *Exceptional Children,* 1970, *37,* 235.

_____. Where do we go from here? In E. Deno (Ed.), *Instructional alternatives for exceptional children*. Arlington, Va.: Council for Exceptional Children, 1973, pp. 167–178.

Dent, H., & Williams, R. L. The psychological testing of Black people—National Association of Black Psychologists: A position statement. Paper presented at the American Psychological Association, Montreal, September 1973.

Dent, H. Assessing Black children for mainstreaming placement. In R. Jones (Ed.), *Mainstreaming and the minority child*. Reston, Va.: Council for Exceptional Children, 1976, pp. 77–92.

Deshler, D. Issues related to the education of learning disability adolescents. *Learning Disability Quarterly*, 1978, *1*(4), 2.

Diana v. *State Board of Education*, Civil Action No. C-70; 37 *RFP* (N.D. Cal., January 7, 1970, and June 18, 1973).

Division for Children with Learning Disabilities. Code of ethics and competencies for teachers of learning disabled children and youth. *DCLD Newsletter*, The Council for Exceptional Children, Author, 1976.

Drotar, D., Bashiewicz, A., Irvin, N., Kennell, J., & Klaw, M. The adaptation of parents to the birth of an infant with a congenital malformation: A hypothetical model. *Pediatrics*, 1975, *56* (5), 710.

Dunn, L. Special education for the mentally retarded: Is much of it justified? *Exceptional Children*, 1968, *35*, 5–24.

Dvoky, A. The way it's going to be. *Saturday Review*, April 1969, p. 61.

Edelman, M. In *Children out of school in America*. Washington, D.C.: Children's Defense Fund, 1974, p. 4.

_____. In *Suspensions: Are they helping children?* Washington, D.C.: Children's Defense Fund, 1975.

Eisenberg, L. Role of drugs in treating disturbed children. *Children*, 1964, *2*(5), 167–173.

_____. Behavior modification by drugs III. The stimulant use of drugs. *Pediatrics*, 1972, *49*, 709–715.

Erickson, E. H. *Childhood and society*. New York: W.W. Norton, 1963.

Erickson, E. *Identity youth and crisis*. New York: W.W. Norton & Company Inc., 1968, pp. 96–114.

Evans, F. B., & Anderson, J. G. The psychocultural origins of achievement and achievement motivation: The Mexican-American family. *Sociology of Education*, 1973, *46*(4), 396–416.

Fair, G. Vocational education programming for special education students in Texas. Austin: Report to the Texas Education Agency, Department of Occupational Education and Technology, Division of Occupational Research and Development, 1976.

Farber, I. E. Sane and insane: Constructions and misconstructions. *Journal of Abnormal Psychology*, 1975, *84* (6), 589–620.

Flores, M. *A study of Mexican-American cultural characteristics as perceived by members of 100 impoverished Mexican-American families, and its educational implications*. Houston: University of Houston Press, 1972.

Flynn, F. R., Gacka, R. C., & Sundean, D. A. Are classroom teachers prepared for mainstreaming? *Phi Delta Kappan*, 1978, *59*, 562.

Fowlie, B. A parent's guide to amphetamine treatment. *Journal of Learning Disabilities*, 1973, *6* (6), 352–354.

Freeman, R. Psychopharmacology and the retarded child. In F. J. Menolascino (Ed.), *Psychiatric approaches to mental retardation*. New York: Basic Books, Inc., 1970.

Freud, A. F., & Dann, S. An experiment in group upbringing. In C. B. Stendler (Ed.), *Readings in child behavior and development.* New York: Harcourt, Brace and World, Inc., 1954.

Freud, S. *An outline of psychoanalysis.* New York: W.W. Norton, 1949.

Freud, S., & Erickson, E. In G. J. Blackham, *The deviant child in the classroom.* Belmont, Calif.: Wadsworth Publishing Company, 1967.

Fusco, G. C. *Improving your school-community relations program.* Englewood Cliffs, N.J.: Prentice-Hall, Inc., 1967.

Gallup, G. H. Fifth Annual Gallup poll of public attitudes toward education. Bloomington, Ind.: *Phi Delta Kappan,* 1973, 38–51.

Gaston, P. M. *The south and her children: School desegregation 1970–1971.* Atlanta, Ga.: Southern Regional Council, 1971, pp. 5–20.

Gay, G., & Abrahams, R. Does the pot melt, boil or brew? Black children and white assessment procedures. In B. Phillips and T. Oakland (Eds.), *Assessing minority group children.* New York: Behavioral Publications, 1973, pp. 330–340.

Gickling, E. E., & Theobold, J. T. Mainstreaming: Affect or effect. *Journal of Learning Disabilities,* January 1976, 321.

Gihool, T. K. Education, an inalienable right. *Exceptional Children* 1973, *39,* 597–610.

Gil, D. G. What schools can do about child abuse. *American Education,* 1969, *5*(4), 2–5.

———. Violence against children. *Journal of Marriage and Family,* 1971, *33*(4), 637–648.

———. *Violence against children: Physical child abuse in the United States.* Cambridge, Mass.: Harvard University Press, 1970.

Gilliam, J., & Dollar, S. The examination of competencies of teachers of the seriously emotionally disturbed. In J. Gilliam (Ed.), *Teaching the autistic child.* Austin: Texas Society for Autistic Citizens, 1977, p. 73.

Giovannoni, J. M., & Billingsley, A. Child neglect among the poor: A study of parental adequacy in families of three ethnic groups. *Child Welfare,* April 1970, *49,* 196–204.

Glaser, H. H., et al. Physical and psychological development of children with early failure to thrive. *Journal of Pediatrics,* November 1968, *73,* 690–698.

Glasser, W. *Reality therapy.* New York: Harper & Row, 1965.

———. *Schools without failure.* New York: Harper & Row, 1969.

Glazer, N., & Moynihan, P. Beyond the melting pot: The Negroes, Puerto Ricans, Italians, and Irish. Cambridge, Mass.: MIT Press, 1963.

Gold, M. *Try another way.* Presentation at a workshop sponsored by the Texas Regional Resource Center, San Antonio, January 1977.

Goldberg, M. L. Factors affecting educational attainment in depressed urban areas. In A. H. Passow (Ed.), *Education in depressed areas.* New York: Teachers College Press, 1963.

Goldberg, S., & Deutsch, F. *Lifespan individual and family development.* Monterey, Calif.: Brooks/Cole Publishing Co., Inc., 1977.

Goldfarb, W. Psychological privation in infancy and subsequent adjustment. In C. B. Stendler (Ed.), *Readings in child behavior and development.* New York: Harcourt, Brace and World, Inc., 1954, p. 85.

Goldstein, K. *Aftereffects of brain injuries in war.* New York: Grune & Stratton, 1942.

Golton, F. In R. Samuda, Problems and issues in assessment of minority group children. *Mainstreaming and the minority child.*

Gordon, I. J. *What do we know about parents as teachers?* Paper presented at the American Educational Research Association, Chicago, April 3–7, 1972.

Gordon, S. A response to Warren Johnson. In F. F. de la Cruz & G. D. LaVeck (Eds.), *Human sexuality and the mentally retarded.* New York: Brunner/Mazel, Inc., 1973.

Gottlieb, J., and Corman, L. Public attitudes toward mentally retarded children. *American Journal of Mental Deficiency,* 1975, *80*(1), 72–80.

Goodlet, A. G. *The family physician.* Nashville: Smith and Nesbit's Steam Press, 1838, p. 85.

Graham, M. D. *Multiply-impaired blind children: A national study.* Philadelphia, Pa.: American Educators of the Visually Handicapped, 1970.

Green, D. R. Racial and ethnic basis in test construction. Final report of the U.S. Office of Education Contract No. OEC 9–70–0058 (057), 1972.

Griffin, H. C. *Attitudes, opinions and general information concerning cerebral palsy.* Unpublished dissertation, University of Texas, Austin, July 1979.

Grim, J. (Ed.). *Training parents to teach: Four Models.* Chapel Hill: N.C.: Technical Assistance Development System, 1974.

Grinspoon, L., & Singer, S. B. Amphetamines in the treatment of hyperactive children. *Harvard Educational Review,* 1973, *43*, 515–555.

Grossman, F. K. *Psychology Today,* 1972, pp. 84–102.

Grotberg, E. *Parent participation. Review of research, 1965–1969.* Washington, D.C.: Office of Economic Opportunity, Project Head Start, Research and Evaluation Office, 1970.

Hamachek, D. E. *Encounter with the self.* New York: Holt, Rinehart and Winston, Inc., 1971, p. 232.

Hammer, E. A time to think: Future needs of deaf-blind persons. In C. E. Sherrick (Ed.), *1980 is now: A conference on the future of deaf-blind children.* Los Angeles: John Tracy Clinic, 1974, p. 83.

_____. *Process teaching: A systems approach to the education of multihandicapped deaf-blind children.* Paper presented at workshop, Collier Center for Communication Disorders, Dallas, Texas, March 1974.

_____. *Behavior and its relationship to deaf persons.* Presentation at Regional Conference on the Deaf, March 6, 1979.

_____. *Families of deaf-blind children: Case studies of stress.* Paper presented at the First Regional American Orthopsychiatric Association Conference, Dallas, Texas, November 17, 1972.

_____. Adolescents with learning disability. In *Learning Disabilities in the secondary school.* Norristown, Pa.: Montgomery County Int. Unit, 1975.

_____. Adolescents with specific learning disabilities: Definition, identification and incidence. In L. Mann, L. Goodman, & J. L. Wiederholt (Eds.), *Teaching the learning disabled adolescent.* Boston: Houghton Mifflin, 1978, p. 38.

_____. Learning disabilities: A definition. In L. Mann, L. Goodman, & J. L. Weiderholt (Eds.), *Teaching the learning disabled adolescent.* Boston: Houghton Mifflin, 1978, p. 31.

Hardy, J. *Report to the Governor's commission on the needs of handicapped children.* Annapolis, Md.: 1965.

Haring, N. G. *Behavior of exceptional children: An introduction to special education.* Columbus Ohio: Charles E. Merrill Publishing Co., 1974, p. 14.

_____. *The application of functional analysis of behavior by teachers in a natural school setting.* U.S. Department of Health, Education, & Welfare, Office of Education, Bureau for Education of the Handicapped. Final Report of Grant No. OEG–0–8–0–070376–1857–(032), 1969.

Haring, N., & Phillips, E. *Educating emotionally disturbed children.* New York: McGraw-Hill Book Co., 1962, pp. 9–10, 240.

Harrington, M. *The other America.* New York: Macmillan Publishing Co., Inc., 1962.

Harrington, S. I can't do it. *Texas Monthly,* October 1978, p. 245.

Hartly, A. Identifying the physically abused child. *Texas Medicine*, March 1969, *65*, 50–55.

Hayes, J., & Higgins, S. T. Issues regarding the IEP: Teachers on the front line. *Exceptional Children*, January 1978, p. 268.

Heber, R. Definitions of mental retardation. In J. Rothstein (Ed.), *Mental retardation: Readings and resources.* New York: Holt, Rinehart and Winston, 1961.

Helfer, R. In M. Soeffing, Abused children are exceptional children. *Exceptional Children*, 1975, *42*(3), 129.

Helfer, R. *Child abuse and neglect: Diagnostic process and treatment programs.* Department of Health, Education and Welfare, OCD, Publication No. OHD 75–69, 1977.

Helfer, R. E. In presentation by McCaffrey at Institute on Child Abuse and Neglect, National Conference, The Council for Exceptional Children, Atlanta, April 6, 1977.

Hewett, F. M. *The emotionally disturbed child in the classroom.* Boston: Allyn & Bacon, Inc., 1968, p. 4.

Hickerson, N. *Education for alienation.* Englewood Cliffs, N.J.: Prentice-Hall, Inc., 1966.

Hill, R. *The strengths of black families.* New York: Emerson Hall Publishers, 1972.

Hillard, A. G. The strengths and weaknesses of cognitive tests for young children. In J. D. Andrews (Ed.), *Outstanding presentations from the NAEYC 1974 annual conference.* Washington, D.C.: National Association for the Education of Young Children, 1975.

Hobbs, D., & Blank, S. *Sociology and the human experience.* New York: John Wiley & Sons, Inc., 1975, p. 286.

Hobbs, N. *The futures of children.* San Francisco: Jossey-Bass, Inc., 1975, p. 10.

————. *Mislabeling of children.* Nashville, Tenn.: Vanderbilt University Press, 1974, p. 6.

————. In J. M. Kauffman & C. D. Lewis (Eds.), *Teaching children with behavior disorders: Personal perspectives.* Columbus, Ohio: Charles E. Merrill Publishing Co., 1974.

————, (Ed.), *Issues in the classification of children* (Vols. 1 and 2). San Francisco: Jossey-Bass, Inc., 1975.

————. Helping the disturbed child: Psychological and ecological strategies. *American Psychologist*, 1966, *21*, pp. 1105–1115.

Hudson, K. Helping parents to help their handicapped child. In *Proceedings of the Institute for Deaf-Blind Studies.* Texas Education Agency and California State Department of Education, 1976, p. 75.

Huntsinger, S. School storm: Drugs for children. *Christian Science Monitor*, October 31, 1970, pp. 1, 6.

Hurley, D. L. *Special education in the inner city: The social implications of placement.* Paper presented at the Conference on Placement of Children in Special Education Programs for the Mentally Retarded, Monte Carono Conference Center, Lake Arrowhead, Calif., March 7–10, 1971, p. 9.

Hurley, R. *Poverty and mental retardation: A causal relationship.* New York: Vintage Books, 1969.

Irvine, D., & Plumpton, R. A. A program for the vocational rehabilitation of emotionally disturbed and brain-injured adolescents in a public school setting. (ERIC EDO57–528).

Jenkins, D. H. The "helping" relationship in education. *University of Michigan School of Education Bulletin*, February 1951, *22*(5), 1–2.

Jensen, A. R. How much can we boost I.Q. and scholastic achievement? *Harvard Educational Review*, Winter, 1969, *39*.

Johnson, J. J. Special education and the inner city: A challenge for the future or another means of cooling the mark out. *Journal of Special Education*, 1969, *3*, 241–251.

Johnson, W. Sex education of the mentally retarded. In F. F. de la Cruz & G. D. LaVeck (Eds.), *Human sexuality and the mentally retarded*. New York: Brunner-Mazel, Inc., 1973, p. 60.

Jones, B. Guidance and individual planning within a computer-monitored system of individualized instruction for grades 1–12. Paper presented to American Educational Research Association annual meeting, Palo Alto, California, 1968.

Jones, P. *Home environment and the development of verbal ability*. Paper presented at the annual meeting of the American Educational Research Association, New York, February 1971.

Jones, R. L. Labels and stigma in special education. *Exceptional Children*, 1972, *38*, 553–564.

_____. Educational alienation, fatalism, school achievement, motivation, and self concept in mentally retarded and nonretarded high school students, 1974. Unpublished paper.

Jung, C. G. *The undiscovered self*. Boston: Little Brown, 1958.

Kauffman, J. M. *Characteristics of children's behavior disorders*. Columbus, Ohio: The Charles Merrill Publishing Co., 1977, p. 15.

_____. Severely emotionally disturbed. In N. G. Haring (Ed.), *Behavior of exceptional children: An introduction to special education*. Columbus, Ohio: The Charles E. Merrill, Co., 1974.

Keel. *Counseling the parents of MR children*. Presentation at the Regional Conference of American Association on Mental Deficiency, Hot Springs, Ark., March 1978.

Kelly, D. H. *How the school manufactures "misfits."* South Pasadena, Calif.: Newcal Publications, 1978, p. 12.

Kelly, E. J. Parental roles in special educational programming: A brief for involvement. *The Journal of Special Education*, 1973, *7*, 357–362.

Kelman, H. R. The function of a clinic for mentally retarded children. *Social Casework*, 1956, *37*, p. 239.

Kempe, C. H., & Helfer, R. E. (Eds.). *Helping the battered child and his family*. Philadelphia: J. B. Lippincott Co., 1972.

Kempe, C. H., Silverman, F. N., Steele, B. S., Droegemueller, W., & Silver, H. K. *Journal of the American Medical Association*, 1962, *181*, 17–24.

Kendall, W. Remarks at the Regional American Association on Mental Deficiency, Hot Springs, Ark., October 1978.

Keogh, B. K., & Becker, L. D. Early detection of learning problems: Questions, cautions and guidelines. *Exceptional Children*, 1973, *40*, 5.

Kidd, J. W., Cross, T. J., & Higginbotham, J. L. The world of work for the educable mentally retarded. *Exceptional Children*, 1967, *33*, 648.

King, J. Remarks in class discussion on "counseling parents with exceptional children," University of Texas, Austin, September 1973.

Kirk, R., & Gallagher, J. *Educating exceptional children* (3rd ed.). Boston: Houghton Mifflin Co., 1979, p. 109.

Kirk, S. A. Speech at the conference sponsored by the Fund for Perceptually Handicapped Children, Inc., Chicago, Illinois, 1963.

_____. Behavioral diagnosis and remediation of learning disabilities. *Proceedings of the Annual Meeting of the Conference on Exploration into the Problems of the Perceptually Handicapped Child*, 1963, *1*, 3.

Klaus, M., et al. Follow-up of low birth weight infants: The predictive value of maternal visiting patterns. *Pediatrics*, February 1972, *49*, 287–290.

Klein, M., & Stern, L. Low birth rate and the battered child syndrome. *American Journal of Diseases of Children*. July 1971, *122*, 15–18.

Klein, W. C. Shopping parents: Patient problem or professional problem. *Mental Retardation*, 1971,

8, 6.

Kroth, R. *Communicating with parents of exceptional children.* Denver: Love Publishing Co., 1975, p. 8.

Krupp, G. R., & Schwartzberg, B. The brain-injured child: A challenge to social workers. In *Casework services for parents of handicapped children.* New York: Family Service Association of America, 1963, p. 46.

Kvaraceus, W. C., & Miller, W. B. *Delinquent behavior culture and the individual.* Washington, D.C.: National Education Association, 1959.

Lain, M. Class lecture, University of Texas, Austin, May 1979.

Larry P. v. *Riles,* Civil Action No. C–71–2270, 343 F. Supp. 1306 (N.D. Cal., 1972).

Larsen, S. The influence of teacher expectations on the school performance of handicapped children. In *Focus on exceptional children,* 1975, 6(8), 1.

――――――. Learning disabilities and the professional educator. *Learning Disability Quarterly,* 1978, *1*, 5–12.

Lax, B. Presentation at the American Association for Mental Deficiency National Conference, Portland, Ore., May 1975.

Lewis, W. Project Re-ED: Educational intervention in children's behavior disorder. *Proceedings: 1967 International Convocation on Children and Young Adults with Learning Disabilities.* Pittsburgh: Home for Crippled Children, 1967, pp. 263–274.

Lippitt, R. Training for Participation. *Adult Leadership,* June 1965, pp. 42–44.

Little, W. J. Lectures by Dr. Little on the deformities of the human frame, delivered at the Orthopedical Institution, Bloombury Square. *Lancet,* 1843, pp. 350–355.

Lowell, E. L. 1980 is now: A conference on the future of deaf-blind children. Los Angeles: John Tracy Clinic, 1974, p. v.

Lowenfeld, B. (Ed.). *The visually handicapped child in school.* New York: The John Day Co., 1973, pp. 117–154.

Lowenfeld, B. Multihandicapped blind and deaf-blind children in California. *Research Bulletin No. 19.* Sacramento, Cal.: American Foundation for the Blind, 1968, pp. 1–72.

MacMillan, D. L., Jones, R. L., & Aloia, G. F. The mentally retarded label: A theoretical analysis and review of research. *American Journal of Mental Deficiency,* 1974, 79(3), 241–261.

MacMillan, D. L., Jones, R. L., & Meyers, C. E. Mainstreaming the mildly retarded: Some questions, cautions and guidelines. *Mental Retardation,* 1976, pp. 3–10.

McCaffery, M. Presentation at Institute of Child Abuse and Neglect, National Conference, The Council for Exceptional Children, Atlanta, April 6, 1977.

McCandless, B. *Children behavior and development* (2nd ed.). New York: Holt, Rinehart and Winston, Inc., 1967, p. 527.

McCarthy, J. J., & Kirk, W. D. *Examiner's manual. Illinois test of psycholinguistic abilities.* Urbana, Ill.: University of Illinois Press, 1961.

McCarthy, J. J., & McCarthy, J. F. *Learning disabilities.* Boston: Allyn & Bacon, Inc., 1969, p. 107.

McConnell, T. R., Cromwell, R. L., Bialer, I., & Son, C. D. Studies in activity level: VII: The effects of amphetamine drug administration on the activity level of retarded children. *American Journal of Mental Deficiency,* 1964, *68*, 647–651.

McLoughlen, J. A., McLoughlen, R., & Stewart, W. Advocacy for parents of the handicapped: A professional responsibility and challenge. *Learning Disability Quarterly,* 1979, 2(3), 52.

McNeil, D. C. *General issues in the education of ED children.* Paper presented at Alabama Conference on Behavioral Disorders, 1974.

McNutt, G., & Heller, G. Service for learning disabled adolescents: A survey. *Learning Disability Quarterly*, 1978, *1*(4), 103.

Madsen, W. *The Mexican-American of South Texas*. New York: Holt, Rinehart and Winston, Inc., 1964.

Mandelbaum, A., & Wheeler, M. E. The meaning of a defective child to parents. In *Casework services for parents of handicapped children*. New York: Family Service Association of America, 1963, p. 5.

Mann, L., Goodman, L., & Wiederholt, J. L. *Teaching the learning-disabled adolescent*. Boston, Mass.: Houghton Mifflin Co., 1978.

Marmor, J. *Psychiatry in transition*. New York: Brunner/Mazel Publications, 1974.

Marion, R. L. Minority parent involvement in the IEP process: A systematic model approach. *Focus on Exceptional Children*, 1979, *10*, 5.

_____. Panel discussions with parents of MR children and adolescents, University of Texas, Austin, October 1975.

_____. Conversation with mother of LD child, Austin, Texas. SCAC, April, 1978.

_____. *Issues in secondary special education*. Unpublished paper, University of Texas, Austin, 1978.

_____. The Adult Performance Level Competency-Based Diploma Pilot Project. Austin: University of Texas Press, 1976.

_____. *Rural education in the South*. Task Force on Southern Rural Development, Atlanta, 1977.

_____. Conversation with Jack King, Chairperson of Special Education Department, University of Texas, Austin, September 1978.

_____. Involvement of minority families in the individual education plan process. Paper presented at the Council for Exceptional Children Institute, Albuquerque, N.M., February 1, 1978.

_____. Recorded conversation with principal of TMR project. Austin, Texas, October 1976.

_____. Conversation with J. Gilliam on survey of institutions of higher education that offered personnel training programs in the southwestern United States, 1979.

Marion, R. L., & McCaslin, T. *Genetic/parent counseling in a tri-ethnic setting*. Unpublished study, University of Texas, Austin, 1978.

Martin, E. W. *Individualism and behaviorism: Future trends in educating handicapped children*. Reston, Va.: Council for Exceptional Children, 1972, pp. 517–525.

Maslow, A. H. *Motivation and personality*. New York: Harper & Row, 1954, pp. 100–101.

_____. *Toward a psychology of being*. Princeton, N.J.: Van Nostrand Co., Inc., 1962, p. 25.

Mayo, L. *National directory of public alternative schools*. Amherst, Mass.: University of Massachusetts, 1974, p. 3.

Mesinger, J. F. Emotionally disturbed and brain injured children—should we mix them? *Exceptional Children*, 1965, *32*, 237–238.

Metz, A. S. *Statistics on education of the handicapped in local public schools*. Washington, D.C.: U.S. Government Printing Office, 1973.

Meyen, E. L. (Ed.). *Planning community services for the mentally retarded*. Scranton, Pa.: International Textbook Co., 1967, p. 33.

Meyen, E. Conversation with Jack King concerning presentation made by Ed Meyen at department meeting, October, 1979.

Meyer, J. *A review of pilot vocational programs for the handicapped in Texas*. Texas Education Agency, Division of Occupational Research, 1972, p. 10.

Midwest Regional Resource Center, *Parent involvement in the IEP process*. Des Moines, Iowa: Drake University, 1978.

Miller, J. M. *Early education of the MH child*. New York: United Cerebral Palsy of New York, 1971, *13*, 137–146.

Miller, S. M. *Breaking the credential barrier*. Address before American Orthopsychiatric Association, Washington, D.C., March 23, 1967. New York: Ford Foundation Reprint, 1967.

Miller, S., & Keene, J. Alternative schools: 10 reasons why they aren't for everyone. *Nation's Schools*. June 1973, *91*(8), 39–41.

Mills v. *Board of Education of the District of Columbia*, 348 F. Supp. 866 (D., D.C. 1972).

Morrow, H., Coulter, A., Gilliam, J., & others. *Making sense of emotional disturbance: Practical approaches for school psychologists*. Paper presented at the annual meeting of American Psychological Association, New York, September 1, 1979, p. 10.

Morse, W. C. Serving the needs of individuals with behavior disorders. *Exceptional Children*, 1974.

————. *Classroom disturbance: The principal's dilemma*. Arlington, Va.: The Council for Exceptional Children, 1971, p. ix.

Morse, W. C., Cutler, R. L., & Fink, A. H. *Public school classes for the emotionally disturbed: A research analysis*. Washington, D.C.: The Council for Exceptional Children, 1964, p. 21.

Morse, W. C., Long, N. J., & Newman, R. G. (Eds.). *Conflict in the classroom* (2nd ed.). Belmont, Calif.: Wadsworth Publishing Co., 1971.

Morse, W. C., Sahler, O. Z., & Freidman, S. B. A three-year follow-up study of abuse and child neglect. *American Journal of Diseases of Children*, 1970, *120*, 439–446.

Mouchka, S. Interpersonal aspects of intervention strategies in the rehabilitation of handicapped children. In *Proceedings of the Institute for Deaf-Blind Studies*. Texas Education Agency and the California State Department of Education, 1976, pp. 79–83.

The National Advocate for deaf-blind children, Mountain Plains Regional Center for Services to Deaf-Blind Children, Spring 1976, III (3), p. 1.

Moynihan, D. P. *The negro family: The case for national action*. Washington, D.C.: U.S. Department of Labor, 1965 p. 5.

Mullin, J. B. *Teacher preparation in COHI*. New York: Columbia University Teachers College, 1970, p. 100.

Munsey, B. The parent's right to read. *Journal of Learning Disabilities*, 1973, *6*, 392–394.

Munuchin, S., et al. *Families of the slums: An exploration of their structure and treatment*. New York: Basic Books, Inc., 1967.

Murdock, G. P. *Social structure*. New York: Macmillan Publishing Co., Inc., 1949, renewed 1977.

Murillo, N. The Mexican-American family. In N. N. Wagner & M. J. Haug (Eds.), *Chicanos: Social and psychological perspectives*. St. Louis: The C. V. Mosby Co. 1971.

Myers, W. *Program in multihandicapped*. University of Texas, Austin, 1978, p. 1.

Myrdal, G. *An American dilemma*. New York: Random House, Inc., 1962.

Nadal, R. A counseling program for parents of severely retarded pre-school children. In *Casework services for parents of handicapped children*. New York: Family Service Association of America, 1963, p. 31.

National Society for Crippled Children and Adults, Inc. *Perspective, 1959: Annual Report*, p. 8.

Nelson, C. M., & Kauffman, J. M. Educational programming for secondary school age delinquent and maladjusted pupils. *Behavioral Disorders*, 1977, *2*, 102–113.

Neuhaus, E. C. Training the mentally retarded for competitive employment. *Exceptional Children*, 1967, *33*, 625.

Newcomer, P. L., & Hammill, D. D. *Psycholinguistics in the schools.* Columbus, Ohio: Charles E. Merrill, 1976.

1969 Advisory Committee on Handicapped Children. Better education for handicapped children. In T. Oakland (Ed.), *Assessing minority group children.* Washington, D.C.: HEW, USOE, 1969, pp. 2–3.

Nondiscrimination Testing Conference, Superintendents. Texas Education Agency, Galveston, 1975.

Noshpitz, J. D. In M. Clark, (Ed.), Troubled children: The quest for help. *Newsweek*, 1974, p. 52.

Oakland, T. Assessing minority group children: Challenges for school psychologists. *Journal of School Psychology*, 1973, 297.

Offir, E. W. A slavish reliance on drugs: Are we pushers for our own children? *Psychology Today*, December, 1974, 49.

Oshansky, S. *Casework services for parents of handicapped children.* New York: Family Service Association, 1963, p. 14.

Outland, R. W. Crippled and other health impaired—Trends in population characteristics and in meeting educational needs. In F. Conners, J. Wald, & M. Cohen (Eds.), *Professional preparation for educators of crippled children.* U.S. Office of Education, Bureau for Education of the Handicapped, 1970, p. 47.

Parsons, T. The American family: Its relation to personality and to the social structure. In Parsons, T., & Bales, R. F. (Eds.), *Family socialization and interaction process.* Glencoe, Ill.: The Free Press, 1955.

Passow, A. H. *Secondary education reform: Retrospect and prospect.* New York: Teachers College Press, 1976.

_____. *Reforming America's high schools.* Phi Delta Kappan, 1975, 590.

_____. (Ed.). *Education in depressed areas.* New York: Teachers College Press, 1963.

Payne, J. E. *Ombudsman and advocate: New roles for social workers.* Unpublished manuscript, University of Texas, 1970, p. 13.

Plessy v. *Ferguson.* 163 U.S. 537 (1896)19, 25, 26, 31, 86.

Pointkowski, T. Mainstreaming—Regardless of law. *Exceptional Parent,* 1978, *8*(5), 3.

President's Advisory Committee on Technical Vocational Education, Washington, D.C.: U.S. Government Printing Office, 1968, p. 122.

President's Commission on Mental Health. *Mental health in America: 1978.* Washington, D.C.: U.S. Government Printing Office, 1978, *1*, 5.

President's Commission on Mental Health. Washington, D.C.: U.S. Government Printing Office, 1978, *1*, 8.

President's Committee on Mental Retardation. *Letter of Transmittal by the Chairman.* Washington, D.C.: U.S. Government Printing Office, March 1974, pp. iii, 18.

Preston, V. J. *A digest of the evaluation of coordinated vocational academic education in Texas.* Texas Education Agency, Department of Occupational Education and Technology, 1974, p. 4.

Prillaman, D. Virginia EMR study. *Phi Delta Kappan.* September 1975, *57*(1), 53.

Qualities employers like, dislike, in job applicants: Final report of statewide employer survey. Austin, Texas: Advisory Council for Technical-Vocational Education in Texas, 1975.

Ramirez, M., Harold, L., & Castenada, A. *Mexican-American values and culturally democratic educational environment: New approaches to bilingual, bicultural education* (2). Austin, Texas: Dissemination Center for Bilingual, Bicultural Education, 1974.

Ravitz, M. The role of the school in the urban setting. In A. H. Passow (Ed.), *Education in depressed areas.* New York: Teachers College Press, 1963, p. 16.

Reisman, F. *The culturally deprived child.* New York: Harper & Row, 1962.

A report on secondary school programs for the learning disabled. Final Report (Project No. H12-7145B, Grant No. OEG-0-714425). Washington, D.C.: Bureau of Education for the Handicapped, 1978.

Reyes, R., & Cezi, K. *Parent and community participation in compensatory education through district advisory committees in California: A progress report.* Reston, Va.: ERIC, Document Reproduction Service No. ED 062 467, 1973.

Reynolds, M. C. A framework for considering some issues in special education. *Exceptional Children,* 1962, *7,* 368.

——————. *Reflections on a set of innovations.* Arlington, Va.: Council for Exceptional Children, 1973, pp. 179–186.

Rhodes, W. C., & Head, S. *A study of child variance: Service delivery systems.* Ann Arbor: University of Michigan Press, 1974.

Rhodes, W. C. The disturbing child: A problem of ecological management. *Exceptional Children,* 1967, *33,* 449–455.

——————. A community participation analysis of emotional disturbance. *Exceptional Children,* 1970, *1,* 309–314.

Rhodes, W. C., & Paul, J. *Emotionally disturbed and deviant children: New views and approaches.* Englewood Cliffs, N.J.: Prentice-Hall, Inc., 1978.

Richmond, J. *The family and the handicapped child.* Paper presented at the Frances Ayres Memorial Seminar on Neuromuscular Dysfunctional Syndromes, Cerebral Palsy Development Center of Northern Virginia, May 24, 1972, p. 159.

Rimland, B. *Infantile autism.* New York: Appleton-Century-Crofts, 1964.

Robbins, L. R., & Kacen, N. M. How should the teacher view the chronically ill pupil? *Today's Education,* May 1971, pp. 28–33.

Robinault, I. *Functional aids for the multiply handicapped.* New York: Harper & Row, 1973.

Robinson, D. W. Alternative schools: Do they promise system reform? *Phi Delta Kappan,* 1973, *54*(7), 443.

Rodin, B. Three degrees of parent involvement in a pre-school program: Impact on mothers and children. Reston, Va.: ERIC Document Reproduction Service No. ED 052 831, May 1971.

Rogers, C. R. The necessary and sufficient conditions of therapeutic personality change. *Journal of Consulting Psychology,* 1957, *21,* 6.

——————. *On becoming a person.* Boston: Houghton Mifflin Co., 1961, pp. 163–198.

Rogers, C. R., & Roethlisberger, F. J. Barriers and gateways to communications. In *How Successful Executives Handle People.* Harvard University Press, July–August, 1952, 28–34.

Rosenthal, A. H. The ombudsman—Swedish grievance man. *Public Administration Review,* 1964, *24*(4), 227.

Ross, A. O. *The exceptional child in the family.* New York: Grune & Stratton, Inc., 1964, p. 8.

Rouche, G., & Mink, O. *Impact of instruction and counseling on high risk youth.* Final report to National Institute on Mental Health, Grant RO1MH 22590, September 30, 1976.

Rowat, D. C. (Ed.). *The ombudsman: Citizen's defender.* London: George Allen & Unwin, Ltd., 1965; Toronto: University of Toronto Press, 1965, p. 7.

Rowat, D. C. The spread of the ombudsman idea. In American Assembly, *Ombudsman for American government.* Englewood Cliffs, N.J.: Prentice-Hall, Inc., 1968, p. 35.

Rubel, A. *Across the tracks.* Austin: University of Texas Press, 1971.

Rubin, R. A., & Balow B. Prevalence of teacher-identified behavior problems: A longitudinal study. *Exceptional Children,* 1978, *45*(2), 102–111.

Rumble, R. C. *A survey of the attitudes of secondary teachers toward the mainstreaming of handicapped learners.* A research project in the Portland, Public Schools, 1978. ERIC Document Reproduction Service No. Ed 162 4T1.

Rusalem, H. Continuing education. In F. Conner, & M. Cohen (Eds.), *Leadership preparation.* New York: Columbia University Teachers College, 1973, p. 64.

Sabatino, D. A. Obstacles to educating handicapped adolescents. In D. Cullinan & M. Epstein (Eds.), *Special education for adolescents.* Columbus, Ohio: The Charles E. Merrill Publishing Co., 1979, p. 336–337.

Sabatino, D., & Mauser, A. J. *Specialized education in today's secondary schools.* Boston: Allyn & Bacon, 1978.

Sagarin, E. The high personal cost of wearing a label. *Psychology Today*, March 1976, *9*, 30.

Salmon, P. B., & Brubacher, J. W. Are compulsory school attendance laws outdated? *Phi Delta Kappan*, December 1973, *55* (4), 230–231.

Salvin, S. T., & Light, B. S. *Curricula methodology and habilitation of the mentally-handicapped.* Los Angeles: University of Southern California, School of Education, 1963, p. xiii.

Sandgrund, A., Gaines, R. W., & Green, A. H. Child abuse and mental retardation: A problem of cause and effect. *American Journal of Mental Deficiency*, 1974, *79*, 327–330.

Satir, V. *Conjoint family therapy.* Palo Alto, Calif.: Science & Behavior Books, Inc., 1967, p. 21.

Satlin, D. B., & Miller, J. K. The ecology of child abuse within a military community. *American Journal of Orthopsychiatry*, July 1971, *41*(4), 675–678.

Schilds, S. Genetic counseling as a part of a mental retardation service: Implications for social work practice, 1968 Available through the author, School of Social Work, Sacramento State College, Sacramento, California.

Screiber, D. (Ed.). *Profile of a school drop-out.* New York: Random House, Inc., 1967.

Seigel, E. *The exceptional child grows up, guidelines for understanding and helping the brain injured adolescent and young adult.* New York: E. P. Dutton & Co., 1974, 176–210.

Shane, H. Looking to the future: Reassessment of educational issues of the 1970s. *Phi Delta Kappan*, 1973, *5*, 326–327.

Sheimo, S. L. Problems in helping parents of mentally defective and handicapped children. *American Journal of Mental Deficiency*, 1951, *56*, 42–47.

Silberberg, N. E., & Silberberg, M. C. *Who speaks for the child?* Springfield, Ill.: Thomas Publishing, 1974.

Siller, J., Ferguson, L., Vann, D., & Holland, B. *Structure of attitudes toward the physically disabled.* New York: New York University School of Education, 1967.

Sills, D. *International encyclopedia of the social sciences.* New York: Macmillan and The Free Press, 1968.

Silverman, F. N. Unrecognized trauma in infants, the battered child syndrome, and the syndrome on Ambroise Tardieu. *Radiology*, August 1972, *104*, 337–353.

Smith, B. Potential of rubella deaf-blind children. In C. E. Sherrick (Ed.), *1980 is now: A conference on the future of deaf-blind children.* Los Angeles: John Tracy Clinic, 1974, pp. 65–70.

Smith, M. B., & Brache, C. I. When school and home focus on achievement. *Educational Leadership*, 1963, *20*, 314–318.

Smits, V., Edwards, L. D., & Conine, T. A. Definition of disability as determinants of scores on the attitude toward persons scale. *Rehabilitation Counseling Bulletin*, 1971, *14*, pp. 227–235.

Soeffing, M. Abused children are exceptional children. *Exceptional Children*, 1975, *42*(3), 9.

Southern Regional Council. *The pushout.* Atlanta: Author, 1973, p. 10.

Sprague, R. L., & Sleator, E. R. Effects of psychopharmacological agents on learning disabilities.

Pediatrics Clinics of North America, 1973, *20*, 719–735.

Steele, B. F. Working with abusive parents: A psychiatrist's view. *Children Today*, May-June 1975, 4.

Stern L. Prematurity as a factor in child abuse. *Hospital Practice*, May 1973, *8*(5), 117–123.

Strauss, A., & Lehtinen, L. *Psychopathology and education of the brain-injured child.* New York: Grune & Stratton, 1947.

Strong, C., Sulzbacher, S. I., & Kirkpatrick, M. A. Use of medication versus reinforcement to modify a classroom behavior disorder. *Journal of Learning Disabilities,* 1974, *7*, 214–218.

Subcommittee to Investigate Juvenile Delinquency. *Our nation's schools—A report card: "A" in school violence and vandalism.* Washington, D.C.: U.S. Government Printing Office, 1975.

Sullivan, H. J. *Effects of parent-administered summer reading instruction.* Paper presented at the American Educational Research Association meeting, Minneapolis, March 2–6, 1970.

Sussman, S. The battered child syndrome. *California Medicine,* 1968, *108*, 437–439.

Swap, S. W. The ecological model of emotional disturbance in children: A status report and proposed synthesis. *Behavioral Disorders,* 1978, *3*(3), 187.

Task Force on Urban Education. *The urban education task force report.* New York: Praeger Publishers, 1970, pp. 82–139.

Task Force II. New York: A working definition of COHI-MH. In *Leadership preparation.* New York: Leadership Training Institute, Columbia Teachers College, 1973, p. 12.

Texas Association for Learning Disabilities. Letters from concerned parents. Austin, 1978.

Texas State Learning Resource Center. *Severely/profoundly handicapped: A definition from BEH.* Austin: Texas Education Agency, 1976, p. 1.

——————. *Notes.* Austin: Texas Education Agency, 1976, p. 4.

Thompson, P. The severely multiply handicapped: What are the issues? Wednesday morning keynote address. In J. Moore and V. Engleman (Eds.). Proceedings from Regional Topical Conference, University of Utah, Salt Lake City, March 6–8, 1974.

Tizard, J. Longitudinal and follow-up studies. In A. Clarke & A. D. B. Clarke (Eds.), *Mental deficiency: The changing outlook.* New York, 1958, p. 442.

Torrie, C. A preliminary report on parent observations and needs as they relate to programs for deaf-blind children in the south-central region. A paper presented to the Regional Advisory Board Meeting, Dallas, Texas, June 15, 1973.

Trexler, G. *Microcommunicating: A manual.* Unpublished doctoral dissertation, University of Texas, Austin, 1974, p. 24.

Turnbull, A. Parent professional interactions. In M. E. Snell (Ed.), *Systematic instruction of the moderately and severely handicapped.* Columbus; Ohio: The Charles E. Merrill Publishing Co., 1978, p. 462.

Turner, K. Conversation with R. L. Marion on Pennsylvania court case that challenged the legality of the 180-day school year, December 1979.

U.S. Bureau of the Census. *1970 Census of the Population: Detailed Characteristics.* Washington, D.C.: U.S. Government Printing Office, 1972.

U.S. Commission on Civil Rights. Pub. L. 86–352, 2 July 1964, 78 Stat. 241, 28 U.S.C. 1447; 42 2000a to 2000hd.

U.S. Commission on Civil Rights. *Toward Quality Education for Mexican-Americans.* Washington, D.C.: U.S. Government Printing Office, February 1974, p. 29.

U.S. Department of Health, Education and Welfare. *First Annual Report of the National Advisory Committee on Handicapped Children.* Washington, D.C., January 31, 1968, p. 14.

U.S. Department of Health, Education and Welfare, Office of Education, Bureau for Education of the Handicapped. *Closer Look,* 1978.

_____. Know your rights. *Closer Look,* Winter, 1976, 2.

_____. What does it take to make a law work? *Closer Look,* Winter-Spring, 1977, 4.

_____. *Standards for rehabilitation facilities and sheltered workshops.* Washington, D.C.: U.S. Department of Health, Education and Welfare, HEW Publication No. [SRS] 72-25010, Rev. Ed. Government Printing Office, 1971, p. 1.

_____. *Entering the era of human ecology.* Washington, D.C.: U.S. Government Printing Office, 1971, p. 13.

_____. Standards for rehabilitation facilities and sheltered workshops. Publication No. [SR 5] 72-25010, Rev. Ed. Washington, D.C.: U.S. Government Printing Office, 1971.

_____. *An overview of the problems of child abuse and neglect: The problem and management.* Publication No. (OCD) 75-30073, 1975, p. 10.

U.S. General Accounting Office. *More can be learned and done about the well-being of children: Report to the Congress.* HEW, Social and Rehabilitation Service, April 1976, p. 1.

Van Dyck, J. New techniques for working with deaf-blind children. In P. Lee, (Ed.), *Co-active movement with deaf-blind children.* Denver: Colorado Department of Education, 1973, pp. 29–32.

Vernon, M. *Multiply handicapped deaf children: Medical, educational, and psychological considerations.* Washington, D.C.: The Council for Exceptional Children, 1969, p. 8.

Vincent, C. E. Family spongea: The adaptive function. *Journal of Marriage and the Family,* 1966, *28,* 29–36.

Wald, J. R. Crippled and other health impaired and their education. In F. Conners, J. Wald, & M. Cohen (Eds.). *Professional preparation for educators of crippled children.* New York: Columbia University Teachers College, 1970, p. 95.

Wallen, J. L. Developing effective interpersonal communication. In R. W. Pace, B. D. Peterson, & T. R. Radcliffe (Eds.). *Communicating interpersonally.* Columbus, Ohio: Charles E. Merrill, 1973, pp. 218–233.

Weber, R. E. *Handbook on learning disabilities.* Englewood Cliffs, N.J.: Prentice-Hall, 1974.

Weintraub, F., & Abeson, A. New education policies for the handicapped: The quiet revolution. *Phi Delta Kappan,* 1974, *55*(8), 526.

Wepman, J. M., & Jones, L. V. *The language modalities test for aphasia.* Chicago: University of Chicago Industry Services, 1961.

_____. *What is the role of federal assistance for vocational education?* Washington, D.C.: Department of Health, Education and Welfare, Office of Education, Office of the Comptroller General of the United States, Report to the Congress, 1974, p. 15.

Wiederholt, J. L. Adolescents with learning disabilities: The problem in perspective. In L. Mann, L. Goodman, & J. L. Wiederholt (Eds.). Boston: Houghton Mifflin Co., 1975.

_____. Educational options for handicapped adolescents. *Exceptional Children,* 1980, *1* (2), 1–11.

_____. *Teaching the learning-disabled adolescent.* Boston: Houghton Mifflin Co., 1978, pp. 1–16.

Williams, W., Brown, L., & Cento, N. Components of an instructional program for severely handicapped students. Paper presented at the Conference on the Education of Severely and Profoundly Handicapped Students, April 1975, pp. 165–166.

Wolfensberger, W., & Zanka, H. *Citizen advocacy and protective services for the impaired and handicapped.* Toronto: National Institute on Mental Retardation, 1973, p. 24.

Writer, J. Behavior management for the deaf-blind. Proceedings of a conference entitled Multidimensional Models for Teaching Deaf-Blind Children. Raleigh, N.C.: Department of Public Education, 1975.

──────. The design and implementation of individualized educational programs for the severely multiply handicapped, including deaf-blind. Paper presented at staff development workshop, Texas Education Agency, April 1977.

──────. The design of instructional programs for severely multihandicapped students. *Educational Methods for Deaf- Blind and Severely Handicapped Students*. Austin, Texas: Texas Education Agency, 1979, p. 17.

Wyatt, K. E. One dickens of a Christmas carol. In F. Conners, J. Wald, & M. Cohen (Eds.), *Professional preparation for educators of crippled children*. West Point, N.Y.: HEW, USOE, BEH, 1970, p. 39.

Wynne, E. A. Behind the discipline problem: Youth suicide as a measure of alienation. *Phi Delta Kappan*, 1978, 307–315.

Yates, & Shirley. Report on statewide pupil personnel needs at departmental meeting, University of Texas, Austin, December 1978.

Yu, M. The causes of stresses to families with deaf-blind children. Paper presented at the Southwest Regional Meeting of the American Orthopsychiatric Association, Galveston, Texas, November 16, 1972, pp. 10–14.

Zander, A. Presentation at the University of Michigan Human Relations Workshop. Ann Arbor, Michigan, August 8, 1961.

Ziring, P. R. Rubella birth evaluation project. In *Current status of the Rubella problem*. Texas Education Agency and California State Education Department, 1976.

Index

A

AAESPH. *See* American Association for the Education of the Severely/Profoundly Handicapped

Abused children

See also Advocate role; Case manager role; Ombudsman role; Special educators; Teachers

behavior of, 197, 199

characteristics of, 192

definition of, 191-192

detection of, 192-193, 201

documenting of, 202

effects on, 200-201

exceptional children as, 196-197

families of, 199, 202-207

history of, 189-190

neglect, 198-199, 202-203

parents of

characteristics of, 193-195, 205-206

crisis periods of, 195-196

feedback for, 206-207

listening to, 203-204

stresses of, 195-196, 205

treatment of, 202-207

physical indicators of, 197-200

reporting of, 202

role discrepencies and, 204-205

sexual abuse, 199-200

teachers and, 189-190, 198, 202-207

Advocate role

See also Case manager role; Ombudsman role; Parent-teacher interaction; Secondary programming; Teachers

attitude in, 49-50, 69

characteristics of, 41, 44-45

ecological approach of, 42, 47

influencing factors, 42

information giving functions of, 45-48, 91, 141, 180

parents in, 42-43

P.L. 94-142 and, 43, 45-47

problems of, 43-44

About the Author

ROBERT L. MARION received a B.A. degree in 1957, an M.A. in 1959, and a Ph.D. in 1973 from the University of Michigan, Ann Arbor. He has done postdoctoral work in family therapy at the Worden School of Social Work in San Antonio, Texas.

Dr. Marion has had extensive practical experience as a teacher, counselor, and administrator in programs for exceptional and culturally different children/youth and their parents. He has assisted in developing programs for culturally different gifted and talented students at the University of Michigan and the University of Texas, Austin. Dr. Marion developed the generic undergraduate special education teacher preparation program and codeveloped the secondary special education program at the University of Texas. He has authored two books and numerous articles on parent involvement in the field of special education.

Dr. Marion is now an Associate Professor of Special Education at the University of Texas.